THE CROOKED MIRROR

The Crooked Mirror

A Memoir of Polish-Jewish Reconciliation

Louise Steinman

Beacon Press

BOSTON

Beacon Press
25 Beacon Street
Boston, Massachusetts 02108-2892
www.beacon.org

Beacon Press books
are published under the auspices of
the Unitarian Universalist Association of Congregations.

16 15 14 13   8 7 6 5 4 3 2 1

This book is printed on acid-free paper that meets the uncoated paper
ANSI/NISO specifications for permanence as revised in 1992.

Text design and composition by Kim Arney

"Reconciliation: A Prayer," from *The Woman Who Fell from the Sky*
by Joy Harjo. Copyright © 1994 by Joy Harjo. Used by permission
of W. W Norton & Company, Inc.

Library of Congress Cataloging-in-Publication Data
Steinman, Louise.
    The crooked mirror : a memoir of Polish-Jewish reconciliation / by Louise
Steinman.
        pages   cm
    Includes bibliographical references.
    ISBN 978-0-8070-5055-2 (cloth : alk. paper)
    ISBN 978-0-8070-5056-9 (ebook)
1. Steinman, Louise—Travel. 2. Jews, Polish—United States—Biography.
3. Jews—Poland—Social life and customs. 4. Holocaust, Jewish (1939-1945)—
Poland—Influence. 5. Steinman family. 6. Poland—Biography. I. Title.
    E184.37.S744A3 2013
    940.53'18438—dc23
                                                        2013013644

For my mother, Anne Weiskopf Steinman,
who believed we must always inquire.

Oh sun, moon, stars, our other relatives peering at us
from the inside of god's house walk with
us as we climb into the next century naked but for the
stories we have of each other. Keep us
from giving up in this land of nightmares which is
also the land of miracles.

—JOY HARJO, FROM "RECONCILIATION—A PRAYER"

CONTENTS

The Country in My Head

Cinders drifted over the heads of family and friends—fire season in Southern California. The rabbi sang so ecstatically from the Song of Songs, some of the wedding guests wondered if he was on acid.

It was 1988, my second marriage, my husband's third. In the past, neither of us had considered a religious ceremony. But all four of our parents were then alive, and we knew it would give them sweet pleasure to see us married under the *chupa,* the traditional Jewish wedding canopy.

When we began planning, knowing our ambivalence about tradition, a friend directed us to Don Singer, "the Zen Rabbi of Malibu."

Don met us at the door of his house with a parrot on his shoulder. He was white-haired, handsome; laugh lines radiated from bright blue eyes. We warmed immediately to his unorthodoxy, his innate joie de vivre.

Don Singer really was a Zen rabbi. His understanding of Buddhism harmonized with his embrace of Hasidic wisdom. His congregation gathered for Shabbat and High Holy Day services in the garden behind the Los Angeles Zen Center, located in one of the city's poorest neighborhoods. On Rosh Hashanah, blasts from the traditional ram's horn (shofar) mingled with catchy tunes from an ice cream truck and the beat of salsa from boom boxes. In Rabbi Singer's eclectic, roaming congregation, I found a contemplative home for my unaffiliated and long-estranged Judaism.

Sometimes at his services, Don spoke about his experiences in Poland. Every winter for five years in a row, Rabbi Singer had served as the principal rabbi for the Bearing Witness Retreat at Auschwitz-Birkenau, an interfaith gathering organized by the Zen Peacemaker Order.

When Don was a teenager in the fifties, his artist father took him to visit the death camp at Dachau. "It is the source of what I am today as a rabbi," he confided. His early experiences led him to explore "the authentic roots of Judaism" and what he considers its most radical commandment: "You shall love the stranger as yourself, for you were a stranger in Egypt, and you know the heart of the stranger."

In one of his Friday night talks, Rabbi Singer mentioned "Polish-Jewish reconciliation." He felt a responsibility to bring Poles and Jews together. I couldn't imagine why.

"When I went to Poland for the first time and met some Polish people, I felt a startling affinity," he said. He took pleasure in the thought that his grandmother came from there. "The Jews were part of Poland's body and soul," he said. "I felt somehow we knew the Poles, that we understood them. I realized they received a bum rap."

I fumed . . . a bum rap? Like so many others, I erroneously assumed the Nazis located their extermination camps in Poland because they expected the Poles would be willing collaborators. I'd heard that Poles murdered Jews even *after* the war ended. The infamous July 1946 pogrom in the town of Kielce, Poland, against Jews who'd returned from the camps, caused mass panic among those Polish Jews who'd survived the war. Forty Jews were murdered in Kielce, despite a large presence of police and army militia. The violence raged on for more than five hours.

The Kielce pogrom convinced many of those Polish Jews who'd survived the war to flee the country. The incident loomed ominously over Diaspora Jews' images of postwar Poland. When I first learned of the Kielce pogrom, in my teens, its logic eluded me. Why would people persecute—rather than protect—survivors who made it back to their homes?

"Polish-Jewish reconciliation" had the ring of a bad joke, like the premise of Philip Roth's novel *Operation Shylock*, in which Israeli Jews emigrate back to Poland in a reverse Diaspora. For my family—as for so many other American Jews of Polish descent—Poland was a black hole, a gnawing void.

I took note that many, if not most, of my Jewish friends had family ties to Poland. An estimated 80 percent of American Jews are of Polish Jewish descent. There was scant generosity in their feelings about Poland; always dependable heat. Most harbored more bitterness toward Poland than they did toward Germany, a fact that I never questioned as odd, misplaced.

The Jews may have once been part of Poland's body and soul, but they'd been excised, cast out.

My own mother could barely utter the word *Poland*. Her grief at the loss of unnamed family in Poland during the Holocaust rendered painful even the sound of where it happened. It was a given that Poland was a country full of people who hated Jews, who allowed and perhaps even abetted an unspeakable genocide on their soil. Bitterness calcified, and in my home and among my generation of comfortable suburban Los Angeles Jewish kids, the very idea of Poland resonated anguish and betrayal in a way it did not for other Americans.

MY MOTHER'S PARENTS EMIGRATED from Poland to the United States in 1906. Back beyond that, silence. Even as a child and without knowing why, the absence of family history on my maternal side was a gap, an ache.

My father's mother, my Russian grandmother, was a gifted storyteller. Rebecca (Becky) Steinman read Hebrew and spoke Yiddish, Russian, Ukrainian, Polish, and heavily accented English.

Becky's stories of flight and migration fascinated me. It was a Polish farmer, she said, who—in 1921 with a civil war raging—smuggled my grandmother with her two children out of Ukraine and into Poland on his horse-drawn cart covered with a bed of straw. In recompense, she gave the Polish farmer the family samovar.

I loved watching my grandmother light Friday night candles—eyes closed, chanting singsong Hebrew and gesturing both arms in wide circles toward her heart to embrace the light. She told tales of "dream peddlers," traveling Jewish merchants who passed through her village selling pots and pans, zippers, combs, ribbons, and special books explaining the meaning of all one's dreams. She advised me to share my dreams "with only three smart people."

But on my mother's side, no one talked. Did they not know about their Polish past? Had it been forgotten so quickly?

I knew that my mother's mother, Sarah Konarska Weiskopf, came from a place in Poland called Czestochowa, and that my mother's father, Louis Weiskopf, came from a town nearby called Radomsk. The word tickled me as a child. *Ra-dumpsk!* I imagined Radomsk as an impoverished backwater, like Dogpatch in those *L'il Abner* cartoons we read on Sunday morning.

I remembered Grandma Sarah as an exhausted old woman who lived in a tiny apartment on Ocean Parkway in Brooklyn, tied her wisps of white hair into a bun secured with bobby pins, and, to my eternal fascination, hid rolls of dollar bills in her oven. Grandpa Louis died before I was born. Four of my generation—including me—were his namesakes.

Growing up in 1950s Los Angeles, in an orderly grid of postwar stucco houses, it wasn't as if I was surrounded by kids who could recite their ancestors back to the Mayflower. Had I queried my playmates, I would have learned that almost all of them had gaping holes in their family histories. My father, like many others on our block, had returned from the war—in his case, combat in the Pacific. The priorities were building economic security, starting families, launching businesses. My dad's new pharmacy in Culver City was open 9:00 a.m. to 9:00 p.m., and he was always there. My mother had three young children to supervise, including my sister who had polio. Being severed from one's family past wasn't supposed to matter.

But at least *I* knew the names of my grandparents. I thought it odd that my mother, if asked, didn't know the names of hers. Nor was she eager to try and fill in the blanks. If asked about her parents' families, names of her grandparents, uncles, aunts, she would only say, "They didn't make it out of Poland." Her huge gray-blue eyes watered, her voice constricted. She didn't want to talk about it.

An incident when I was eight shifted the axis of my world. I was watching my favorite TV show in the family room. My usually permissive mother barged in, abruptly switched the channel, and issued an order: "You watch this!" Then she left the room.

It was a black-and-white documentary on the camps, the naked bodies stacked like cordwood, the emaciated striped-suited survivors unrecognizable as human beings. I heard my mother sobbing on the other side of the closed kitchen door.

The next day I took odd and spontaneous revenge—ripping up the pages on Hitler in volume H of the *Encyclopedia Americana* shelved next to my desk in the fourth-grade classroom at La Ballona Elementary. A classmate—Jewish, no less—betrayed me. Later, after recess, while I lined up with the rest of my class, my teacher handed me the mutilated book and grimly dispatched her gold-star student to the principal's office.

From a framed portrait over the principal's desk, President Eisenhower bore silent witness to my interrogation. "Why this page? Why not this one?" I wanted to tell the principal that those dead people on television could be my unnamed relatives—great-aunts, uncles, cousins—in Radomsk, the town in Poland with the funny name. But I could not coax a single word to come out of my mouth.

My mother was summoned. She conferred with the principal behind the frosted glass door, emerging with red, wet eyes. She took my hand and we walked outside into the bright glare of the afternoon. We drove home in silence.

Low voices rumbled in my parents' room that night. My mother did not apologize for having made me watch the program about the camps, but she did let me stay home the next day, as if I had a fever. We never discussed the torn pages of the H encyclopedia volume. There were feelings neither of us could put into words.

IT WAS RABBI SINGER who summoned me to engage with that ache about my family's missing past in Poland.

In the winter of 1999, he called out of the blue. Don was excited. A woman in his congregation had made a donation so that a writer could attend the Bearing Witness Retreat at Auschwitz-Birkenau, and I was the writer, he said, who came to mind. The stipend would cover the cost of the retreat, the plane fare to Krakow, travel expenses. "After the retreat," he urged, "take time to travel in Poland."

I was not eager to go. Wasn't a week in Auschwitz a form of masochism? A communal identity based on a legacy of victimhood made me uneasy. The idea of meditating on the train tracks at Auschwitz-Birkenau terrified me.

I was disconcerted by Rabbi Singer's contention that the Poles had received a "bum rap"; but his other claim—that he felt a "startling affinity" to the Poles—intrigued me. I'd grown up with the phrase "Never forget" imprinted on my psyche. Its corollary was more elusive. Was it possible to remember—at least to recall—a world that existed *before* the calamity?

I accepted Rabbi Singer's invitation with a mixed sense of anticipation and dread. I took comfort knowing that he would be there. The retreat was almost ten months away.

SEVERAL MONTHS BEFORE DEPARTURE, I went to an exhibit at a local museum on the "History of the Jews in the West." A yellowed map of mid-nineteenth-century Europe caught my eye. I scanned the map. I found Radomsk. But where was Poland?

I knew that Poland had been partitioned in 1795—Prussia taking the areas in the west, Austria the south, Russia the east. It's one thing, however, to read about a country's historical fate at the hands of occupying powers and another thing entirely to *see* that it has vanished from the map.

My first history lesson about Poland sank in: it has no natural borders. No major mountains or rivers define its physical edge. Catastrophic geography plus ruthless neighbors equals invasion, occupation, oppression.

In 1918, at the Paris Peace Conference following World War I, Poland reemerged as a state after turbulent diplomacy. But during the 123 years (1795 to 1918) it was erased from the map of Europe, and later under Nazi and then Communist subjugation, Poland existed only in memory and through the verses of its exiled poets, in the nocturnes of its composers. The country became, as the great Polish poet Adam Zagajewski notes, "a chimera." Without a government, Poland's artists were its spiritual rulers, providing a sense of national identity.

For the citizens of this noncountry that had disappeared at the end of the eighteenth century, a strong independent Poland existed only as a state of mind. A French journalist referred to this conceptual Poland as "*un pays dans la tête,*" a country in one's head.

Until I went to Poland, I hadn't realized that it was a country in my head too.

CHAPTER 1

The Memory Book

Close to my departure for Poland, I typed "Radomsk" into Google. My hard drive rumbled. The words *Sefer-yizkor li-kehilat Radomsk veha-seviva* (The memorial book of the community of Radomsk and vicinity) materialized on my screen.

I was stunned. I never imagined that six hundred pages about the town of my ancestral past might be available at the click of a mouse.

The memorial books (*yizkor bukher*) were all written in the wake of the Shoah. Few of them had been translated from the original Yiddish and Hebrew. That was one reason why descendants of Polish Jews—like me, not versed in those languages—were excluded from this extraordinary effort in memory gathering, cut off from our ancestral past.

But I was fortunate. A dedicated New Yorker named Gloria Berkenstat Freund, whose mother came from Nowo-Radomsk (the name of the town under Russian rule), was hard at work translating the Yiddish sections of the Radomsk Yizkor. As Gloria completed a chapter, she posted it online. It was like reading a serial novel. Over the next several months, I downloaded pages.

I visited Gloria at her Upper West Side apartment near Julliard. She was a slim, elegant woman in her sixties. Wire-rimmed glasses framed a serious, delicate face. She sat down at a computer in her office and within minutes she pulled up the name of my great-grandfather Kopel (Yakob) Konarski, and the whereabouts of the graves of my maternal grandparents in Mount Hebron Cemetery in Queens, in a section reserved for Radomskers. Gloria had recently bought herself a plot.

I associated *genealogy* with a friend's father who was forever firming up his lineage to William the Conqueror. Gloria's dedication to family history was mystifying. Her relatives often asked her, "Did you find anyone famous? Anyone important?" Gloria believed every person she uncovered was important; she was "giving testimony to their lives."

My visit to Gloria in New York was part of a tradition of Radomskers and descendants of Radomskers seeking each other out. The Nowo-Radomsker Society in the United States was founded in New York on February 6, 1898. The first sixteen members, the yizkor duly records, "held their first meeting in the apartment of Schlomo Zilberzatz." Every Radomsker landsman (townsperson) and landsmen from towns in the vicinity could join upon payment of one dollar in dues.

Over the next decades, when new immigrants from Nowo-Radomsk arrived in New York, "they found an address to which they could turn." Members of the Nowo-Radomsker Society tried to provide help to every member in need and—by sending funds to Nowo-Radomsk—they played a crucial role in the lives of those who remained behind. They were "like a big family. . . . When someone had a happy occasion, everyone rejoiced. And when, G-d forbid, there was bad luck, everyone shared in the grief."

There were no photos in the digital version of the Radomsk Yizkor, but I located an original in Los Angeles in the archives of the Simon Wiesenthal Center. A librarian took my request, disappeared into the stacks, and reemerged with a thick, oversized book.

Embossed on the maroon leather cover was a synagogue in flames. I carefully turned the brittle paper to page 501, a photo of the 1916 Relief Committee for the Jews of Nowo-Radomsk. There in the second row was a dapper, mustachioed young man: my grandfather Louis.

The authorship of the Radomsk Yizkor Book—like that of the more than one thousand other yizkor bukher published for other Eastern European communities—was a wholly democratic enterprise with "some one hundred collaborators, most of them townspeople, of all strata and of different ages." Just a few were writers. Others were housewives, carpenters, watch repairmen, butchers, doctors. The contributors were scattered around the globe: New York, Toronto, Tel Aviv, Buenos Aires.

Bringing the memorial book to fruition over twenty years required "an inconceivable super human effort," wrote one editor. That effort showed. The number of voices, the sheer volume of information, was intimidating.

There were useful facts—for instance, how Radomsk got its name from the little Radomka River, which flows through the region. There were delightfully odd bits of information, like the one noting that Radomsk had fifty-two kosher butchers, all of them surnamed Ofman. There was mention of a satirical Yiddish newspaper, with the evocative title *Der krumlikher shpigel* (The crooked mirror), "in which Jewish life was featured with all its difficulties and achievements." One writer, Sarah Hamer-Jacklyn, recalled the organ-grinder in the town square. The monkey panhandled the crowd while his master creaked out a melody that young Sarah knew by heart:

Red little cherries tear me away
And green let me stay
Pretty girls take me,
And ugly ones let me go.
Oy! Woe is me!

The different modes of storytelling were confusing. Some voices were intimate and arresting, others pedantic and tedious. Some were passionate, some wracked with bitterness over what had been lost. The memorial book was a patchwork without a discernible pattern.

One thing was very clear: Radomsko was no backwater. In the period between the world wars, the town had literary circles, sports clubs, large communal libraries, and professional unions. The affection former inhabitants held for the town was palpable. The fortunes of the town burgeoned when the express rail line between Warsaw and Vienna was established, with Radomsko as a stop. In the mid-1800s, the Thonet Brothers of Vienna established a furniture factory in the town. I had Thonet bentwood chairs in my dining room!

The city of Radomsk (its Yiddish name) endured while its rulers (and its suffixes) shifted. After Poland was partitioned in 1793, the city was at first under Prussian control. The Russians—who renamed the city Nowo-Radomsk—ruled from 1816 to 1914, when Austrian forces took the city. In 1918, when the Polish Republic was reestablished in the wake of World War I, Nowo-Radomsk once again became a Polish city: Radomsko.

But Poland's independence was short-lived. The regimes of Hitler and Stalin had found common ground, as historian Timothy Snyder writes, "in their mutual aspiration to destroy Poland." The Molotov-Ribbentrop Pact, negotiated in the Kremlin, sealed Poland's fate. At dawn on September 1, 1939, Nazi Germany invaded Poland from the north, south, and west. A few weeks later, the Soviets invaded Poland from the east.

From 1939 to 1945, Radomsko was part of the Generalgouvernment, under German occupation. By the end of June 1943, the Nazis declared Radomsko *Judenrein*, "free of Jews." Eighteen thousand Radomsko Jews had been deported or shot, part of the three million Polish Jews murdered by the end of the war. In the words of the great writer Rafael Scharf, himself a Polish Jew, "What flourished and what died in Poland was unique and unrepeatable."

Gloria Freund told me, "Any American Jew who says they didn't lose family in the Holocaust just doesn't know." I had no names for those family members lost in Radomsk, the ones who "never left Poland," the very mention of whom caused my mother tears.

Reading the yizkor whetted my curiosity to know more about what had preceded the cataclysm. My grandparents' town began to morph from black and white into color in my imagination. One writer recalled the main synagogue, completed in 1898: "the blue sky painted on the ceiling, with the stars, the small clouds, and the flying angels." Another rhapsodized that "when the lights were lit one got the impression of finding oneself in another world."

In the yizkor I encountered a lively Jewish community where assimilationists, traditionalists, communists, socialists, and Zionists lived their lives shoulder to shoulder with Polish Catholics, where a Polish Catholic painted the synagogue's blue ceiling and a Jewish tinsmith roofed the spires of the Catholic church.

The idea of going to Poland grew in its appeal. My extended family was not enthusiastic. My uncle Al, then ninety-three, wrote from Florida, "It is my understanding that all Weiskopfs and Konarskis in Radomsk and Czestochowa were killed in the Holocaust. Whether they were marched to Auschwitz or some other hellhole (with the help of the Poles) is unknown. Have a safe and good trip."

My grandmother Rebecca would have said, in Yiddish, "*Du darfst forn keyn Poyln punkt vi du darfst hobn a lokh in kop.*" (You need to go to Poland like you need a hole in the head.)

I could not yet articulate the reason, but I did need to go to Poland. The call from Rabbi Singer initiated a decade-long conversation with Polish compadres who were seeking the truth about the past, however painful, creating their own rituals to honor the memory of and teach their towns about the history of their lost Jewish neighbors. Though we had yet to meet, we were already reaching toward one another across an abyss of loss, constructing a collaborative skein of memory.

CHAPTER 2

Warum? Why?

Rabbi Singer, as it turned out, did not go to the Bearing Witness Retreat that fall in 2000. He was still exhausted from the previous trip, his fifth. Each time, it had taken him months to recover. For various reasons, none of my Zen Center friends who'd planned to go were able to follow through. I would have to make friends among strangers.

In the boarding lounge of the Zurich airport, I waited for my flight to Krakow to be called and speculated who among the milling passengers was on his or her way to attend a Zen retreat at Auschwitz. The gum-chewing teenager with the bright yellow backpack? Doubtful. The gray-haired woman in the green loden coat? Maybe. Certainly not the statuesque young brunette wearing high heels, tight jeans, and a fur coat, toting a shopping bag stuffed with duty-free cosmetics.

At takeoff, I zeroed in on a tall, pale, serious-looking man across the aisle from me. Thin, with curly salt-and-pepper hair, he wore wire-rimmed spectacles. As the plane accelerated, he sat ramrod straight, his long fingers gripping prayer beads, his eyes shut. After the stewardess delivered his special-order vegetarian meal, I leaned across the aisle and whispered, "Are you going to Auschwitz?"

He startled. How, he wanted to know, had I figured it out?

There were eighty-four of us—Americans, Germans, Poles, Swiss, Brits, Italians, Dutch, French, and Israelis. Every day during that week, morning and afternoon, no matter the weather, the entire group—Buddhists, Jews, Catholics, Protestants, Muslims, and one Native American from Pine Ridge, South Dakota—practiced sitting meditation together at Birkenau in two long, parallel lines, facing each other across the same railroad tracks where the infamous Doctor Mengele once made his life or death selections.

The natural beauty of Birkenau disturbed me. The documentaries I'd seen as a child were in black and white. Survivors' testimonies mentioned mud, dirty snow, and ice. Nothing prepared me for lush green grass carpeting the ground around the children's barracks or the shimmering gold leaves of birch trees (*Birkenau* is the German word for "birch") on the outskirts of the crematoria. Wounded land has a powerful will to heal over.

In our shared room at the Oswiecim youth hostel, my roommate Debra and I conferred on how many layers to wear that day. Silk long johns, lined jeans, turtlenecks, wool sweaters, Gore-Tex down jackets, fleece hats. The prisoners at Auschwitz-Birkenau labored outside without any protective clothing. They wore thin cotton in the winter and were lucky to have shoes.

We began each day at 7:00 a.m., meeting in small groups at the youth hostel. We sat in a circle of chairs and, if anyone managed to give voice to the complex emotions they were experiencing, to what they had observed, the rest of us listened.

"Speak from the heart," urged Eve Marko, our group leader. Her other piece of advice, based on past experiences at the retreat: "Take it all in now . . . sort it all out later."

Each morning at Birkenau, we pulled our meditation cushions out of a storage room and walked out along the railroad siding, the tracks where prisoners arrived after their harrowing journey in packed cattle cars. We carried red plastic bowls clipped to our belts or stored in our packs for the hot vegetable soup ladled out from the back of a truck at lunch by stout Polish farmwomen.

Andrzej, one of the Polish members of the Zen Peacemaker Order, cranked up an old air raid siren as a signal. The siren howled its melancholy crescendo before fading back to silence. Then, at each of the four cardinal points of the vast ellipse formed by the meditators, participants took turns chanting the names of those who died here at Auschwitz-Birkenau. The names came from a list compiled by the Gestapo.

Sometimes you heard the same name—many people in a family— over and over and over. Sometimes you heard the name of someone you knew back home, back in your "real" life. Glassner. Krasnow. Oschkowsky. Posner. Zweig. Zweig. Zweig. The list was long. There were plenty of names to go around. As I did not yet know the names of my own family members who had perished, I did not know to listen for Libeskinds or Wilhelms or Zilbermans.

I participated in prayer services led by imams and pastors, swamis, rabbis, and roshis. I joined rabbis wearing phylacteries and prayer shawls in chanting the name Allah thirty times. I sang hymns with the Swiss Protestants. I inhaled the scent of burning sweetgrass that the Lakota healer from Pine Ridge wafted around my body with an eagle feather. I gratefully absorbed his invocation: "I asked the grandfathers to pity those who died here, to honor those who died here. To honor those who lost loved ones they knew or did not know."

After two days of following the schedule of group rituals, Eve reminded us that we were free to go off on our own. "There are eighty-four participants here, and eighty-four different retreats."

Could I comprehend the sheer physical size of the place by walking the entire circumference? Under a gray sky, I walked slowly across the landscape of forlorn chimneys, muddy walkways, decomposing wooden barracks. I ended up in front of the brick building located on the grounds of what the inmates called Canada.

You were lucky if you worked in Canada, where slave laborers sorted the victims' confiscated possessions. You might scrounge some marmalade or bread or vodka. You could eat, but you'd also go mad. And you'd soon be a victim yourself—the Germans could not afford witnesses to their crimes.

I paced back and forth in front of the brick building. A metallic taste of anger burned my throat. Why? *Warum?* The writer Primo Levi asked that same question early in his internment at Auschwitz, when a German guard snatched out of his hand an icicle he'd hoped might slake his thirst. *Warum?* The guard's reply? "*Hier ist kein warum.*" (There is no why here.)

There is no relief; there is no answer. But why?

I stomped the gravel with each step, so absorbed I didn't at first notice I was not alone. Not far away, Allan Whiteman—whom I'd met on the plane from Zurich—sat cross-legged on the grass in meditation.

The restless souls of both victims and perpetrators inhabited his body as he meditated that day. "Packed in like a subway car," he told me later. "They wanted to talk. Some wanted to scream, howl." The experience wasn't mystical or metaphysical, he insisted, rather as mundane as could be. "They told me where to go. I was called like you call a dog. You couldn't ignore them . . . you could not turn it off."

The next morning when we all sat down together on the railroad tracks, I tried meditating on the word *why*. Breathe in why, breathe out why. No answers. More questions. I watched my anger form and dissolve, form and dissolve.

My mind resisted a simple truth: the elite SS officers who planned the genocide and the lowly guards who carried it out were human beings, not monsters. It was much easier to think of perpetrators as separate from the human sphere. In Rwanda, neighbors attacked neighbors in a murderous rage. In Bosnia, the snipers firing on Sarajevo from the surrounding hillsides were neighbors of the people they were firing on.

In an essay on ethnic strife in Kosovo, the Polish priest and philosopher Józef Tischner writes, "When reflected in a crooked mirror the face of a neighbor is distorted. The neighbor is always worse than we imagine, he is false, treacherous evil." Any ideology can be that mirror. The Third Reich propagandists, the Rwandan politicians, the Serbian nationalist media were all adept manipulators of mirrors.

What allows human beings to turn off their conscience? What does it take to see clearly—to divert yourself from the lynch mob, to defy the system, to see through the propaganda?

Rudolf Höss, the commandant of Auschwitz, perfected the killing capacity of the ovens at Birkenau while living just outside the grounds of the camp with his wife and four young children. I'd walked past his attractive two-story brick house, surrounded by a garden where late autumn roses bloomed.

Under German occupation, any Pole who sought to save the life of a Jew risked not only his or her own life but the lives of everyone in his or her family as well. Of all the countries in Nazi-occupied Eastern Europe, Poland was subjected to the most severe and sadistic repression. Yet some found a way: Irena Sendler, a Polish Catholic social worker, managed to save the lives of more than twenty-five hundred Jews—most of them children—imprisoned in the Warsaw Ghetto. "I was taught that if you see a person drowning," she said, "you must jump into the water to save them, whether you can swim or not."

Why does one person reject the view reflected in the crooked mirror and another accept the distortion?

Breathe in why.

Breathe out why.

So simple. So difficult.

CHAPTER 3

In Block 11

In the evenings, at the Oswiecim youth hostel, I longed to sit immobile with a hot cup of tea or, better yet, a cold beer. This never happened.

One night, after an austere meal of cabbage, rice, and scrambled tofu, all eighty-four of us boarded buses for the two-mile drive back to the camp to hear a talk by an Auschwitz survivor.

Enthusiasm was in short supply. We were all bone tired; an incident earlier in the evening had wrung me out.

I was reading on my cot when my roommate, Debra, burst into the room, distraught. She'd asked Dorota, a young Polish woman, to translate some letters written in Polish by her father—Arnold Unger—when he was fifteen, soon after his release from Dachau. For two hours, she listened:

> After three years of dangers, bondage, dark roadways, my memories break my heart. . . . The long-awaited freedom, instead of happiness, fills me with sorrow and sadness and terrible pain. Without joy or hope for a future, broken in spirit.

Debra paced between our cots then collapsed onto the floor, groaning. It wasn't right that the sun was shining on these winter days in Birkenau. It wasn't fair that we had warm food and dry beds. It wasn't right. It was all a blasphemy of her father's experience.

"I don't want this story to be mine," she sobbed. Her father's words had left her fearful of going to sleep, afraid of waking in the morning with a broken heart.

—w—

WE DISEMBARKED AT THE camp under a moonless sky and walked onto the deserted grounds of Auschwitz 1. Upstairs in the drafty attic of a brick building called Block 11, a tall, elderly man leaned against a pillar, waiting. He had sad, drooping eyes and the lined face of an eloquent clown. His name was August Kowalczyk. Recently retired, he'd been an actor and director of some note at the Polish National Theater in Warsaw. He'd played Cyrano de Bergerac, Mefisto in *Faust*.

August waited patiently while everyone settled in, or tried to. We were packed in, knee against knee. Why couldn't we have gathered to listen to August's story in a room with some heat? I glanced over at Debra. She sat shivering, her eyes downcast.

"The question . . ." August began, "is why have I come here? I arrived here the first time to leave through the chimney. But I did not leave through the chimney, I left to freedom. The second time, I come here to bear witness. I try to live up to that role."

In 1940, when he was nineteen, August—a Polish Catholic—was arrested by the Germans while attempting to join the Polish army being formed in France. He endured a five-month interrogation by the Gestapo, who deported him to Auschwitz. There he joined the very first prisoners at the camp—a group of Polish intelligentsia (including some Jews) from the Gestapo prison at Tarnow, who had arrived six months earlier.

August was number 6,804—the six thousand eight hundred fourth prisoner out of what would eventually be three million inmates at Auschwitz.

Block 11, known as the Death Block, was the most feared place at Auschwitz 1. Outside Block 11 was the wall where prisoners were summarily executed. In the cellar of Block 11 were the *Stehbunkers*, the infamous "standing bunkers" where four prisoners were forced to stand all night in an airless cell that measured three feet by three feet.

During his eighteen months at Auschwitz, August toiled as a slave laborer. In his nightmares he was always running, the guards always pursuing him. The center of his nightmare was always Auschwitz. In the dream, he didn't succeed in escaping. In real life, he did.

While laboring on a drainage ditch on June 10, 1942, August's work detail of fifty prisoners took advantage of a guard's distraction to flee. "Nine of us, including myself, got away," he said, "thirteen were shot that day, and twenty were recaptured." On the following day, when none of the remaining prisoners in the camp would reveal who organized the escape, the camp commander personally shot seventeen prisoners. He then ordered three hundred Poles from the penal company driven to a bunker at Birkenau where they were gassed.

Dorota, who had earlier translated Debra's letters, was the patient translator for August's long talk. If I hadn't been tightly packed in next to my fellow listener, I would have keeled over. There was only so much I could absorb in a day. My butt ached. My teeth chattered. My goose-down parka was insufficient insulation. She continued with August's story.

In reprisal for an earlier escape attempt by another inmate, August explained, he had been hung from a pillar, "the punishment post." He smacked his large hand against the wooden pillar behind him.

I lurched to full attention.

There was a reason we had to hear August's story in *this* place, not in some comfortable lounge with upholstered chairs. It had happened *right here*. *This* man was strung up on *this* pillar and lived to tell us the tale.

"Incredible pain," he continued. "Sweat falling onto the floor. Two other men hung from the other two pillars in the room. An SS officer sat next to a heater with his dog, reading the newspaper. One of the hanging prisoners yelled out, 'Mother, you whore! Why did you give birth to me?' before he lost consciousness. They put him on a table and the guards beat him. When he regained consciousness, they hung him again."

August's chest crumpled forward slightly. The flesh on his face grew slack. "August is very tired," Dorota advised. "He will take just a few questions."

Eve raised her hand. Her aunt had died here at Auschwitz. "August," she asked politely, "you said that it made survival more possible to know that there was family, community on the outside who loved you, were waiting for you. Was this also true for the Jews?"

August answered. Dorota translated, "No, this was not the same for the Jews. The Jews were resigned to their fate."

No more time for questions. People helped one another up off the floor, shook out numb, stiff legs. Everyone wanted to get warm, to get some rest.

As we walked out, into the cold night air, I was zapped by a bolt of anger. I could feel the blood rushing into my head. Had August really said what I thought he'd said? How dare he?! The person walking beside me was also agitated, muttering to himself. It was dark, but I recognized the voice—a psychologist named John, also from LA. "Why didn't I challenge August about his last statement?" he fumed. "It's a canard!"

He was right. The anti-Semitic stereotype among Polish Home Army fighters was that Jews were passive, would not fight. Yet those who said the Jews "allowed" themselves to be led "like sheep to the slaughter" were misinformed, or they blasphemed. Or, their understanding had not been updated from the immediate postwar period.

People used the phrase "like sheep to slaughter" before they understood how the Nazis lied at every part of the extermination process, how they brutalized people, starved them, robbed them of their dignity, duped people into believing they were going for resettlement. Those going to their death in the ovens were handed bars of so-called soap for "showers," deceived to the very end.

Jewish partisans joined resistance movements against the Nazis. There were armed uprisings in the Warsaw ghetto, in Treblinka, in Czestochowa, in Bialystok, in Minsk. For the Sonderkommando uprising in Birkenau in 1944, the inmates—who shoveled out the ashes of their fellow Jews before their own certain death—set Crematorium 4 on fire. Jewish women prisoners smuggled gunpowder for the uprising—obtained from the munitions plant where they worked as slave laborers—in their hollowed molars.

Hiding or evading deportation was itself a potent form of resistance, and resistance could have unintended consequences. On November 7, 1938, a young man named Herschel Grynszpan, whose family came from Radomsko, walked into the German foreign office in Paris where he shot Nazi foreign service officer Ernst vom Rath twice in the abdomen. Vom Rath died two days later. His death provided the Nazis with justification for a massive, already-planned attack—the infamous Kristallnacht, "Night of Broken Glass," against the Jewish community inside the Third Reich.

The Radomsk Yizkor is not ambivalent about whether Herschel Grynszpan was a heroic martyr or a misguided pariah: "The Jews of Nowo-Radomsk were proud that from their environment had come the avenger."

JOHN AND I WERE not the only ones who were upset that night after August's talk in Block 11. In the dark there were many murmurs, which reverberated throughout the next day as well. In our morning council meeting, I wanted to argue. I wanted give and take. Eve decided no, we would stay with the council form. She understood people were angry. That night, she told us, a meeting for all eighty-four participants in the retreat was scheduled in one of the wooden barracks at Birkenau. We would speak one by one so that we could really listen to one another.

It began to rain lightly when we climbed down off the buses in front of the gates of Birkenau. There were no night lights and no moon. Few people had flashlights. People groped along in the dark. Jakov, a Dutchman, escorted elderly Zofia, a Polish survivor of Ravensbruck, trying to prevent her from falling into a muddy ditch.

The wind howled. The barracks at Birkenau have flimsy wooden walls, no insulation. We plopped our cushions on the cold ground where the wooden bunks for inmates used to be. Participants placed votive candles on the concrete structure—once the inmates' latrine—extending down the middle of the barracks. Signs everywhere admonished, "No candles in the barracks." There were no museum officials or security guards around anywhere. I couldn't shake the fear of being trapped in a fire in a wooden barracks in Birkenau.

The lit candles dispelled the gloom. Faces glowed in the soft flickering light. A microphone was set up at the far end of the hall. Eve spoke first. Her voice, as ever, was calm and measured. People could speak about whatever they wished, she said. The idea was simply to speak from the heart. "Stay with the difficulties," she urged, then opened with a question: "When someone makes anti-Semitic, or anti-German, or anti-Polish remarks, how will we respond?" I looked around. August was not in the group tonight.

John, who'd been so stirred up the night before, approached the microphone. "I was stricken to hear—in the most unexpected place— a falsehood, a demeaning representation. I say to August, 'Check the facts. Check the facts.'"

One of the Polish women entreated the assembly "not to let the flames of anger become hate." She tried to give context to August's remarks. "We Polish people are different from Jewish people. Poles think of themselves as heroes because of our struggle, our background. We are filled with these stories about resistance from childhood."

The subject of resignation and passivity was a potent issue for all Poles—Catholic and Jewish both—in the context of their unprecedented historic persecution. Armed resistance to occupiers was a long tradition. The Jews, a subordinated minority within Poland, historically chose accommodation as a survival tactic.

Though Poland had been home to Jews as far back as the twelfth century, they were always a distinctive presence. They had different customs, religious rituals, dietary restrictions. Many spoke only Yiddish. Whether, how, and when the Jews saw themselves as Poles and whether, how, and when the Poles regarded Poland's Jews as Polish has always been a complicated equation.

Suddenly the door to the barracks swung open and two burly security guards stood backlit in the opening. Were we busted?

The guards were escorting Andrew—a disabled participant—to the barracks. He'd been stumbling around in the dark without a flashlight. Having delivered Andrew the officials vanished, to my disappointment, concerned neither with our after-hours presence nor potential fire danger to us and these historic structures. Council continued.

Then Bettina spoke. She was a young German woman I'd noticed all week, the one with the tender, stricken face.

At first she spoke in a subdued, girlish voice. "Today when I chanted names, I added twenty names of Jews who were murdered from my town. My town in northern Germany had 120 Jews at the time of the war. Three survived. They were deported from the town in October 1941. One hundred were deported to Holland. Twenty others went directly to Auschwitz. The mayor of the town arranged the deportations. He took their property." She paused, took a breath. "He was my grandfather."

When she'd first arrived at Auschwitz, haunted by the restless soul of her grandfather and the souls of the 117 Jews who had died, Bettina hadn't been sure she wanted to live. As she spoke, her voice gained confidence. "The more I begin to understand, the more I can ask for forgiveness. May these wounds never end to hurt." She sat down.

I was stunned by what I'd heard, exhilarated that we could allow each other the uninterrupted space in which to say it.

The last speaker of the evening was Levana, an Israeli. August was not an evil man, she told us. He was not an anti-Semite. "This incident invites us to have a new language," she proclaimed. "We are on the verge of finding this new language to talk to each other."

Her excitement was contagious.

CHAPTER 4

Among the Living

My attempts to call my husband in Los Angeles from the pay phone in the Oswiecim youth hostel were futile. For the most emotionally intense week of my life, I'd been completely out of touch with my closest confidant. I'd have to wait until the retreat ended. As the week progressed, it became increasingly urgent that I see Lloyd's breathing, teasing self. When he stepped into the lobby of my hotel in Krakow, jet-lagged from a seventeen-hour journey from LA, I flew across the worn carpet and burrowed into his embrace.

The next afternoon we rented a car and set off for Radomsko via Czestochowa, the industrial town where my maternal grandmother was born. Our hotel, a 1960s Communist-era high rise, was located across a busy boulevard from Jasna Góra, Czestochowa's most famous—perhaps its only—attraction.

The Monastery of Jasna Góra ("bright mountain") dominates the entire town of Czestochowa. Every year millions of pilgrims from all over Poland visit this most important shrine of Polish Catholicism. During the German occupation, Hitler forbade the faithful to make pilgrimages there, but many did anyway as a sign of defiance. During the Cold War, the shrine was a center of anti-Communist resistance. The beloved Polish pope delivered several important homilies from a specially constructed platform on the grounds of the monastery during his reign.

For six hundred years the monastery has been the home of the famous Black Madonna icon—Our Lady of Czestochowa.

There are hundreds of legends about the Czestochowa Madonna. One of the earliest, dating back to 1430, tells how robbers broke into the monastery to steal and vandalize the precious image, which they broke into three pieces. Adding insult to injury, one of the robbers inflicted two gashes on the Virgin's face. Raising his dagger to strike again, he dropped dead.

The intimate chapel was thronged with worshipers on the weekday morning we visited. There were no pews: all of us stood facing the icon. Most worshipers fingered their rosaries, murmured prayers. Over the years, generations of these believers had left evidence of the icon's miraculous healing powers. Hanging from the chapel's walls were abandoned crutches, braces, and canes, all darkened with a patina of soot from candles and incense.

The Black Madonna did look sorrowful, with jagged scars like tears on her dark brown face. The icon, framed in silver, hung high over an ornate black baroque altar. Pearls, sapphires, rubies, and diamonds encrusted the Madonna's midnight-blue robe. The Christ child's robe was embroidered with gold thread. Thousands of necklaces of hefty red amber beads adorned the walls surrounding the altar.

I did not find it comforting to be in the presence of the Black Madonna of Czestochowa. My mother never forgot to remind us that each spring—in the hazy imagined Poland of our grandparents' early lives—pogroms against Jews clustered around the Easter holiday celebrating Jesus's resurrection. For centuries, Catholic liturgy singled out the Jews for responsibility for the death of Jesus Christ.

I learned this firsthand as a young child, when two girls from our neighborhood, wearing the plaid uniforms of St. Augustine's School, informed me that I'd killed their Lord. I reported this stunning news to my mother. How had I killed Jesus? When? She responded with such uncharacteristic ferocity that I regretted having let her in on the secret.

No, the Madonna's sorrowful visage did nothing to comfort me. Listening to the sweet counterpoint between the priests and the faithful, I heard my mother's voice whispering in my head: "The Poles never prayed for the Jews in Radomsk!" If they did, no doubt they prayed for them to find the true way to Christ.

—ɯ—

"IT'S BEEN MY BELIEF for some time," writes the essayist S. I. Wisenberg, "that part of the American trauma is our shared sacrifice of leaving behind. Language, family, community, land. Gone. Gone. Gone."

Now I was in Radomsko, an actual place. Here. Here. Here. Yet I had no idea what I hoped to find in this provincial Polish town. The only features I recognized from old photographs were the Catholic church and the clock tower on the old town hall. It was no use looking for the beautiful Radomsko synagogue with its blue ceiling and painting of the zodiac. The Germans blew it up in 1941. I knew no one who lived here now. My grandfather Louis Weiskopf, for whom I was named, died before I was born. I knew next to nothing about him and, now that I wished to know more, there were few I could ask.

Louis Weiskopf, the son of a rebbe, was a devout, good-humored Jew who davened (prayed) every morning in the traditional tefillin, leather straps, which he wrapped around his arms, a small leather box containing scriptures on his forehead.

Uncle Al had written me that his father Louis's reputation with his landsmen was based on his being a *shtarker*, a "strong man." Once when the circus came to town, he volunteered to wrestle with its strong man. I imagined my grandfather stepping into the ring to face his opponent in a crowded canvas tent while his friends cheered.

During the time Louis was a young man in Nowo-Radomsk, the famous Jewish strongman Zishe Breitbart was performing with the little circuses that crisscrossed Poland. Breitbart, dubbed "The Ironman," was a blacksmith's son from the city of Lodz. Jewish children all over Eastern Europe idolized him.

Whether or not it was the Ironman my grandfather challenged, the story—passed down to his son—shows the man's moxie. Louis took risks (though they rarely panned out). In 1913, together with a group of his Radomsker landsleit from New York, he bought part ownership in a watermelon farm in Alabama, sight unseen. Louis, Sarah, and their two young sons, Simon (Cy) and Albert (Al), took the train south to the small town of Bay Minette, where Louis also opened a cabinetry shop.

Uncle Al told a story of his brother being struck by lightning during an Alabama thunderstorm, of running, terrified, from his lifeless brother to fetch his father. Louis bent over his inert eldest son and shook him hard. "Come back!" he commanded, and he did.

Both the farm and the shop went bust, and the Weiskopf family returned to New York. "From the slums back to the slums," Al laughed.

These were the few facts I knew about my maternal grandparents' past. Within the next year, I learned more from a woman named Laura Mendley. In the course of her own family research, Laura sought out Gloria Freund, the translator of the Radomsk Yizkor Book. Gloria noted that Laura and I were both researching the same family name and put us in touch.

Laura was my second cousin. Our families had lost contact. Our grandmothers, Rose and Sarah Konarska, were sisters. When my young grandparents emigrated from Nowo-Radomsk, Laura's grandmother Rose traveled with them aboard the *Furnessia*, a Scottish freighter. They arrived at Ellis Island on September 11, 1906. Another sister, Leah, arrived later.

Laura and I began to put the pieces together. I learned for the first time all the names of my Polish great-grandparents. Grandma Sarah's parents were named Kopel Konarski and Dvojra Libeskind Konarska. *Libeskind* means "love child." My grandfather, Louis, was the son of Abram Wajskopf and Golda Zylberman Wajskopf. My siblings and I had never heard these names before.

Our amazement deepened when we learned that our grandmothers had a fourth sister—Fayga Konarska, "the kid." In 1911, five years after two of her older sisters emigrated, she married Fayvel Wilhelm, a tailor from Nowo-Radomsk. No one in the family had known that Fayga even existed.

Tucked into a 1935 diary of her mother's cousin, Laura had found, were several addresses in Nowo-Radomsk. There was an address for Yankel Grynszpan, grandfather of the firebrand Herszel Grynszpan, the legendary young assassin of the Nazi officer vom Rath. There was an undecipherable address for Fayga and Fayvel Wilhelm.

Perhaps Fayga had stayed behind to look after the elderly parents? Laura, born in 1927, remembered from childhood that her grandmother sent packages of clothing to Poland and received letters in return. "Then it stopped."

Though it was nearly sixty years after the end of the war, our new-found curiosity about lost relatives came at an auspicious moment. In newly democratic Poland, regional archives were opening up for the first time. An enterprising Radomsko descendant, a music professor named Dan Kazez, organized the Czestochowa-Radomsk Area Research Group. He sought contributions from Radomsko landsleit all over the country to cover the cost for a researcher to type archival lists in the Radomsko City Hall. Donations flowed in. E-mails began flying.

As the anonymous Polish typist clacked away at his typewriter in Radomsko, my inbox flooded with my great-grandfather's marriage record, cemetery archives showing that my great-grandmother Golda Zylberman Wajskopf was buried somewhere in the Radomsko cemetery, the 1841–1860 Book of Residents, the 1939 Radomsko List of Jewish Residents, 1929–1934 identity cards.

One day Dan Kazez sent a message: "This is a list of persons who perished in the Holocaust in Radomsko. We have found no other copy of this document anywhere in the world." I scanned down to the *w*'s.

Wilhelm, Genya
Wilhelm, Lulek
Wilhelm, Fela
Wilhelm, Hershlik
Wilhelm, Rozya
Wilhelm, Henok
Wilhelm, Shrpinca, and children
Wilhelm, Aron
Wilhelm, Yentla
Wilhelm, Fayvel
Wilhelm, Fayga
Wilhelm, Bluma

There they were. We'd found them and lost them in the space of weeks. My aunt Fayga, her husband. And the others? Siblings? Children? Grandchildren? Cousins? Nephews? Nieces? How old were Yentla and Bluma? And Lulek, a beautiful Polish diminutive for Lucian.

It hadn't occurred to me that *not* knowing the names of family who "hadn't made it out of Poland" conferred immunity to a specific kind of pain. Washing dishes or driving to work, my mind wandered to the lost Wilhelms.

THE LOVELY NINETEENTH-CENTURY TOWN hall on the corner of the main square was now the home of the Radomsko Regional History Museum. During the German occupation, the building housed the Gestapo torture chamber. After 1945, the Communist authorities used it as a prison for members of the AK, Poland's army of resistance against the Nazis.

We were the only visitors that cold winter day, perhaps the first in a long while. Our entry caused a minor flurry. None of the staff spoke English, but after a brief huddle, they received us graciously. One of the women secured a large clutch of keys, and motioned for us to follow her up the stairs. She opened up the display rooms and turned on the lights.

We walked through the museum's permanent exhibits. All the wall texts were in Polish. We viewed collections of pottery shards from archeological digs, displays of nineteenth-century butter churns, exhibits of roof thatching and farm implements. Each time we left a room, our guide turned off the lights, then flipped on the switch in the next.

We paused in front of photos of Radomsko citizens deported to Siberia under Russian rule, infantry helmets from the First World War, then moved on to the displays about World War II. There were gruesome pictures of Polish partisans from the town, standing in front of pits before their execution by German soldiers.

The guide paused in front of the one glass case containing artifacts from the Jewish community of Radomsko: a set of tefillin, just like the one belonging to Grandpa Louis, in an embroidered velvet bag; a pair of silver kiddush cups; silver candlesticks; and two small oil paintings. Just one glass case?

The two paintings evoked the ambience of the town's prewar Jewish life: well-worn wooden benches in an intimate little prayer house; a water carrier lugging his bucket up a crooked staircase rising from a cobblestone street. The name of the artist was Natan Szpigel.

The yizkor revealed that Szpigel had achieved some success in his day, exhibiting in galleries in Warsaw, Lwów, and London. He married a local eye doctor and they had two children. The Szpigels had the means to leave Radomsko in 1939, but they decided to stay. Szpigel's rationale: "In a war, no one knows when he will die." A Nazi officer shot the painter's youngest son for sport. Szpigel, his wife, and other son died in Treblinka.

The yizkor also offered a clue to the provenance of those two Szpigel paintings in the Radomsko museum. After liberation, a camp survivor named Mrs. Kesselman returned to Radomsko and found, in place of her two Szpigel paintings, two portraits of German soldiers displayed on the wall of her dining room. On the back of each canvas, she discovered splatters of blood. Suspicious, she began scratching at the paint "and then the real pictures were revealed—two images by Natan Szpigel." A painting hidden in a painting.

We stepped outside the museum. It had been my intention to look for the Radomsko Jewish cemetery. But it was suddenly clear that I didn't want to spend the little time we had in Radomsko with the dead.

So Lloyd and I strolled arm in arm down Reymonta, the street where my courting grandparents promenaded, where young mothers pushed their prams to show off their new babies. I bought a turquoise beret at the market, tart apples from a local farmer. We eyed jars of pickled wild mushrooms we would have loved to try but didn't dare. We browsed a stationery store for notebooks and stood in line at the post office for stamps. We walked near the little Radomka River, where traveling circuses set up their tents and a young Louis Weiskopf, my grandfather, stepped forward to wrestle the strong man.

For now, that was enough.

THE HUNDREDS OF RADOMSKERS who collaboratively wrote the yizkor book agreed on one central admonition: "Please! Descendants of Radomsk, wherever you are in the world; teach your children and grandchildren about our town and its people."

On my first reading, it didn't cross my mind that the varied authors of the Radomsk Memorial Book could be addressing me. Me? A secular American Jew who attends Yom Kippur services at a Zen Center? I don't read Hebrew. The only Friday night prayer I've been able to convince my areligious Jewish husband to recite with me is from Joyce's *Finnegan's Wake*. I have no children of my own to teach. My connection to this town has been obscured by emigration, time, and trauma.

My unconscious, however, was undaunted by the intangibility of an evaporated life. Soon after I returned home from that trip in 2000, I dreamed about Radomsko. Not only was it *my* first dream about the town, but I can claim with reasonable confidence that no one in my family had dreamed about Radomsko for at least a generation.

In the dream, Lloyd and I walked the streets of Radomsko. On a side street, we found the Great Synagogue solid and unscathed. It was an impressive old stone building with a handsome arch defining its portals. We walked through the archway, but there was nothing inside. There *was* no inside. The front wall of the building was a façade.

We found ourselves in open space, standing on an intimate town square in a comfortable neighborhood of old half-timbered townhouses in soft pastel colors. There were leafy sycamores and paths leading off into surrounding meadows. Through the windows I saw, to my astonishment, several of our friends: sculptors, dancers, filmmakers, a jazz pianist. They were all absorbed in their work. Children darted across the square. Savory cooking smells wafted out of kitchens. Of course Lloyd and I wanted to live there. It was familiar, embracing.

In writing about his Jewish heritage, the Egyptian writer Edmond Jabès uses the phrase "permanent rupture." "I don't believe in continuity," he wrote. "Continuity is made of ruptures, and we ourselves are this rupture."

When I woke up, I realized that the writers of the Memorial Book of the Community of Radomsk, *were* addressing me.

I was the rupture. I was the continuity.

CHAPTER 5

Wannsee

In June 2002, a year and a half after the retreat, I stepped out of a taxicab onto the gravel driveway of a stone villa in a leafy Berlin suburb called Wannsee. I entered the lobby, suitcase in hand, unsure of myself, out of place. I knew nobody.

I'd gone to Birkenau as a skeptic. I came away confused and inspired by the dialogue among the interfaith and international gathering. On that dramatic last gathering in the barracks, I'd discovered my lack of knowledge about Polish history and the Poles' own narrative of resistance, as well as the encumbrance of my own unexamined prejudices. The desire to unravel those prejudices brought me to this special gathering in Wannsee.

The name Wannsee is forever linked to an infamous gathering on January 20, 1942, when the Nazi elite, under the chairmanship of Reinhard Heydrich, head of the Reich security office, and his "Jewish expert," Adolf Eichmann, gathered in another villa overlooking the lake. The buffet lunch was delicious, the cigars and Cognac superb, the work pressing. The officers were there to discuss implementation of the "final solution to the Jewish question."

I was here for the biannual conference of a group whose very existence would have dumbfounded those Nazi officers. One by One was founded in Germany in the early nineties by descendants of "survivors, perpetrators, bystanders, and resisters" to explore the legacy of the Holocaust and the Nazi regime. In their literature, they defined themselves as "a group of people called upon—for particular reasons—to break 'the conspiracy of silence'" endemic in postwar German society.

Primo Levi wrote of "the deathly silence of the perpetrators." There was also the conflicted silence of the survivors, who wished to spare their offspring from learning about their humiliation, their torment. Teams from One by One visited German schools to lead workshops; members from both the perpetrator side and the victim side spoke to students. Another team from One by One had recently led workshops with Croat and Muslim women in Bosnia, exploring the possibilities for reconciliation after the bloody war in the former Yugoslavia.

Among the participants were the granddaughter of a German antifascist, the grandniece of the SS commandant of France, a South African woman whose baptized Jewish father was murdered in Auschwitz, a former member of the Wehrmacht, and an elderly Polish survivor of Ravensbruck. There was a sturdy German Jewish woman who wore a bowler hat on her shaved head and worked with tough neo-Nazi teenagers in Berlin, as well as a Dutch woman whose Jewish parents had managed to place her, a baby of nine months, with Christian neighbors before they were deported.

Most of the people gathered here had listened to one another's stories during intense, weeklong dialogue groups in years past. Some of them had heard apologies offered for the first time. There was a familial air, like a reunion of summer campers, among those who'd traveled from New York and Johannesburg and Berlin.

At breakfast, I learned that the polite, white-haired gentleman sitting beside me had once been a member of the Wehrmacht. The hair on my arm stood up. I couldn't wait to leave the table. I confided my distress to a grandmotherly South African woman named Bina. Her Jewish father had died in Auschwitz. "Aha! You must mean our dear Otto," she said. "If you knew his story, you wouldn't feel you wanted to avoid him."

Otto was one of three brothers. The oldest brother was an enthusiastic Nazi until he was sent to the Russian front, witnessed the burning of Russian villages, and was commanded to join the Einsatzgruppen in the murder of Russian Jews. He protested the horror, was sent to punishment camp, then committed suicide. The youngest brother enlisted early in the war and died immediately at the Russian front. Near the end of the war, Otto was seventeen. The Germans needed cannon fodder. He was ordered into the Wehrmacht. The alternative was a punishment camp.

Bina visited Auschwitz, where her father was murdered, together with Otto. There, she told me, "I experienced the grief of the victims and the grief of the perpetrators. I realized that grief is grief."

What kind of moral choices could one expect of a seventeen-year-old boy in Nazi Germany? Sophie Scholl, a German college student, was only twenty-one when she was executed for her participation in White Rose, the nonviolent German Resistance movement. Bina's story, however, eased some of my wariness about Otto.

We convened that afternoon in a room with French windows opening onto a view of the lake. Less than a year had passed since the terrorist attacks on the World Trade Center, and participants from Europe and the United States struggled to find language to discuss their responses. An East German woman described how she wept as she watched the burning towers—and how bewildered she was to hear her teenage son cheering in the next room "because the Americans got what they deserved."

The woman sitting beside me in the circle of chairs spoke next. Her beguiling outfit suggested she was French: black leggings with zippered ankles, a black stretchy tunic with asymmetrical pockets. I was wrong; she was American. "Right after the planes hit the towers," she said, "I dreamed that I—that my whole life—was in a bullet heading a zillion miles an hour to Afghanistan. Just before I got there, I turned into a vitamin."

The group collectively startled at her pungent condensation of images. She continued undeterred. "My explanation of this dream is that the bullet and its speed were my extreme *anger* at everything and everybody responsible. But my unconscious compassion won. I really believe that even acts of atrocity are, really and truly at core, manifestations of human helplessness." She sat back in her chair, crossed her arms.

A bullet? A vitamin? I made a mental note: this woman not only had great fashion sense; she was also a gifted dreamer.

Eva Madelung, a therapist from Munich, joined us the next morning to demonstrate family constellation therapy, a technique devised by a German psychologist who'd spent decades studying how the prejudices and traumas of one generation are passed down to the next. My father's combat experience in the Pacific war was a shaping force of my childhood. My mother's unexamined fury toward Poles was deep in my bones.

Eva's iron-gray hair was pulled back severely from her gaunt face. Her eyes were so deep-set, I thought at first she was blind. You could feel her penetrating focus, even with her eyes closed. Our entire group assembled again in a circle. Eva asked for a volunteer. Cheryl, the woman who'd dreamed of herself as a vitamin, promptly rose from her chair.

Eva asked her basic facts about her family. Were there any premature deaths? Were there any family members no one talked about, hidden away? Was there anyone who'd been cast out of the family?

In a matter-of-fact tone, Cheryl recited a hair-raising litany of events. Eva listened, eyes shut.

Cheryl's parents were both from Poland. Her maternal grandmother was deaf and mute. Her grandmother's first husband abandoned her, but she married again. She and her second husband lived in Tarnopol, a good-sized town in what was then Poland and is now Ukraine. On the day the Nazis rounded up the Jews of Tarnopol, Cheryl's mother came home from school and hid. She escaped into the woods with a school friend and kept running. She never saw her family again.

Both Cheryl's parents survived the war in Russia. Both of them spent time in labor camps there. They met in her father's hometown of Kolomyja after the war, and soon after they emigrated to New York. They told their two daughters very little about their past in Poland. "It was as if I had hatched out of an egg," Cheryl said.

Eva asked Cheryl to choose representatives for her family drama, casting from our group of witnesses a mother and a father, grandparents, and a woman to play herself. She asked Cheryl to physically place the characters in the space according to her own inner picture of their relationships. Eva then added another character. She asked Cheryl to choose someone in the room to personify Poland.

Cheryl quickly chose her parents and grandparents. Otto, the former Wehrmacht soldier, played her father. She took a long time picking Poland. She stood in the center of the room, rotating, looking carefully from face to face in the circle. She settled on a heavyset woman whose broken leg was in a cast.

Eva moved the other characters around, changing their positions relative to each other and to the space. She asked Cheryl to move them closer or farther apart, facing each other or facing away. Poland always stood in the back of the room, behind the family drama. Poland never budged.

From time to time, Eva asked the different characters how they were feeling. "Unwell," Poland told us.

Poland was in obvious discomfort. She shifted from leg to leg trying to get comfortable. Her alignment was off. She rubbed her aching neck. Poland was unbalanced. She had no one to lean against, no source of support, and no way to offer support to others.

Cheryl kept a wary eye on her.

LATER THAT DAY WAS the session with the awkward title "Tabus Zwischen Deutschen, Polen, und Juden?" (Taboos between Germans, Poles, and Jews?) that had inspired me to buy a plane ticket to Berlin. At Birkenau on the last night, there had been mention of Jews and Poles finding a new language to talk to each other. I was eager to speak it.

A German woman named Mona was the workshop leader. Mona's mother had been an SS officer in Warsaw, and it had long been Mona's passion to bring together Germans, Poles, and Jews in dialogue as personal reparation for her mother's complicity. She told us how her SS mother turned her twisted rage against her own daughter. Mona fled home at fourteen. Over the next two decades, with a lot of good therapy and the help of One by One, she'd constructed a healthy life for herself and her daughter in Berlin's gritty Kreutzberg neighborhood. If neo-Nazis ever threatened the local synagogue, you could count on Mona and her friends to stand vigil through the night.

There were fifteen of us at the session, ranging in age from thirty-two to eighty-six. Each of us briefly stated why he or she was here. When it came to Zofia, an eighty-six-year-old artist from Warsaw,

Dorota, the young Polish woman who'd translated at Auschwitz, translated first from Polish to English then from Polish into German.

Zofia, a Polish Catholic, was held at Ravensbruck camp for five years, then led on a forced march in the snow at the end of the war. Alongside the emaciated women prisoners marched the German Army, fleeing the Soviets. From above, Allied planes dropped bombs on soldiers and prisoners both.

"I looked at the faces of the soldiers," said Zofia. "I saw the depths of their suffering—these people who destroyed my life, my country. I thought, 'This is the fate of all humanity sent to war by fanatical leaders.' Dialogue is a necessity—the only way for us to be saved."

Cheryl walked in after we'd begun. Mona asked her why she'd come. She began guardedly, picking up steam as she spoke. "Both my parents were Polish. My father's family owned the Grand Hotel in Kolomyja, a small town in Poland. After the war, when my father straggled back home from a labor camp in Siberia . . . his childhood friends shot at him. My question is, Do the Poles want us back?"

Mona placed stacks of index cards on the table and asked each of us to write down, in a few sentences per card, the emotions, historical issues, disputed issues we thought essential for any future dialogue.

After my return from the retreat at Birkenau, I'd begun devouring the work of some of the many writers who'd delved into the history of Polish-Jewish relations. By the time I arrived at Wannsee, I was primed to ask questions and seek out discussion. I eagerly began scribbling topics: the Kielce pogrom; Jan Karski, the Polish courier to the West; the possibility of restoring Jewish cemeteries and historical monuments together. I wanted to know the texture of life for Jews and Poles living side by side in towns like Radomsko. I wanted to talk about the boycotts of Jewish businesses during the interwar period, the exclusion of Jews from Polish universities. By the last card, my manic enthusiasm was ebbing: "What is the point, really, of discussing all this?" Jewish history in Poland was over and done with. Wasn't all this just a futile exercise?

Magda, one of the Poles, wanted to discuss the sensitive charge that Polish Jews had welcomed the hated Red Army into eastern Poland in 1939. The Russians were the Poles' historic enemy and this perception of Jewish behavior still rankled.

Dorota, the translator, wrote on one of her cards, "Compassion is a very small cake" (*Wspolczucie jako bardzo male ciastko*), her handy metaphor for the way Poles and Jews compete for the ownership of their suffering. Comparative victimhood had poisoned relations between Poles and Jews for decades.

We filled many hours and hundreds of index cards in the stifling heat. Just before our dinner break, Cheryl, visibly upset, bolted out of the room. I had no idea why.

After the exhausting session was finally over, I looked for Cheryl. She sat on a bench smoking, staring out at the rowers skimming the lake in the late afternoon light. She looked miserable. I couldn't tell whether or not she was grateful I'd come looking for her. Nevertheless, I invited her to walk into town with me, to unwind, debrief. She agreed to come.

It was a relief to step out of the villa and the grip of those intense group dialogues into the balminess of a Berlin summer evening. It was still light at 9:00 p.m. We found an Italian restaurant open. Over a glass of chianti, I learned that Cheryl was a poet, that for many years she'd been a set and costume designer for films, that she was married to a film director. She had a grown daughter and she'd recently moved from New York to a small town in the south of France. It was easy to talk to Cheryl; she was quirky and familiar.

She'd decided to join the workshop just minutes before it began. "I was already conflicted. I even phoned a friend of mine in Colorado—another daughter of survivors—and asked, 'Are we Polish?' 'Why?' she answered, 'Who wants to know?'"

After a second glass, Cheryl confessed that the person who'd made her most uncomfortable in the workshop was *me*. I was incredulous. Why? "Because you had so many strong feelings about Poland. Issues you wanted to discuss. Questions you wanted to raise." Until this moment, I hadn't considered how my obsession might unsettle someone with a more fraught (dis)connection to her family's past than my own. "I have *no* relationship to Poland," she continued. "Poland is where everything was lost."

What was it like for her during the family constellation exercise? What was she thinking when she chose *her* Poland?

"My Poland was both reassuring and frightening. Big, solid, and unmovable. A large country who couldn't protect me. But I felt proud that among my family, my own ancestral country was in attendance."

She heated up. "The fact is . . . Poland permeated my parents' hair, their breath, humor, worldview, food, attitude, dreams, expectations. You can't imagine what comfort I felt, finally, that Poland stood up for me with my family—took its place in my life for all of those in the room to see and I could claim my Polishness."

She sank back into her chair. We sat for several moments, neither one speaking, sipping what was left of our wine.

IT WAS MIDNIGHT WHEN we returned to the villa. The front door was locked. We contemplated throwing pebbles at someone's window. On the back terrace, we discovered Dorota and Magda, the two young Poles, smoking in the dark. We joined them. At first we all sat in uneasy silence. Up to now, all our interaction had been in structured groups following a prescribed form.

Dorota asked shyly, "Cheryl, why did you leave the workshop before we finished?"

Cheryl was surprised. "Did you notice I wasn't there?"

"Yes," Dorota said. "I missed you." A pause. "I was so happy when you said that you were Polish."

I asked Dorota, "You were born after the war. What did it feel like to grow up in a Poland without Jews?"

"You could feel the absence," she said softly. "It was like being part of a fabric where there's a huge hole torn out of the middle."

We talked quietly long into the night, the glowing embers of cigarettes moving as each person spoke. For both Cheryl and me, it was our first conversation with Poles of our generation. Moonlight shimmered off Lake Wannsee. We began to grow comfortable with one another. It helped that we could see each other only in silhouette.

After our goodnights, I walked Cheryl to her room in the villa. She paused before the open door. "I will *never* step foot in Poland," she said. I nodded, turned to go.

"Unless . . ." she said, "unless someone takes me."

I'd found a partner for my own Polish quandary.

CHAPTER 6

Walking Papers

Cheryl and I sat side by side on a hard wooden bench in a small drab office in an obscure neighborhood of Warsaw. We thumbed anxiously through pages of applications: List your friends. List your mother's maiden name. Your occupation. Your reason for visit. Your passport number.

The radiator hissed. In the center of the room, a stout man pecked at a manual typewriter. He paid us no attention. "Excuse me," I ventured. "We didn't bring our passports." The stout man took a drag on his cigarette. "You should have thought of that," he said, without looking up.

We returned with the necessary documents. A steady, cold rain spattered down—not auspicious weather for tramping around a cemetery. Nevertheless, when the stout man buttoned up his moth-eaten black overcoat and battered fur cap, we followed him out to his van. We drove a winding road through the city streets.

The cemetery stretched out for miles around. In the distance, men hunted deer with crossbows. Who'd ever heard of Jews hunting? I noticed one of the hunters loading a fawn into his SUV. Was this the right cemetery? Our guide gestured toward the acres of graves: "Pay attention to what your friends are afraid of," he said sternly.

I WOKE UP. Cheryl was curled up in the armchair by the window in the living room of the flat we'd rented in Warsaw in the fall of 2002. She inhaled her morning Marlboro, sipped from a mug of coffee.

"The tour agency called," she said. "We're to meet this guy named Christopher at 9:00 a.m. We'll recognize him by his overcoat and beret."

For the rest of our travel in Poland I'd arranged for a guide, but he wouldn't arrive from Krakow for another two days. Anxious to see what was left of Jewish Warsaw, I'd called a local travel agency. We were assigned Christopher.

I told Cheryl our dream exploits in the Jewish cemetery. She'd been busy in the Other Realm as well. In the medieval Polish town of her dream, ragged soldiers of the emperor arrived on horseback, demanding she sew them new uniforms.

Cheryl had a strategy in mind. "Everybody in my family was afraid the soldiers would attack us, so I instructed the tailor to make the uniforms out of itchy fabric to distract the soldiers and put them off guard." She stubbed out her cigarette, laughed, pleased with herself.

Cheryl grew up in Long Island suburbs hearing Polish from both her parents. Her mouth can make those impossible sounds my mouth, one generation later, cannot form. She can sing, in Polish, and to the hilarity of our Polish friends, a nasty song about Polish soldiers she learned as a child from her mother. Her mother cooked that heavy, heavenly Polish food—pirogi, fried croquettes, cabbage rolls, kasha, sour rye soup, dark breads—against which my stomach often rebels.

I opened the shutters, gazed out across the damp Old Town square at the reconstructed medieval buildings opposite ours, soft pastels reflecting morning light. Men, women, children bundled in overcoats—carrying briefcases, shopping bags, backpacks—strode purposefully across the square. Pigeons congregated by the fountain with the statue of the Syrene, the mermaid symbol of Warsaw with her upraised sword.

Cheryl liked to imagine that our rented apartment in Warsaw's Old Town was our apartment before the war. Two Jewish girls in Warsaw. Two Jewish women writers. According to this fantasy, we would have managed to flee our provincial hometowns—Radomsko in central Poland and Kolomyja in Polish Galicia, near Ukraine—for the intellectual and artistic capital of the country. We would have worn beautiful, pleated woolen coats like the fashionable women were wearing on Nowy Swiat, Warsaw's elegant shopping street. My grandmother Rebecca used to rave about the elegant coats worn on the streets of Warsaw.

The Radomsk Yizkor Book pays homage to the many "provincial youth" of Radomsk who left their hometown for Warsaw's literary culture to "breathe the air of their beloved poets and columnists."

In the vibrant, hopeful years after World War I, when Poland was reestablished as a nation with Field Marshal Józef Pilsudski as head of state and the legendary pianist Paderewski as prime minister, we might have done just that.

At the famous meeting hall of the Warsaw Literary Union at Tlomackie 13, we might have slipped in to see our heroes. On a given afternoon, the Radomsk Yizkor tells us, "the esthete Yosef Heftman could be seen eating marinated herring and the essayist J. M. Neuman drinking tea with challah. The poet Y. Segalowitch sits in a corner with a 'literary supplement' (as the young women who attached themselves to the writers were called)."

On the stage, Jewish musicians play an Argentine tango and the small, blond, pale Hersh Dovid Nomberg, the great poet from Radomsk, dances "as if someone were haunting him, placing his feet like a zealot who has been told by the dance teacher when a turn needs to be made to the right, a thump to the left," while two of his Radomsk landsleit, "the agile photographer Lukwik Wajnberg and his eccentric daughter Tusye," sit at a table, drinking tea and "observing Nomberg's balletic troubles."

Would we have written in Yiddish or Polish? Would our lovers have been Jewish or Polish? This speculation was part of Cheryl's ongoing research, which she summarized in two questions: Are we Polish? and, Do they miss us?

IN OCTOBER 1944 THE city of Warsaw ceased to exist. Hitler, enraged by the Warsaw Rising in which the Polish Resistance battled the SS and the Wehrmacht in cellars and sewers all over the city for sixty-three days, ordered Warsaw—with its six centuries of history—destroyed "stone by stone." The job of the "burn squad" (*brennungskommando*), like that of the firemen in Bradbury's *Fahrenheit 451*, was to destroy property, not to save it. They numbered all the buildings still standing in order of their importance to Polish culture. Then they dynamited them. Only 35 of 780 buildings on the Warsaw historic register survived intact.

Any life in the Warsaw Ghetto had been extinguished a year earlier, after the Nazis quelled the unexpected resistance from those Jews who decided to fight to the finish rather than submit to deportations to the camps. Those two separate Warsaw uprisings, a year apart—the first in 1943 by the incarcerated Jews and the second in 1944 by the Polish Resistance—are frequently confused.

The Warsaw Ghetto Uprising began on April 19, 1943, and lasted twenty-seven days. The ghetto was reduced to a smoldering ruin. In Radomsko, the last few dozen Jews learned about the uprising on a contraband radio tuned to the "Free Poland" station. News of this Jewish resistance bolstered the courage of the survivors.

The 1943 ghetto uprising astonished the Germans, who responded to the under-armed and outnumbered Jews with ferocious savagery. Historian Norman Davies, in his book *Rising '44: The Battle for Warsaw*, notes how the audacity of the ghetto fighters provided a moral lesson to those Varsovians who saw it happen: "The cause was hopeless: their courage magnificent. They set an example: some would say, a very Polish example."

Whether or not the subsequent 1944 Warsaw Rising was advisable, in the long run, is still debated. The human toll—not to mention the obliteration of Warsaw's physical structure—was horrific.

Neither Britain nor the United States intervened in the destruction of Poland's capital. And, while the *brennungskommando* did their work, Red Army soldiers in thick overcoats lit cigarettes and stamped their feet in the snow fifteen kilometers from Warsaw on the other side of the Vistula.

The Soviets waited out the three months it took for the Nazis to decimate the city and subdue the stubborn Poles before marching into Warsaw as "liberators." No Pole tells the story of Warsaw's destruction without mentioning that fact.

With Poland under Stalin's rule, heroes of the 1944 Warsaw Rising were arrested, stripped of their medals, smeared as Nazi collaborators by the Communist regime, interned as political prisoners. Their true story was erased from textbooks.

—w—

POLAND HAS BEEN BATTERED. Sliced. Pounced upon. Many Poles are skeptical that anyone who isn't Polish would even *try* to understand their history. One night we walked to a smoky café in Old Town with Dorota; her husband, Lech, a journalist; and several other new Polish friends. Dorota was the young Polish woman I'd last seen at Wannsee, when we sat and talked in the dark.

En route to the café, we stopped in front of the monument to the 1944 Warsaw Rising. Lech told me his uncle had died in the violence. "Did the Polish Underground try to help the Jews in 1943, during the Ghetto Uprising?" I asked. He struggled to explain, then begged off. "It is complicated to explain in Polish," he said, "and impossible for me in English." We heard this over and over—how complicated Polish history is.

For several days, Cheryl had admired an old print in the window of an antiquarian bookstore in the Old Town. It was a bawdy political cartoon featuring Poland's prewar socialist leader, Marshal Józef Pilsudski, dancing a wild line-dance with other politicos in a surreal cabaret. When Cheryl inquired about buying it, the proprietor of the shop raised his eyebrows: "Polish history. You wouldn't understand."

Dorota, who grew up in Warsaw, was defensive about the fact that modern Warsaw was built over the ruins of the ghetto. "The whole city is a graveyard," she explained. "If we didn't build over the past, we wouldn't have a city."

WE WAITED FOR OUR guide beside the Syrene statue, clapping hands together to keep warm in the frosty morning air. I admired Cheryl's stylish Polish winter ensemble: a fitted black boiled wool coat with a cinched waist and ankle-length wool skirt that hung in scallops, a fur cap with earflaps.

Within minutes, a heavyset, white-haired man wearing an old navy peacoat, tinted glasses, and a black beret and clutching a heavy black satchel appeared. Christopher Huszczanowski, a walking encyclopedia of Warsaw Jewish history, was a dead ringer for the grumpy man in my dream of the night before.

How do you tour a city that no longer exists? Christopher had much to impart in five hours and he wasted no time in beginning. His satchel was full of evidence: maps, diagrams, photocopied photographs of an invisible city. He knew exactly where everything that was gone was once located. Each time he wanted to show us one of the maps, he set down his satchel and pressed open the lock with a satisfying "click."

His callused finger, stained with nicotine, outlined the borders of the Warsaw Ghetto on a map. He laid out a photograph of the famous carousel that operated on the Aryan side of Warsaw, a powerful symbol in Czeslaw Milosz's 1943 poem "Campo dei Fiori," which I'd read aloud to Cheryl the night before. The poet recalls the hideously cheerful melodies of the carousel drowning out the rat-tat-tat-tat of German machine-gun fire behind the ghetto wall.

In the chaos of August 1942, a former Polish Army officer and member of the Polish Underground named Jan Karski disguised himself as a ragged ghetto inmate and, with the help of the Jewish Underground, entered the Warsaw Ghetto through a tunnel under an apartment building at 6 Muranowska Street. Karski's mission was to bear witness to the terrible suffering of the starving ghetto inmates.

"To pass through that wall was to enter into a new world utterly unlike anything that had ever been imagined," he wrote in his memoir. Karski's guide urged him, "Remember this! Remember this!"

Christopher overwhelmed us with numbers, dates, names. A blizzard of disparate facts. I tried to absorb it as my feet walked the memory of the ghetto. Cheryl, wrapped in her thick coat, asked no questions.

Christopher wasn't Jewish. How had he found his way to this line of work? In the fifties he worked for a travel agency. They assigned him the least desirable task: assisting Hasidic Jews in finding the graves of their holy rabbis in ravaged Jewish cemeteries.

To the Hasidim, the grave of a holy rabbi is a sacred—even healing—place of visitation. "The location has to be exact," he told us. "Not one inch off." He stood up to his ankles in the mud with measuring tape and yardstick in gray provincial towns, listening to Hasids from Williamsburg decipher anecdotal descriptions of their rebbes' burial places. And, what do you know? He fell in love with the work, with the community.

He started to study the Jewish history of Warsaw, no easy task under Communist rule. It was easier—much more advisable—to forget all about Poland's Jews. Polish sociologists call it programmed amnesia.

Christopher was a bitter man shaped by the grotesqueries of those years. His fellow Poles, he said, "don't want to remember about the Jews." And his daughter, he said, couldn't care less too.

Christopher claimed to know Jewish cemeteries all over Poland. When I mentioned Radomsko, once one of the most eminent Hasidic dynasties in Poland, Christopher dropped to his knees and clicked open his satchel. "I have a map to the rebbe's grave in Radomsko," he declared, rummaging through his papers, then concluding it wasn't there. "I will leave it for you later today at the Orbis Forum Hotel. Ask for it at the front desk."

Did Christopher routinely make drop-offs at this hotel? Was the desk staff familiar with his shabby black coat, his thick envelopes containing measurements and evidence?

Our next destination was the Umschlagplatz, where Warsaw Jews were ordered to assemble for deportation. From there, the cemetery on Okopowa Street.

It must have been the mention of the cemetery. "I've had enough," Cheryl announced. She had no intention of visiting any cemeteries on this trip: "I've grown up with the living dead."

Christopher wilted. The tour was not yet complete.

Before I could talk her out of it, Cheryl hailed a cab, dove into the back seat, slammed the door shut. "A pity, a pity . . ." muttered Christopher as the taxi disappeared into Warsaw traffic.

He pulled yet another map out of his satchel. We continued walking. This area of the ghetto was once composed of narrow streets, two- and three-story buildings, a mix of apartments and stores. The rebuilt area consists of drab, gray eight- and ten-story-high superblocks built by the Communist regime for "the working man."

One of the few original ghetto buildings still standing once served as the hospital where Janusz Korczak, born Henryk Goldschmidt, visionary pediatrician, writer, and pedagogue, had practiced. He came from an assimilated Jewish family who spoke Polish and considered themselves Poles.

Korczak dedicated his life to caring for children, particularly Jewish orphans. Dom Sierot, his Warsaw orphanage, was a children's republic—with its own parliament and newspaper. On August 5, 1942, when the Germans soldiers came to collect his wards, Korczak would not abandon his children. He accompanied them to the Umschlagplatz and from there to Treblinka.

We reached the cemetery on Okopowa Street, the oldest Jewish cemetery in continuous use in Eastern Europe. More than 250,000 people are buried here. No one knows the exact number; the Nazis burned the cemetery records. We were the only live ones in the vast necropolis.

There were elaborate tombs that belonged to notable Warsaw writers like S. Ansky, Isaac Leib Peretz, and Ludwig Zamenhof, the Polish Jew who invented the international language called Esperanto. Korczak, gassed at Treblinka with his orphans, is immortalized in bronze. Cradling a little girl in his arms, the good doctor leads his young charges on their dignified last walk through Warsaw to the trains.

Early on in the war, ghetto residents who died were buried in individual graves, but deaths in the ghetto were soon so numerous that the dead—among them the last Radomsker rebbe and his entire family—were buried in mass graves. Christopher pointed out those markers as well.

We walked the wide lanes limned with willows, old oaks, and sycamores. I admired the beautiful, old, engraved Jewish gravestones, or *matzevot*: fierce protective lions, kneeling rams, tender hands of blessing. I'd seen exquisite black-and-white photos of these Jewish grave markers in the book by the artist Monika Krajewska, *Time of Stones.*

During the Communist era, Monika and her husband, Staszek—friends of Rabbi Singer's—crisscrossed Poland to neglected Jewish cemeteries, documenting the stones sinking into the ground, reclaimed by nettles and blackberries. They were among Poland's memory workers.

We walked on a thick carpet of damp leaves. "Do you smell that?" Christopher waited for the odor to prod my brain. Unmistakable: the sewer. Christopher pointed to an open hole. "The Germans were leery about letting Jews in the cemetery," he said, "because they could escape through the sewer system."

I tried to imagine fitting my body into that narrow sewer pipe if my life depended on it. "Unless you were a dead person," he added, "you needed a pass to go to the cemetery."

Last night's dream clicked into alignment with historical truth. I shivered. There *were* hunters in the Jewish cemetery. You *did* need a passport to enter. And it was well worth paying attention to what it was your friends were afraid of.

Christopher escorted me to a bus stop. We stood there silent for several minutes as he checked for the right bus to take me back to the Old Town. "By the way," he suddenly asked, "do you know anyone whose family was from Lodz?" Yes, I did. He thrust an envelope at me. "I was instructed to pass it to someone whose family came from there." The bus arrived. Christopher grabbed my right hand and kissed my wrist, like I'd only seen men do in movies.

I took my seat next to a weary Warsaw matron. I tore open the envelope and stared at the contents: a stack of Lodz ghetto money, fifty pfennig notes—the paper soft and crumbling. What would fifty pfennigs have bought in the Lodz ghetto? I missed my stop. The bus roared across the Vistula.

An hour later, I returned to our apartment on the square. Cheryl was curled up in the comfy armchair, calmly smoking a Marlboro.

While Christopher and I tramped around muddy Okopowa cemetery in the cold rain, Cheryl had directed the cabbie to Fukier, a prewar holdover and still one of the classiest restaurants in Warsaw. She commandeered the best table by the window and ordered a lunch of roast goose stuffed with apples, wild mushrooms, kasha and hot beets, and a fine old bordeaux.

In that beautiful room, in fin-de-siècle elegance, framed by red velvet curtains, surrounded by old china and fresh flowers and glowing candles, to the strains of Chopin, the murmurs of Polish voices, and a talkative parrot in a cage, the daughter of the former proprietors of the Grand Hotel of Kolomyja savored the best of what Poland had to offer.

CHAPTER 7

A Young Man from Oswiecim

I pulled open the heavy oak door of our Warsaw flat and looked into the startling blue eyes of a slender young man. His delicate face was fringed with a faint blond beard.

"Tomek!" he said amiably. I stared, uncomprehending. "Tomasz Cebulski! Your guide. Just arrived from Krakow!" In our e-mails between California and Poland, our future guide had displayed a mature grasp of the complicated nature of Polish-Jewish dialogue. He hadn't mentioned he was just twenty-three.

I'd found Tomek through a chain of recommendations, beginning with Princeton professor Jan Tomasz Gross, the author of the 2000 book *Neighbors*, about the massacre of Jews in Jedwabne, Poland, under Nazi occupation. Gross's scholarship revealed that the atrocity was perpetrated by the Jews' Polish neighbors, not German soldiers, as had been previously assumed. His book set off an anguished debate in Poland and caused a sea change there in thinking about the Holocaust.

I asked Professor Gross to recommend a guide for a personal journey through Poland. He recommended Robert Gadek, the director of the Judaica Center in Krakow. Gadek recommended Tomek, then a history student at the Jagiellonian University writing a thesis about prewar Jewish life in Poland. In addition to his excellent English, Tomek was fluent in French and German. He'd studied Hebrew, traveled to Israel. I was intrigued.

I brewed a pot of dark tea while Cheryl sized up Tomek in the front room. I could tell she was skeptical. This skinny kid was going to escort two premenopausal Jewish women around provincial

Poland? How would he protect us if anything went awry? I couldn't really imagine, however, anything going seriously awry. Poland was not Colombia or Iraq. But Cheryl's fears about Poland, I reminded myself, were not rational.

I had tried to explain that to our friend Dorota when, on our first night in Warsaw, she and Lech drove us to Lazienki Park in the center of town. They wanted to show us the beautiful vintage gas lamps lighting a walkway through the park. Cheryl had no intention of walking in a shadowy Warsaw park in the night. "It's perfectly safe," an exasperated Dorota whispered in my ear. How was I to explain that Cheryl's sense of vulnerability in Poland had been honed in childhood through the tales she heard and overheard from her survivor parents?

That afternoon Tomek escorted us to the Jewish Historical Institute on Tlomackie Street. Before our appointment with the genealogical researcher, we looked at a photo exhibit about historical Jewish Poland. Cheryl looked for familiar faces. It exhausted her.

We were ushered into the tiny office of the researcher, Yale Reisner, whose cluttered desk was piled high with dusty ledgers, note cards, old coffee cups, memory books. We sat uncomfortably on three hard chairs while Yale searched computer databases for traces of Cheryl's mother's family. All Cheryl knew fit on one small scrap of paper.

Yale, an American Jew from Philadelphia, was like a fortune-teller, although his focus was the past rather than the future.

"What was your grandmother's name?" Yale asked Cheryl. She burst into tears. "I don't know," she wailed. "I don't know enough to be here." She told what she knew of her family's story. How her father's Polish friends had shot at him when he returned to Kolomyja, his hometown, from exile in Siberia. I glanced at Tomek, noting the dismay on his face as he registered this information.

Yale pulled a 1929 Warsaw phone directory off the shelf, a business directory that listed a stationery store on Grzybowska Street with the proprietor's name Koch. Cheryl's mother's family name. It was something.

Dorota and Lech had driven us in their battered Toyota to this same Grzybowska Street the night we'd arrived. Cheryl's mother, as a young woman, had lived in an apartment there. We drove down the dark streets in the rain, but where the address should have been, the street now ended. Cheryl was bereft.

She was also disappointed our trip would not include a visit to neighboring Ukraine, to Kolomyja. Those who knew the Ukrainian countryside had warned against traveling there in November: "It will be a sea of mud." I was secretly relieved. Visiting Kolomyja was Cheryl's ardent desire and her worst fear. I was terrified how she might respond to the town that so haunted her. What would I do if she fell apart?

When Yale learned we were leaving Warsaw for Radomsko the next morning, he pulled a small box from under his desk: a tin Hanukah menorah and enough candles to last through the holiday. Sundown the next day would be the first night.

As we packed, we traded first impressions of Tomek. It bothered Cheryl that Tomek had been with us at the historical society that afternoon. She felt exposed, humiliated as she faced the void in her family history.

I found Tomek charming and enthusiastic; she found him obnoxious. I saw his smile as radiant; she saw it as cloying. I saw him as a smart kid with a genuine interest in Jewish history. She saw him as an arrogant young Pole preying upon her "sad reason for coming to Poland," as she termed it. "He's made a job taking advantage of Jews looking for family roots," she fumed. He charged too much, she said, though I pointed out that what he charged was the going rate.

In the morning we rolled our suitcases over the cobblestones to the edge of Old Town, climbed into the comfortable Daewoo sedan Tomek had borrowed from his father, and set off on the long drive to Radomsko. On the outskirts of Warsaw, I remembered the map to the tomb of the Radomsker rebbe that Christopher, my surly Warsaw guide, had promised to leave for me at the front desk of the Orbis Forum Hotel.

Cheryl whipped out her cell phone and handed it to Tomek, who—ever helpful—explained to the desk clerk what we were looking for. No one there knew what we were talking about. Tomek, unfazed, assured me we'd find the tomb without any problem.

I could already see that sunny Tomek was the polar opposite of Christopher, who had been shaped by the Second World War, the

Cold War, the rigidity of the Communist regime. Tomek came into adulthood under a nascent democratic government. Christopher was disillusioned by his country and his countrymen. Tomek was deeply proud of Poland and its traditions. Christopher was the Old Poland. Tomek was the New.

While Cheryl sat in the back staring glumly out the window at the foggy Polish landscape, I quizzed Tomek as to how he'd come to focus on Jewish history in Poland. He'd grown up in Oswiecim, the town synonymous with Auschwitz. His parents, both chemists, worked at a chemical plant on the same territory once occupied by the infamous I. B. Farben compound. Conversation stopped.

I remembered my walk around Oswiecim on the last morning of the retreat two years earlier. I'd glanced at the faces of the townspeople going about their Monday morning shopping routines, feeling a mixture of bewilderment and loathing. As we rode the bus each morning from the youth hostel to the camp, I'd look out the window at farmers tilling their vegetable gardens. Their fields must have been fertile with all that ash from the crematoria.

Yet the Germans had imposed the concentration camp on this small Polish city; the Poles hadn't built it. It was either misinformation or sloppy thinking to assign blame for the concentration camps onto the Poles who were themselves victims of the Germans. What happened at Auschwitz was also a Polish tragedy.

Tomek was familiar with my silent response, as well as with the inevitable question: "How did it feel to have grown up in such a place?"

"If I hadn't been brought up in Oswiecim, I wouldn't be doing this work now. But to be honest, growing up, I felt nothing special about Oswiecim. It was a town like a thousand others."

Tomek learned in school that Poland had suffered devastating losses, that the Nazi occupation was exceedingly cruel, and that the Poles had resisted heroically. But there was also a lot of history he *didn't* learn. For instance, he did not officially learn about the 1944 Warsaw Rising, nor about Katyn, the 1940 Soviet massacre of twenty-three thousand Polish officers—among the best-educated men in Poland—an event officially and violently denied by the Communist government and attributed to the Nazis.

For those who knew and refused to accept the lie about Katyn or who spoke of it publicly, the punishment was harsh. But the truth of the massacre at the hands of the Soviets was transmitted within Polish homes, and Katyn became a symbol of Soviet oppression of Poland.

As far as memories of minorities, especially Poland's Jews, only the very negative stereotypes lingered. "Fifty years of Communism served the Polish people as a real brainwash," said Tomek.

As part of a devout Catholic family, Tomek attended Sunday masses. In 1965—before Tomek was born—Pope Paul VI issued the proclamation "Nostra Aetate," repudiating the idea that Jews were Christ killers. Yet accusations against Jews were common in the Catholic liturgy throughout Tomek's childhood. "Among kids, nasty jokes about Jews and concentration camps were very popular," Tomek explained.

Tomek's readiness to acknowledge and openly examine the bigotry of his youth was startling. His candor reassured me. He'd emerged from his socialized brainwashing with his intellectual curiosity intact.

In Oswiecim, as in most provincial Polish towns, there were few activities for teenagers. Tomek gravitated to the International Youth Meeting Center, sponsored by the German government with the mission of encouraging Polish-German reconciliation. Eager to travel abroad, he signed on for a "seminar" in Germany. It didn't matter to him that the destinations of these trips were the camps at Dachau and Bergen-Belsen.

In Culver City, where I grew up in the fifties, local kids scaled the fences of the MGM studio lot to play on the set of World War II movies. In Oswiecim, kids climbed over the fences of Birkenau to fish in the ash ponds. Tomek hadn't been lured by these escapades. He missed the optional field trip to the camp with his school class. He wasn't particularly interested in history. After all, he was going to be a chemist like his parents.

When he finally made his first visit to Birkenau with his youth group, his initial impression was shock. Even though he'd lived in close proximity, he'd never imagined the scale of the camp. The tour guide rattled off dates, but the meaning escaped him. "Only the space itself was telling its story."

Even if Tomek had been one of those Polish schoolkids paraded past heaps of shoes, hair, and eyeglasses on their school trips to Auschwitz in the eighties, he would not have learned they came from Jews. Compulsory Holocaust curriculum wasn't instituted until 2000. At the Auschwitz museum, established by the postwar Communist regime, the victims were then listed only by nationality. Last in the alphabetized roll call of the dead was *Zydowski*, Polish for Jewish.

In his late teens, Tomek became involved with a German non-profit that dispatched student volunteers to work on cleanup projects in former concentration camps or in present-day Jewish communities in Central Europe. He enrolled because it was a cheap way to travel. His first two choices were to go abroad. He was disappointed to be assigned to Warsaw, his third choice. "Warsaw is nothing special for a Krakow-born boy," he laughed, referring to the rivalry between the two cities. In Warsaw, his group was assigned to clean the Jewish Cemetery at Okopowa Street. The cemetery that Tomek encountered in the early 1990s looked very different from my recent visit there with Christopher.

The general disorder overwhelmed him. "There were twenty of us and the cemetery had thirty-three hectares and two hundred fifty thousand tombs. All our lifetime would be not enough to clean the cemetery! But we started."

Little by little his work group uncovered old *matzevots* (tombstones) from the bushes. On the stones, Tomek read the names of Jewish Poles like Zamenhof, the inventor of Esperanto, and Korczak, the visionary educator. Until that moment, these were all what he called "100 percent Polish" names. Knowing they were Polish, he'd assumed they were Catholic. Tomek was suddenly inundated with questions that challenged what he'd been taught about his country's history.

"Why were Poles like the hero Janusz Korczak buried here? What was the language written on the stones? Why did no one bring flowers and candles here? If this was such a big cemetery, then this must have been a big community! Who were the Jews and what happened to them exactly? Why did it happen?"

There was no one to whom he could pose his questions. Discussion of the fate of Poland's Jews was still taboo. There were no books available on the subject. Widespread popular opinion held that the Jews had not only welcomed the despised Communist takeover, they also had actually helped facilitate it.

Tomek and his companions managed to clean only about thirty square meters during their two-week stint. By the time they were finished, he recounted, "We were changed." While they were clearing tombstones, an American rabbi came by the cemetery to see what they were doing.

Tomek was extremely nervous. He'd been nurtured on those old, negative stereotypes. "Jews kidnapped children, they dealt with money, they couldn't be trusted."

To his surprise, the rabbi was friendly, and moreover, very grateful. He told the students the job they were doing was highly respected in the Jewish world. Tomek asked if I knew why.

I did. But I wanted to hear Tomek say it.

"Because you will never hear 'thank you' from the dead."

There was no sound from Cheryl, but I knew she was listening.

CHAPTER 8

Keys

We settled into silence as Tomek navigated pea-soup fog. It was dusk when we approached Radomsko; a hard, steady rain hammered the roof of the car. The town looked gray and mean, leached of whatever charm I'd imagined on my visit two years earlier. I was full of doubt about bringing Cheryl and Tomek here. My anxiety mingled with doubt about how we'd find our way into the Radomsko Jewish cemetery. I was intent to visit it this time. We had to find the person who had the key.

Tomek was in a lighthearted mood. Tonight was St. Andrew's night, a Polish fête celebrated with a quaint ritual. The custom was to take a big skeleton key, "like they use to open the door in an old church," and pour hot melted wax through the bow of the key into a dish of cold water. You held the hardened wax up to the light and divined the future from the shapes of the shadow cast on the wall.

I fixated on the image of a key. I'd been reading about Jan Karski, the risk-taking Polish courier for the Polish Underground. All the testimony and documents meant to convince the West that the Germans were carrying out a genocide against the Jews of Poland had been photographed and shrunk onto a microfilm, then placed inside a hollow house key, which Karski carried with him on his dangerous mission across Hitler's empire.

Karski landed outside London on November 25, 1942. The microfilm in the key—handed off en route—reached London a week before him. Officials of the Polish Government-in-Exile condensed the information into a two-page report in English, which began,

"News is reaching the Polish Government in London about the liquidation of the Jewish ghetto in Warsaw."

In the end, few believed Karski or the information contained in the hollow key. Few were willing to admit to what was happening at that moment, let alone divine the future: that a mass extermination of European Jewry was well in progress. One who did believe was Szmul Zygielbojm, a London representative of Poland's Jewish socialist Bund movement. Karski's account shook him to the core. Not long after his meeting with Karski, Zygielbojm read a speech on the BBC, declaring, "It will be a shame to go on living, to belong to the human race if steps are not taken to halt the greatest crime in human history." Five months later, Zygielbojm committed a very public suicide—setting himself on fire in front of the British Parliament, leaving behind a note with one last plea for the world to take action on behalf of the Jews.

WHO HAD THE KEY to the Radomsko cemetery? My discomfort coalesced into that one worry as we pulled into the driveway of the Hotel Zameczek. The architecture looked intriguing from the outside, but gave no hint of the decorative abominations within: fluorescent lights, plastic flowers, pink frilly curtains, a superfluity of mirrors. "Baroque shell with post-Soviet folk interior," quipped Tomek.

The Zamaczek (small castle) was built in the nineteenth century by an aristocratic family who were also owners of the local brick factory. The Communist government appropriated it after the war and divided it into small apartments. The building gradually fell into ruin. In 1988 Andrzej Kopiec, a local wheeler-dealer, managed to buy it and began a renovation.

Tomek quickly established that burly Andrzej, his ear glued to his cell phone, was the keeper of the keys to the Radomsko Jewish cemetery. In fact, Andrzej, it turned out, was involved in many ways with the remnants of Radomsko's Jewish past. When I signed the guest book, I noticed the signature of Sigi Rabinowicz, Brooklyn scion of the last Radomsker rebbe.

The Radomsko town manager had introduced Sigi to Andrzej in 1988, when Sigi had come to town looking for a local Pole to take care of the cemetery and do so discretely. "This was not something you wanted to show off back then," Andrzej admitted. Every year since then Hasids from Israel, Brooklyn, and Argentina make their pilgrimage to visit the *ohel* (tomb) of the Radomsker rebbe. They always stay at the Hotel Zameczek. They don't mind the ghastly décor, and Andrzej koshers the place for them.

With my primary worry set to rest, we retired upstairs. We uncorked a bottle of sweet Bulgarian wine—the best we could do—and assembled the menorah from our Warsaw care package. All three of us chanted the blessing over the wine and clinked glasses. I lit the candles for the first night of Hanukah.

Hanukah celebrates a miracle, the burning of an oil lamp for eight days and eight nights when it was supposed to burn for just one. "I bet this is the first Chanukah candle lit in Radomsko for a long time," Tomek said softly. He was probably right. The glow from the candle flickered on the faces of my two companions.

"To your family," Cheryl offered with a smile. It was a small miracle, but still . . . a miracle: to light a Hanukah candle in my grandparents' town with my Jewish friend and my Polish friend.

IN THE MORNING, ANDRZEJ drove us through rainy Radomsko, pointing out a wooden house: "The last Jew in Radomsk lived there," he announced over the whine of the windshield wipers. The man's name was Borkowski. He died in a car accident in Radomsko in 1993.

The yizkor made note of the "last Jew in Radomsk to die a natural death in his own bed," on January 2, 1943, in the midst of the deportations. He cheated the Nazis and was considered blessed.

When we reached the cemetery on the edge of town, Andrzej pulled out his clutch of big keys and opened the iron gate. A red-cheeked old caretaker emerged from his ramshackle house, yapping dogs at his heels.

Andrzej led us through the tall, wet grass to the ohel of the Radomsker rebbe and his descendants. Another special key among the dozens of others on Andrzej's key chain opened the metal. Though Cheryl had warned me she would not set foot in any cemetery in Poland, she stayed by my side for moral support.

The whitewashed walls that held the remains of the great Radomsker tzaddik, the wonder rabbi Shlomo Hakohen Rabinowicz, known as Tiferes Shlomo (Shlomo the Magnificent), his wife, and a few other prominent rabbis were illuminated by a single lamp. Stubs of memorial candles as well as paper scraps—notes written by pious Hasidim—were scattered on the tombs, as if we'd arrived a few days after a party.

Tiferes Shlomo, born in 1801, was known for performing miracles. According to the yizkor, his penetrating eyes hypnotized the sick, relieving them of their pain. He knew how to handle demons and ghosts, evil spirits and dybbuks, troubled spirits of the dead who possess the bodies of the living.

Young Shlomo was still a rabbinical student when he made his first unwitting acquaintance with those phantoms. As he stood in the prayer house reciting the Zohar (a mystical text of the Kabbalah) and gazing out at the old cemetery, he took out the sacred ram's horn (shofar), sounded only on High Holy Days, and bugled the ritual call.

In response, the hollow-eyed dead—mud clinging to their shrouds—rose from their graves, banged their bony knuckles against the windows of the prayer house, crying, "Is this the call of the Messiah?" Scared out of his holy wits, Shlomo threw down the shofar and ran "where his eyes carried him." The corpses then returned to their eternal rest.

The rabbi was also known for civic miracles, redeeming Jewish men from inordinately long Russian military service by intervening with the proper officials. He composed and sang rapturous melodies. He was a "wisecracker, a great wit." During the winter he collected donations for wood for the poor. The yizkor book is full of stories about the great tzaddik; both religious and secular Jewish descendants of Radomsko recalled him with immense affection.

The space inside the vault was damp, the plaster infused with mold. I felt like a character in E. M. Forster's *A Passage to India*, faint within the Marabar Caves. I half-expected the door to fly off, a fiery blast from beneath the tomb, Tiferes Shlomo hypnotizing me from the beyond.

If the rebbe could perform miracles, what would I ask him to do? Those two paintings by Natan Szpigel were still luminous after years hidden under the portraits of German soldiers. Could the rebbe peel back the veneer of grim repression that sixty years of totalitarian rule had layered over this town? Could I glimpse an ordinary morning when my great-aunt Fayga Konarska Wilhelm rose from bed, put a teakettle on to boil?

Just months before our visit, a group of Polish students from the Korczak Foundation in Warsaw had cleared away the heaviest growth in the cemetery. After their efforts, a group of Israeli students from a Gimnasia in Tel Aviv had arrived to make the first attempt to record and photograph the information on the headstones.

Cheryl slipped outside and I soon followed. We walked the rows of old stones in the wet, thigh-high grass, stumbling occasionally over thick berry vines. My great-grandmother Golda Wajskopf was buried here somewhere. No telling where. The date of her death—1925— was a comfort of sorts. She was already in her grave in 1944, when fifteen hundred Radomsker Jews were executed in this cemetery by the Germans.

The previous night at the Hotel Zameczek, five young men ate together at a table near ours. Their cheeks were pinker than the walls of the gaudy dining room. They made loud cell-phone calls to make-believe girlfriends. One of them was celebrating his birthday, which fell on St. Andrew's Eve, the holiday of keys and fortune-telling. It was also the birthday of Andrzej, the proprietor, who was whooping it up at a long table of his relatives in a private suite. Vodka flowed.

"Who are your foreign friends?" one of the ruddy young men asked Tomek, noticing that we were all speaking English. "Writers," Tomek replied, not eager to chat. More words were exchanged, followed by peals of laughter from the drunken men. I asked Tomek to translate. He did reluctantly: "Are your friends Jews? Well, if they want to talk to a Jew in Radomsko, tell them to talk to Andrzej, he's the Jew of our town."

Yes, they were just boisterous young men celebrating a feast day, but I couldn't help wondering what they knew or didn't know about the Jews who once made up a sizable portion of their town. In Yad Vashem there are more names of Poles on the list of Righteous Gentiles than from any other country. Jan Karski thought young people should draw great comfort from the fact that "there existed such people in the world." Who in Radomsko risked their lives to save their neighbors? Did these young men know any of them? Might I be able to meet any rescuers from Radomsko?

ONE DAY AND ONE night in Radomsko was all I could bear to inflict on my uncomplaining companions. I couldn't pinpoint the source of the discomfort that gripped me so intensely. I wanted to get out of gloomy Radomsko and head on to Krakow. Cheryl begged me not to leave on her account, yet she perked up at the prospect of an earlier departure.

Before leaving, I wanted to revisit the Regional History Museum I'd visited two years earlier. With an English-speaking guide, I'd be able to make more sense out of the displays. Cheryl stayed in the car, which Tomek parked on the main shopping street. Half an hour later when we returned, having determined the museum was closed for renovation, she was gone.

We looked in all directions before noticing her waving at us from the window of a bakery across the street. She sat at a little table nursing a Styrofoam coffee cup and a piece of poppy seed strudel, watching the Saturday morning promenade—mothers and kids, furniture factory workers in blue overalls—all enjoying a moment of ease. From Tomek's car, she'd observed a young couple exit the bakery, embrace in the doorway before parting. She decided the bakery was an important Radomsko gathering place and went to investigate.

Inside, she watched a woman and her grown daughter whose animated intimacy reminded Cheryl of time spent with her own daughter. The bakery lifted her spirits. "It expanded the movie in my head beyond the one of you traipsing around in the rain in an overgrown cemetery looking for a trace of family. In the mud."

We ordered two more kinds of strudel: cherry and chocolate. I bit into the sweet, flaky pastry. "My mother made strudel just like this," Cheryl said delightedly. "So did mine," added Tomek. She marveled at his appetite. We watched Radomskers settle down at the tables to exchange gossip. It was a relief to sit in the steamed-up bakery with rain streaming down the windows, a relief to calm emotions churned up in the cemetery.

The recipes my grandmother learned in Radomsko accompanied her to the Lower East Side, where she baked hamantaschen for Purim and honey cake for the Jewish New Year. My mother replicated those sweets a generation later for her children in Los Angeles.

Cheryl's gut instinct for how to *be* in this town of my ancestors did not involve trekking around the tombs of wonder-rabbis. It was as simple as the recipe for strudel passed down by Bessie Tomashevsky, the great Yiddish theater performer born in the Ukrainian borderlands not far from here. Generations of women in Radomsko must have followed it:

"Wash your face, put on a clean apron, then go into the kitchen and make the strudel."

CHAPTER 9

"Do You Miss Us?" Cabaret

Unlike the city's rival, Warsaw—which the Germans had bombed to smithereens—the magnificent architecture of ancient Krakow, once Poland's royal capital, survived the German occupation intact. After bleak Radomsko, it was a relief to wander such a masterful conception of a city—organized, embellished, yet human-scaled.

"A ready model of the cosmos" is how Polish poet Adam Zaga-jewski describes his favorite city, noting how the two main gates of the fortified walls enclosing the Old Town open "like the valves of a human heart."

In the Planty, the greenway park encircling the Old Town center, matronly women walked dachshunds in plaid raincoats. Near the Jagi-ellonian University, a sculpture of Copernicus watched over students reading physics texts and chatting on cell phones. On street corners, spirited young violinists played Bach and Chopin. There was a thrill-ing abundance of bookstores and art galleries. And brooding over the city was the magnificent Wawel Castle, where Poland's great kings, statesmen, and poets are buried.

All roads lead to the Rynek Główny, the market square, laid out in 1257. The arcades of the fantastical Renaissance Cloth Hall domi-nate the spine of the square. It reminded Cheryl of a landmark from her itchy-coat dream, where she'd used a clothier's strategy and skill to protect her family from military menace. "I must have bought my yardage here," she joked. Inside the building were craft stalls catering mainly to tourists. I noticed carved wooden replicas of the Last Supper sitting next to carved wooden Hasidic musicians. Collectibles.

Between the Cloth Hall and St. Mary's Church loomed the larger-than-life bronze of Adam Mickiewicz, Poland's larger-than-life epic poet. Every schoolchild in the country knows his masterwork, *Pan Tadeusz*, a Polish *Iliad*.

Mickiewicz's life would make good fodder for a Hollywood blockbuster. The romantic poet was born on Christmas Eve in 1798, on his uncle's estate in the wooded borderlands Poland currently shares with Lithuania and Belarus. Three years before Mickiewicz was born, the Republic of Poland-Lithuania ceased to be—partitioned among the Austrians, the Prussians, and the Russians—and this region came under the rule of the czar.

Mickiewicz was a patriot who lived his life exiled from a land that did not exist, where writing in Polish was a risky patriotic act. He was a socialist before socialism, a political activist, a plotter. He was an intimate of Alexander Pushkin, a friend of Frederic Chopin and George Sand. He tried to organize militias to bring down the Russian Empire, to hasten the rebirth of a Polish state.

During the Crimean War, Mickiewicz, together with his friend Armand Lévy, a Polish Catholic of Jewish descent, traveled to Turkey as part of a wild scheme to organize a "Hebraic" regiment recruited from Polish Jews dragooned into the Russian army and taken prisoner by the Turks. This Polish Jewish legion, supplemented by Ottoman Jewish volunteers, would be mustered to support France and Britain in defeating Russia. Mickiewicz, who died in Constantinople of cholera in 1855, was a mad dreamer.

The Nazis took great pleasure in dynamiting Krakow's statue of Mickiewicz. Restored in 1949, during the years of Soviet oppression it was a beacon of hope, a vision of a man who kept his faith in what Poland could be again—a free and democratic society.

By some accounts, Mickiewicz's mother was from a family of Jewish converts. In his rural childhood, young Mickiewicz moved among Jews and his lawyer father took their cases. In his university days in Vilnius, the city hummed with Jewish life and scholarship. Jews were part of the landscape of his life.

In Mickiewicz's *Pan Tadeusz*, a Jewish innkeeper named Jankiel is one of the principal characters. Jankiel is both an observant Jew and an ardent Polish patriot, a combination of loyalties not uncommon among Poland's Jewish citizens who fought for Polish independence alongside their Catholic neighbors. Many of them considered themselves Jewish Poles, not Polish Jews.

The stirring political manifesto at the heart of *Pan Tadeusz* is the ballad that Jankiel sings to entertain the wedding guests at his rural inn. Historian Simon Schama considers Jankiel's performance "a musical history of Poland's sorrows and defiance." Another critic suggests that Mickiewicz, by presenting a wise Jewish elder as comfortable in the Polish landscape as a hunter or a woodsman, was indulging in mere poetic wish fulfillment.

Schama credits Mickiewicz with far deeper insight. "Where so many of his contemporaries saw the history of the two nations (Jewish and Polish) as necessarily alien to each other, Mickiewicz from the beginning saw just how snarled up they were in each other's fate."

"Snarled up . . . in each other's fate"—I'd return again and again to Schama's useful phrase over the years, as I thought and wrote about Poles and Jews.

THE CAVERNOUS FLAT CHERYL and I rented for our week in Krakow was on the second floor of an old building on Józef Dietl Street, which bordered Kazimierz, the old Jewish section of town. The stately houses on Dietl, now divided into flats, were once mostly inhabited by Jewish families. From our front windows, I watched yellow trams glide down the center of the boulevard under bare sycamores festooned with crows' nests.

On our first night, I heated a can of soup, sliced bread, opened a bottle of red wine. Cheryl lit a second-night Hanukah candle and put on a CD she'd brought from France: Charlie Haden's *Nocturne*. The yearning romanticism of Haden's instrumental ballads fit the moment exactly.

The next afternoon, while Cheryl wrote in her journal and sipped hot tea with cherries at Café Camelot near the main square, I walked over to St. Mary's Cathedral, paid my ten zlotys, and climbed the several hundred spiral stairs to its tower. I wanted to feel the city in my muscles.

In the small room at the top, a calm, blue-eyed man in a military uniform pulled on the huge rope eleven times to ring the cathedral bell. Then he bugled a melancholy phrase four times to each cardinal direction, abruptly breaking off each time. His caesura commemorates a Polish guard silenced by an arrow to the throat during a thirteenth-century Tatar invasion. This poignant and somewhat macabre ritual is performed around the clock; history contained in the heralding of each hour of the day. The bugle sound defines Krakow to Krakovians.

That night Tomek, eager to show us the sights of his own city, came by to escort us to a klezmer concert at the restored Temple Synagogue in Kazimierz. The main sanctuary was already packed when we arrived, but Tomek charmed his way to three seats near the stage.

Built in the 1860s, this handsome building was once attended by the bankers, businessmen, writers, and musicians of Krakow's progressive Reform Jewish community. During the occupation, the Nazis used it as a stable. It had been rededicated just two years earlier, after a six-year international restoration effort. Its ceiling had been replastered, delicate Oriental Moorish motifs painstakingly repainted, stained glass windows reglazed, cornices regilded. Now the glow of chandeliers was amplified by klieg lights installed by a television crew from Polish national TV.

Tonight's concert commemorated the music of Leopold Kozlowski, one of the few Jewish klezmer musicians to survive the war. A native of Lwów, he settled in Krakow after the war and taught his music to Polish musicians who regarded klezmer as an indigenous regional style. Kozlowski, an endearing fellow with white muttonchop sideburns and a sense of humor that needed no translation, emceed the concert.

Polish actors dressed like Hasids in black silk jackets sang Kozlowski's songs. Was this some kind of minstrel show? "Are they playing our music because they miss us?" Cheryl whispered.

The audience in the packed hall was attentive, respectful. There were middle-aged couples, teenagers, children. Tomek looked as rapturous listening to these old Yiddish songs as I imagined a twenty-three-year-old should look when listening to his favorite rock band.

In our kitchen the next morning, Cheryl contemplated her last night's dream. We had attended a performance at a club called the "Do You Miss Us?" Cabaret. A large Plexiglas box encased the stage. Inside were artifacts belonging to rich Polish émigré Jews: gold watches, elegant shoes, stacks of books. Displaying these material artifacts was risky—others might covet them. One must avoid ostentation.

"It comes down to this," she said. "Poland, you didn't want us. Poland, we've done quite well without you . . . thanks very much!"

THE CENTER FOR JEWISH CULTURE occupies a gracious building in the heart of Kazimierz. Its bold interior architecture features a glass atrium shaped as a square. Robert Gadek, Tomek's friend and the center's program director, was a tall, thin young man in his thirties with a warm, intelligent face. Robert escorted us to a table inside the glass cube of the central atrium and ordered espresso all around.

Cheryl wasted no time. Gesturing toward the glass cube above us, she began describing the "Do You Miss Us?" Cabaret dream to Tomek and Robert. I calmed down once I saw that Robert was nodding enthusiastically as if he too had attended this dream cabaret. He didn't consider it odd or offensive when Cheryl asked, in all earnestness, "Do the Poles miss us?"

"There's no yes or no answer," he replied. "It's complicated."

Robert's own history was a case in point. He'd grown up in Nowy Sad, near Tarnopol on Poland's postwar eastern border. "My parents' attitude about the Jews was 'chapter closed,'" he said. At university in Krakow, as part of his coursework in linguistics, he discovered Yiddish. "I was naïve enough to go searching for the people who were speaking this dialect. I thought they were some kind of minority who lived in isolated circumstances. Why were they hidden from me?"

The Center for Jewish Culture, where Robert had worked for almost a decade, was the brainchild of Polish intellectuals living abroad. One of the center's most important supporters, its "good ghost," as Tomek called him, was Rafael Felix Scharf, a Polish Jewish native of Krakow who became an English journalist and diplomat. Scharf devoted his life to mending fences between Poles and Jews.

Scharf grew up on Dietl Street, where our apartment was located. Kazimierz was his neighborhood, where he went to school, helped his mother shop, attended synagogue, visited friends. In 1930, after receiving a law degree from the Jagiellonian University, he left Krakow for London for postgraduate studies. He became a journalist and ultimately a diplomat. During the war, he served in the British Army, and after the war ended, he was a member of the British War Crimes Investigation Unit. Though his mother survived the war in hiding, the entire Jewish community of Krakow that had nurtured Scharf—"family, friends, teachers, neighbors, shopkeepers, beggars"—was completely wiped out.

At the Judaica Center I'd bought Scharf's only published book, a collection of his essays titled *Poland, What Have I to Do with Thee?* Cheryl and I took turns reading sections aloud to one another in the evenings during our stay on Dietl Street.

In the keynote he delivered at the dedication of the center, in 1993, Scharf explained that he would not dwell on the reasons he left Krakow in 1930. He would not talk about the quotas for Jews at the university, the nationalist rhetoric that suggested Jews emigrate to Madagascar. "When I am thinking of those times as I often do, the idea occurs to me—when it was so bad, why was it so good?"

That question—so deftly articulated—was one that haunted both Cheryl and me. It was part of what drove Tomek to study Jewish culture in Poland. He'd told me that it sometimes pained him that Jewish visitors to Poland focused only on those "five years . . . not the whole length of the history of the Jews in Poland."

Tomek had a point. But those five years were not like any other five years. As the writer and Holocaust survivor Jean Améry wrote, "If in five years, all Poles had been murdered, those five years would not equal any other five years, any other eight hundred years." Tomek countered, "But without those eight hundred years of Jewish life in Poland, you cannot understand what was lost in those five."

On a 1992 visit to Krakow from London, Scharf paid a visit to the Cathedral of St. Mary's on Krakow's main square. He shared his pew, he recalls in an essay, with a young man who was praying with great fervor. "At the end of the service, as we were leaving the church together, we got talking, with growing sympathy and openness—two authentic Krakovians, spanning two generations."

The young man confided in Scharf, that, as a believer, a student of ancient history and a practicing Catholic, it no longer caused him any difficulty to accept that Jesus was a Jew. "But in no way," he said, "am I able to accept that Our Holy Virgin Mary, the Queen of the Crown of Poland, as we like to call her, was a Jewess."

"I didn't know what to say," wrote Scharf. "To understand these things, on a level which does justice to the depth and complexity of these predicaments, is too difficult for me, for most of us."

But helping people to understand "these predicaments" was precisely, Robert explained to us, what the center was attempting to do. The idea behind the center was to attract non-Jews and hidden Jews (those who converted to evade detection), "to educate, give facts, change minds."

The center was founded in 1989, at the end of Communist rule when all discussion of the absent Jews was taboo. The Kazimierz neighborhood was then derelict, its residents living in extreme poverty. Few had their own toilet. No one had a phone.

Tomek's grandfather lived in Kazimierz, and he remembered on one visit how a car burned out of control on the street outside his grandfather's flat. "Such an ordinary sight; no one paid it any attention. Kazimierz was the scariest part of Krakow."

Most of the residents were elderly. "The old ones," Robert said, "are victims of the old system. But you cannot blame the old system for everything. Anti-Semitism is not the only barrier . . . Poles have trouble with any 'otherness.' I call it their identity anguish. They feel superior and inferior at the same time."

The center first had to win the trust of these elderly neighbors, who feared losing their homes to returning Jews. Soon after they opened, they installed a pay phone in the building as a way to attract suspicious, poor neighbors to come inside the new building.

"Most of the houses—not only in Kazimierz, but in Krakow—had been Jewish houses," Robert explained. "When Poland was born after the war, everything was nationalized and belonged to the state. There was no more private property. Any papers you had claiming ownership were worthless."

After 1989 people started to talk about lost property. Property restitution, after the injustices of the Nazi and Communist regimes, was a bureaucratic nightmare. Property appropriated from dead Jews or expelled Germans was often seized by the Communist regime in the name of socialism. Some properties had been lost and claimed several times over. There were moral, legal, and political issues to be navigated in each instance—a hopeless tangle to which no nationwide solution has yet been found.

In Kazimierz, where most of the properties had originally been owned by Jews, the fear of losing homes was mixed in with a twisted prewar notion, as Robert described it, "that awful proverb 'Ours are the streets, and yours are the houses.' In other words, you Jews, foreigners, capitalists—you own the houses and we poor Poles have no place to live *in our own country*."

I felt hot under my collar. I thought of the character of the Polish woman in Philip Roth's *Operation Shylock* who founded a chapter of "Anti-Semites Anonymous." Perhaps parody was the most honest response. Those who suffered from the disease of anti-Semitism needed a twelve-step program to wean themselves from the habit of blaming Jews for their problems.

Yet, even as I bristled at his account, I admired Robert Gadek's lucid analysis and matter-of-fact approach. It was only natural that these elderly Polish pensioners—who weathered the Communist secret police, the Nazi occupation, and a hundred disappointments and humiliations—feared the loss of their homes.

"People really started to be afraid in 1997, when the state declared that they would respect prewar ownership of communal properties, like former synagogues, cemeteries, prayer houses," he continued. "People here thought that Jews will come and they'll remove us from our houses." As it turned out, none of the drafts of restitution legislation about private property were passed until 2001, and then the Polish president promptly vetoed it.

The Jewish Center organized a meeting with a lawyer to explain the proposed statutes. "We were afraid no one would come. But they came, and you could really feel the tension, the anger." The lawyer explained that it wasn't that easy to throw people out of their houses. By giving access to information and resources, the center created one of those "moments," Robert explained, "when the people thought, 'Aha! The center is trying to do something for us.'"

Now, more and more neighborhood residents come here with their guests, their families. "They come to use the pay phone. They sit down in the coffee shop. They come after Holy Mass to have a look at the exhibition." The center deals with Jewish issues first of all, but it has also become a place for neighbors to speak about their problems, their issues.

"We have become a part of this landscape," said Robert. "I don't know how much it changes their attitudes toward Jews. But this is not a project for just ten years, it's a process for generations."

I thought it strange yet poignant that Poles were running the Center for Jewish Culture. "I'm asked, sometimes twice a day, 'Are you Jewish?'" sighed Robert. "Of course, the answer is no."

"Maybe some of them have this notion—in back of their head— that Poles are all anti-Semitic. That if Poles are running the Center for Jewish Culture, there must be some 'dirty business' behind it.

"We know perfectly well that if the Holocaust hadn't taken place, then this place would be run by the Jewish community. But unfortunately, we cannot change history. The only chance for such a center to exist is to be run by Poles."

I asked about Krakow's hidden Jews, whose parents had converted to Catholicism after the war or abandoned their religion under the Communist regime. Many of them did not discover their parents were Jewish until they were adults themselves. Did they come here also?

"Yes, they say it is one of the few places where they are able to feel openly Jewish. They're not religious, so they don't feel comfortable with a religious community. They say, 'Here we feel like we're part of a society, not in the ghetto. We're among non-Jews, not only among Polish Catholics, but other groups who are coming here—Armenians, Ukrainians. This is how our fathers described life before the war. Jews were the biggest minority—but one of very many in Poland.'

"That's why I call this process a two-way street," he concluded, "because we learn from each other."

THE DARK DECEMBER CITY was covered with snow. Cheryl and I spent that last Krakow afternoon in our flat, reading, writing, listening to music, napping. Cheryl dreamed the closing night's performance of her "Do You Miss Us?" Cabaret. The Polish dream actors were dressed in Hassidic garb, singing in Yiddish, as they had been in the Temple Synagogue. The stage curtain at the back of the set slowly opened. A gasp from the audience. Backstage, tied and gagged, were Jewish prisoners with tubes and wires coming out of their heads.

"Their music was being siphoned out of them," she said.

"But they were still alive," I said, reaching for an optimistic interpretation. The absent Jews were still a lifeblood of this place. At Wannsee, Dorota had said, "You could feel there was a hole cut out of the whole fabric." Young people like Robert and Tomek went looking for us.

We ate dinner with Tomek. Delicious. Two hot soups—cucumber with dill and sour rye soup (zurek) with cabbage. Cheryl was ecstatic—the tastes brought her back to her childhood, when her mother used to make three pots of soup for the week. I asked Tomek to teach us some Polish words.

Tomek held up a spoon. *Wish-kah.* Then he picked up a smaller spoon. "A little spoon is a *wish-ah-chkah.*" Here was one of the things I loved about the Polish language, how almost every noun was bestowed with a tender diminutive, as Rafael Scharf called it, "a caressing gradation."

Cheryl didn't want to love her Polishness, but she did. "Poland is in me," she admitted. "I was bitten at birth."

CHAPTER 10

Poland, Peyote

Kolomyja had always been Cheryl's primary reason for wanting to travel to Poland. She'd accompanied me to Radomsko, comforted me there in its bleakness. Now, in the spring of 2004—a year and a half after our first Polish journey—Cheryl would finally travel to Kolomyja. She called it "the town that unloved me." She'd longed to go there her entire life; she also feared it. We would go there together.

I tried to sleep off jet lag in a Warsaw hotel room. Cheryl was en route from Nice. I expected her knock at any moment. It had been unclear whether our Polish collaboration would have another round. For months, Cheryl's ambivalence had stalled our travel plans. "The pickle on Poland," she wrote from France, "is that it's not the country of caricatures I grew up picturing. Annoyingly, I feel drawn."

I knew better than to pressure her. Our partnership had been spontaneous, its duration unstated. But the idea of traveling to Poland without her was dispiriting. I depended on her intuitive genius for exploring unfamiliar situations. I loved the questions she asked, the parables she dreamed.

Hoping to jostle our travel stalemate, I accepted Cheryl's invitation to the old city of Nice, in the south of France, to join her and her husband for New Year's 2003. That first night Cheryl and I went down to the harbor for a sunset walk, what the Central Europeans call "shpatziering"—a promenade meant for intimate conversation, taking in the sights, nodding at acquaintances. She was excited to show me their adopted city.

I filled her in on how, since our last trip, I'd continued to search out information on my family in Radomsko, how pieces of information about heretofore unknown family appeared in my inbox without warning.

Cheryl listened sympathetically. My story resonated. In a recent dream, an old Native American man had cautioned her that going back to Poland "was like taking peyote." Delving into the family past was like a mind-altering drug. You'd better know what you were doing, you'd better fortify yourself with ceremony and steadfast guides, because otherwise, you could get "lost in it."

I'd ingested the drug. Not long after I'd first learned of the existence of my great-aunt Fayga Wilhelm, I'd found her name on the list of those from Radomsko who'd perished during the Shoah. For weeks afterward—standing in line at the ATM, driving to the grocery store—I'd burst into tears. On another list, I noted the name Adam Wilhelm, who'd survived the war and been repatriated in Stockholm. I wrote to the Swedish Consulate and for weeks entertained hopes that one of Fayga and Fayvel Wilhelm's children might still be alive. No, it was a different Adam Wilhelm, from Lodz. More recently, I'd found a seventeen-year-old cousin, Dvojra Gitla Konarska, listed on a 1942 German roster of "designated laborers"—upending my workday.

Poland had insinuated itself into my conscious and unconscious life. I'd even dreamed a map of Poland etched on the palm of my hand. I wrote to a Polish friend about it.

"Map of Poland on your palm? With all the border changes?" he wrote back. "Nightmare!"

WHEN MAX BLITZ, CHERYL'S father, lived in Kolomyja, it was a Polish town. With borders redrawn after the war, Kolomyja was in Ukraine. To travel to Ukraine, Cheryl needed extra reassurance. We'd heard various reports about the safety of traveling there. One woman whose business was to lead "roots" tours there (and who charged high fees to do so) claimed that you needed a driver and a bodyguard, your own toilet paper, water, food. You needed to have a special relationship with the police. Every cautionary tale amplified Cheryl's unease.

Cheryl contacted the history department of the University of L'viv, the cultural capital of Ukraine. She netted a response from a historian and genealogy researcher named Alex Dunai. He was experienced at guiding foreigners, he spoke the language, he knew the history of the place. He assured her that it was not dangerous to travel in Ukraine. "Would it be possible to be shown one's family house by its present occupants without fear of being attacked?" she wrote him. No, that was not a worry. He also described himself as large of build, much heftier—Cheryl assumed—than our dear Tomek. Alex was the ticket. We made our travel plans.

As our departure date grew closer, Cheryl staged some dream masterpieces, casting her anxieties as beasts of prey in a dangerous landscape. Her encounter with a resourceful lion in a dangerous town was the standout. "How do you deal with the anarchy?" Cheryl asked the lion. "Look at my ruff," the lion instructed her, "but do not touch it." Razor blades were woven into his dark mane. "It doesn't help being a lion in a lawless place," the king of beasts explained. "Now if anyone tangles with me, he'd get sliced up."

Cheryl took heed. The morning after, she purchased an international cell phone that worked in Poland and Ukraine. If the situation in Kolomyja overwhelmed her, she could call her husband, Henry, or her daughter Anna. She needed an edge, a way to obtain comfort. The cell phone would be her concealed weapon.

CHERYL ARRIVED AT THE Warsaw hotel exhausted, long after dark. She brought a French repast: crusty bread, soft goat cheese, a bottle of bordeaux. We sat on the big hotel bed, clinked glasses to celebrate our reunion, caught up on family stories. Her spring wardrobe was streamlined—four interchangeable, black, stretchy outfits that folded up to practically nothing.

After two glasses of wine, she confided what was uppermost in her mind: "My father called from New York last night."

Cheryl's father had long begged her not to go to Ukraine. He'd always told her he didn't know what had happened in Kolomyja while he'd been in the camps in Siberia or what had happened before he'd come home and his neighbors—his soccer friends—had shot at him. He said there wasn't anyone alive who had seen what actually took place. He wanted to protect his daughter from what he knew, protect her from those images he could not stop seeing.

But now he told her that, in fact, he *did* know what had happened in Kolomyja. Cheryl's cantankerous aunt Jean—her father's sister, then a young girl—had seen it all. Jean had survived Auschwitz, where she'd been one of Doctor Mengele's "experiments." Months earlier, when Cheryl had informed Jean of plans to visit Ukraine, her aunt had been irate, dismissive: "There's nothing there for you! This has nothing to do with you!"

For Cheryl's father, the reality had finally sunk in that, despite his entreaties, his daughter was going back to his hometown. Even though she'd never been there before, she was "going back." If he would never step foot in that town again, she was going back for him.

He called to ask her to do two things for him while she was there: "Go to the site of the former synagogue where your grandfather Sandor was burned alive. Go to the place in the forest outside the town where my mother and my sister were shot and are buried in a mass grave with other women from Kolomyja."

Aunt Jean also finally accepted that her headstrong niece was *really* going to Kolomyja. "Jean said to tell you to look for our house at 28 Walova Street. That house was supposed to have been her dowry."

While Cheryl was still reeling from the shock of hearing, for the first time, any specifics of the family calamity, her father added a parting piece of advice: "Don't tell anyone your family name is Blitz. They might shoot you."

The next morning we left Warsaw for Ukraine.

CHAPTER 11

An Orange Room in L'viv

From the tarmac of the L'viv airport, I peered out the round window of our small plane. Four gigantic Soviet Realist, cast-concrete personae—a factory worker, a peasant woman, a soldier, a pilot—adorned the columns of the Art Deco terminal.

L'viv, the largest city in western Ukraine and its cultural capital, would be our staging ground for the trip to Kolomyja, one hundred twenty-five miles away at the base of the Carpathian Mountains.

The Ukrainian customs official possessed the charm of a street mugger. "How much money do you have?" she snarled. Cheryl dumped all her euros on the counter. The functionary wasn't pleased. "No dollars?"

While they negotiated, I studied my first Ukrainian bill, a five hryvna banknote that featured a grizzled Ukrainian national hero. Using my rusty high school Russian, I painstakingly sounded out the Cyrillic letters: they spelled Boh-dan Ch-miel-nick-i.

Bohdan Chmielnicki was a hero of Ukrainian nationalism, but no hero to Poles or Jews. In 1648 he led a Cossack uprising against the Polish nobles who ruled Ukraine, a campaign that degenerated into an anti-Jewish crusade. According to the great Jewish scholar Gershom Scholem, the Chmielnicki catastrophe of 1648 "fell as a stunning blow upon Polish Jewry." Over one hundred thousand Jews were massacred before Polish forces suppressed the insurrection.

I tucked the wrinkled bill in my wallet.

Past the baggage claim, a friendly face was waiting: our stalwart Ukrainian guide, historian Alex Dunai. He was bear-like in build, sunny in temperament, warm and funny. Driving into the city, he told us about his Ukrainian family. "The Germans and Soviets were equally evil to my family," he told us. The Nazis deported his grandfather's sister to Auschwitz; the NKVD (the Soviet secret police) dispatched Alex's great-uncle to Siberia.

As we entered L'viv, I felt an instant affinity with this proud, old city with its wrought-iron filigrees on balconies from its Hapsburg days, its Art Deco gargoyles, the young lovers necking under blooming chestnut trees. Old women with faces wrinkled like potato skins sold bouquets of fresh dill and lilacs and white coral bells on almost every street corner. Alex bought a fragrant bunch that I zipped into my backpack, the protruding blossoms attracting an honor guard of honeybees.

The city's architecture was an improbable yet harmonious blend of styles, from the medieval to the modern. According to Alex, people were now starting to buy the enormous, mainly eighteenth-century flats in the deserted center of town. It was an expensive proposition; under Soviet rule, nothing got repaired here. The floorboards were usually rotted, the plumbing useless.

Alex, a budding entrepreneur, wanted Cheryl's opinion about real estate as an investment. She had successfully renovated several flats around Nice. Maybe L'viv was the place for a second home?

Under the rule of the dual monarchy of Austria-Hungary, as capital of the crown land of Galicia, the city was known as Lemberg. In 1919 it reverted to Poland and was known as Lwów. After the Second World War, it became a Ukrainian city, renamed L'viv.

The Poles still consider this city, in fact all of western Ukraine, to be part of their "Lost Lands." Between the wars Lwów was cosmopolitan, a seat of Jewish learning; its population, 40 percent Jewish. Several memoirs about life in prewar Lwów mention ethnically mixed neighborhoods where Jews and Gentiles lived side by side, with no apparent enmity.

At the beginning of September 1939, Lwów was part of the Polish territory annexed by the Soviet Union. One has to bear in mind, as historian Timothy Snyder points out in his epic work *Bloodlands,* that the double occupation of the lands on the western border of Russia, first by Soviet, then German armies, "made the experience of the

inhabitants of these lands all the more complicated and dangerous. . . .
It created risks and temptations that were unknown in the West."

If you were a Polish Catholic family living in western Ukraine
in 1939, you were subject to vicious repression by the NKVD, as
part of Stalin's anti-Polish repressions designed to eliminate Polish
intelligentsia. At that same time if—like Cheryl's family—you were a
family of Polish Jewish hotel owners, your business would likely have
been expropriated as part of Stalin's anticapitalist repression. For Polish citizens deemed a possible security danger to the Soviet state—this
included such likely suspects as military veterans, civil servants, policemen, *and* their families—the NKVD arrived at night to remove you
from your home at gunpoint, then loaded you on an unheated freight
train bound for Siberia.

As the Russians withdrew and the Germans pushed into western Ukraine in 1941, all Poles—Jews and Catholics both—were in a
quandary. They were glad to be rid of the Soviets and the murderous
NKVD, but terrified of the Germans. Stay or go? Either way, you
took your chances.

Cheryl's grandfather in Kolomyja was advised by one of his close
friends, "a Communist big shot," as her father tells it, to take his
dreamy elder son, Andrzej, who'd joined the Communist youth
league during the Soviet occupation, and flee east to the Soviet
Union. "When the Germans come in, he will be the first target,"
his friend warned.

Her grandfather took heed. He ordered his younger son Max
(Cheryl's father) to stay home, promising he'd return from the east
in a few weeks. But Max had his own ideas. In the predawn dark,
fifteen-year-old Max stowed away in the back of the wagon. His
father and brother were already fifteen kilometers outside Kolomyja
before he was discovered. "So . . . you will come with us," his father
said simply.

They crossed the border into the Soviet Union with thousands
of others heading east under German bombs, alongside the retreating Russian Army. Though they endured the privations of hunger,
the backbreaking routine of labor camps, and many other misfortunes, Max, his brother, and his father survived the war. Few Jews in
Lwów, or Kolomyja, or Kiev, or elsewhere in Ukraine survived the

Nazi years. Soviet occupation had been terrible. Nazi occupation was worse. For the large Jewish community in Lwów, it was a disaster.

At the end of the war, in 1945, Lwów became a Ukrainian city, part of the USSR. The surviving Polish population, as part of the forcible uprooting of millions of Europeans, were forced out of their ancestral homes and deported west with Poland's new borders. Lwów was renamed L'viv after Ukrainian independence in 1991.

Among those Poles displaced from their home was the family of poet Adam Zagajewski. The future poet, then an infant, together with his sister and parents traveled west for two weeks in a cattle car from their home in cosmopolitan Lwów, with its cafés, opera house, and grand university, to the ugly industrial city of Gliwice, in Poland. In a succinct description of the capricious nature of those mass postwar deportations that inflicted misery on so many, Zagajewski writes in an essay, "Millions of families were forcing resistant suitcases shut with their knees; all this was happening at the behest of three old men [Stalin, Churchill, FDR] who had met at Yalta."

That first night Alex walked us back to the Grand Hotel. In the lobby, burly businessmen from Kiev smoked their Cuban cigars, blonde *prostitutkis* on their laps. Cheryl and I fell asleep to CNN footage of mass graves in Sudan, children starving, animals torched. There was no remote control and we were both too exhausted to budge from our bed to turn off the TV.

WE WERE ON OUR way with Alex to the History Museum the next morning when an old white-haired gentleman appeared out of no-where, wearing a striped tie and a stained trench coat of another era. He tipped his hat and introduced himself as "the last Jew in Lemberg." Cheryl greeted him in Yiddish and his leathery face broke into a grin. He kissed her hand. Alex told us this old man—well known to him— had a daughter in Israel, but that he still needed help. In post-Soviet Ukraine, pensioners received less than seventy-five dollars a month, no medical care. Life was very hard. We offered the Last Jew of Lemberg a fistful of dollars and good wishes.

In the History Museum, you could view 1920s black-and-white photos of old Lwów on a stereopticon. Through the lens was a vibrant city populated by Poles, Ukrainians, Jews, Armenians, Ruthenians

(Catholic, as opposed to Orthodox Ukrainians), Turks, Hungarians, Roma. Now L'viv was populated only by Ukrainians. The stereopticon animated the flatness of the photo, as if bringing that pluralistic culture back into three dimensions.

After shuffling across the waxed parquet floors of the museum in obligatory one-size-fits-all boiled-wool slippers, we went outside into the Italianate courtyard. Alex and I ordered coffee while Cheryl slipped away to browse the antique shop next door.

At the adjacent table, a Ukrainian woman, her bouffant dyed dull bottle-orange, fussed over her young daughter who was happily spooning ice cream into her mouth. Workmen in overalls shuffled through the courtyard. They stooped to their knees and, grunting, hoisted open a heavy wooden trapdoor set into the stone floor, revealing a dark void into which they disappeared.

The young girl watched the ground open up with some amazement, then dropped her spoon and began screaming hysterically. Her mother tried in vain to shush her. The child looked betrayed. If you couldn't count on the ground to be solid, what could you count on? Her sobs did not subside until the workmen reemerged and closed the trapdoor. The child's distress was uncanny. She was too young to know that some Jews from the Lwów ghetto—including young children—survived fourteen months in the rank sewers beneath these very streets.

Cheryl rejoined us just as the child's wails subsided. The girl's existential terror was no mystery to Cheryl. When her daughter Anna was little, Cheryl told us, she was afraid of taking baths. Her fear was that she might be sucked down the drain by the swirling pull of water. Cheryl played games with Anna, rendering the drain harmless, amusing. She had a gift for concocting playful solutions to comfort the fears of others.

Cheryl unwrapped three porcelain eggcups she'd liberated from the dusty shelf in the antique shop. Each four-inch figurine was a rotund, squatting Ukrainian woman, hands in her pockets. The tips of her black slippers poked out from billowy, red harem pants. Her blouse was egg-yolk yellow with black dots. An orange-red target decorated her stomach. Below her black collar, a white ruffled lace bib.

The cup balanced on the woman's sturdy head was cheerful too: orange and yellow dots, each looped by a delicate broken line. The Eggcup Woman was probably from the 1940s, Russian constructivist in style but authentically Ukrainian, the woman in the shop had informed Cheryl.

I imagined the artisans in that factory in some Ukrainian city, painting stripes on the red harem pants of a cheerful eggcup at the same time agents of the NKVD arrived unannounced in their black police vans (the infamous *chernyj voron*, or "black crows") to arrest scores of Ukrainians on nonexistent charges.

Upon entering any bleak hotel room for the rest of our trip, our first act was to set up an Eggcup Woman. She was our Ukrainian Quan Yin, our Constructivist Buddha, our polka-dot Humpty Dumpty, our talisman of good cheer.

LATE IN THE AFTERNOON the second day, Alex drove us to the outskirts of town to the site of a concentration camp named Janowska. Few in the west have heard of it. By 1944, when the Red Army liberated Lwów, between one hundred thousand and two hundred thousand people had died in the city, the great majority of them Jews. Many of those casualties died in Janowska.

"I'm very tired," Cheryl announced. She slid down into her seat, closed her eyes, and folded her arms across her chest.

Alex and I ignored the Restricted Entry sign and walked past the gate toward the settling pond containing the ashes of victims. Cheryl had once asked me, "How do you have a past if your parents never tell you their story?" Looking out over the pond, I realized it made no sense to tell your story when you didn't want to remember what had happened.

That night Cheryl and I ate our cabbage borscht in tired silence in the hotel bar. There was one more event on our agenda. Before leaving the United States, an artist friend had pressed into my hand a scrap of paper with the scribbled phone number and name Natalka Polovynka. She was an actor-singer at the National Theater in L'viv. Alex had placed the call, as Natalka spoke little English. She promised Alex she would come by our hotel after dinner.

With no word from the mysterious Natalka, we retired to our room and turned out the lights at 10:30 p.m. Half an hour later, we were startled awake. A woman was in the lobby asking for us. We changed out of pajamas and ran downstairs.

The stately Natalka—fine-boned, tall, and blonde—waited for us. With sign language and a smile she invited us to follow her. She walked briskly through the dark and winding streets to the entrance of an old stone apartment building. There were no lights. It looked abandoned.

We climbed five flights of worn stone stairs, trusting our feet since we could see nothing. I placed my hand on Natalka's slender waist. Cheryl placed her hand on my back as our trio ascended. "They really like the dark here," Cheryl muttered. Finally, Natalka put her key in a lock and opened an unseen door in the hallway, which now flooded with light from the small room beyond. She welcomed us inside.

The room was daubed in hues of rich terracotta. Enormous surreal sunflowers were impastoed on the walls—ecstatic blooms responding to an unseen breeze. Natalka's eight-year-old daughter, Hannah, blonde like her mother, smiled shyly at us, then resumed embellishing the flowers on the wall with paint and a delicate brush.

Natalka's fellow artists, five women and a bearded Russian director named Sergei, welcomed us. They offered cushions for sitting on the bare wooden floor. Sergei brought us each a mug of hot herb tea.

One of the women, Yelena, spoke English, so we were able to exchange some essentials. They were curious: what had brought us here? Cheryl told them we were going to Kolomyja, her father's town. She told them that many in her family had been murdered there by the Germans. I told them my mother's family was from Radomsko, in Poland; my father was born in Zhitomir, in Ukraine. Sergei lit up; he was from Zhitomir. We told them we were learning about this place, about our family stories, about our Jewish history intertwined with the histories of Poles, with the history of Ukrainians such as themselves.

They would sing ancient songs for us, gleaned from ethnographic recordings of Ukrainian peasant women. These songs were vanishing from the earth. The melodic structures are more than one thousand years old, Yelena explained, "but we treat them as if they are living things."

Their songs began low and slow, the women slumped against the orange wall. They had all worked during the day at their various jobs and they had already rehearsed several hours.

They sang of a girl waiting for her Cossack lover, a crow in a tree. Out of their weary bodies came ethereal, dissonant melodies.

With eyes closed, I saw my Ukrainian grandmother, as a young woman, running in a field. On her deathbed, she'd told a story of how her father-in-law once sent her from Zhitomir to Kiev "to exchange Czarist rubles for gold." "If you see soldiers, throw the money off the train," her father-in-law told her.

For the return trip, she pinned the gold in a muslin sack inside her dress. My grandmother was accompanied by two of her brothers-in-law, but the story made clear that she was the one entrusted to bring home the family valuables.

As the melodies rose and fell, I heard the story in my grandmother's voice:

> We are on the train going home to Zhitomir. So crowded on the train. Then, we hear soldiers. They search everybody, moving from car to car. We hide behind a sack of wheat. Quietly, our hearts pounding, we climb to the roof of one of the cars. Itzhak pulls my hand. We jump.
>
> We walk back to Zhitomir. Everybody there stands around crying and crying. They scream, so happy to see us. Why are you crying? We ask. Soldiers, they say. They murder everyone on the train, everybody in the station.

My grandmother could come up with a story peopled with corpses, but she would also light up in delight when she recalled the Ukrainian countryside. No sunset was ever as vivid, no butter as sweet, no birdsong as thrilling, no bread as substantial as had existed in Ukraine. There was much here that she had loved. There was much here that Cheryl's parents had loved. This music must have been part of that. I glanced over at Cheryl. Her face was rapt, her focus deep inside her own experience of the melodies.

The songs moved through the women's bodies, animating chests, straightening spines, lifting heads. The silences between songs was charged, all of us breathing in that room with the crazy flowers on the orange wall, the young girl with pigtails slumbering behind her mother, the scent of mint tea, the dark night outside.

They performed the entire cycle of songs, two hours worth, just for us. By the end of the performance, well past midnight, the sad elation of these complex rhythms brought the singers to their feet. They spun with arms outstretched, the fatigue no longer visible in their bodies.

THREE OF THE WOMEN walked us back to the hotel. Yelena locked her arm inside mine. She was a schoolteacher by day, an artist to the core. "I want to live in the paradise we make with our songs," she told me.

We said our reluctant goodnights to the three Ukrainian women in front of the doorway to the Grand Hotel L'viv. Before leaving, Yelena turned to Cheryl and embraced her. "Welcome home," she said.

CHAPTER 12

"The Town That Unloved Me"

The breakfast buffet in the ornate dining room of the Grand Hotel was lavish—smoked fish, crepes cooked to order. I planned to eat heartily; we'd need plenty of energy on the day we set out for Kolomyja. When I asked Cheryl to pass the jam, she looked at me oddly, then made the following bizarre pronouncement: "Just as you wouldn't expect spaghetti to be like fishing line and cut up your insides, you wouldn't expect your neighbors to do what they did." I nearly choked on my blini.

"That's all I remember from my dream this morning," she said.

I made her repeat it.

"Why would anyone expect pasta to be dangerous? But then again," she paused, "why would you suspect that your neighbors would shoot you, take your house?"

Max Blitz, Cheryl's father, couldn't have anticipated that after he straggled home from a Soviet labor camp and finally approached the Grand Hotel that had belonged to his family, his friends from the soccer club would shoot at him from the upstairs window. What kind of crooked mirror were those friends of Max Blitz looking into?

The tried-and-true tactic of divide and conquer is one possible explanation for why so many Ukrainians and Poles vented their fury on their Jewish neighbors. In Ukraine, Stalin spread rumors that the Jews were responsible for the catastrophic famine of the 1920s and '30s (caused by his own policies). As soon as the Germans arrived in eastern Poland and Ukraine, they spread false rumors that Jews were responsible for the NKVD executions of thousands of prisoners.

After Max Blitz came home from four years of war and saw how people behaved, said Cheryl, "he wanted to throw a bomb on Kolomyja."

Cheryl had the long car ride ahead to mull over her dream image. By 9:00 a.m. we were on the road to Kolomyja, the town—as she'd told me repeatedly—"that had unloved her."

I was dazzled by the spring beauty of the Ukrainian countryside. We drove past fields of bright-yellow mustard, safflowers. Geese with goslings strutted along the side of the road. Calves, goat kids gamboled beside their mothers. Horse-drawn carts laden with milk cans clattered along the asphalt. Onion-shaped domes topped the wooden churches. In Ukraine, the little towns, shtetls, were years behind Poland in modern improvements. Signs of urbanization became more and more rare the farther we drove from L'viv toward the Carpathian Mountains and the border with Romania.

The sound of the name Kolomyja was soft. Feminine. Sometimes Cheryl called it Kolomay. The town was spelled Kolomea in German, Kolomyya in Ukrainian, Kolomyja in Polish. And there were other variants, origins unknown: Kolomiya, Kolimeya, Kolomey, Kolomyia, Kolomaya, Kolomay. According to one local tradition, there used to be an ancient Roman settlement, or *colonia*, in the town, thus the rhyming name Kolomea. *Kolo* in Polish can mean "wheel" and *myje* means "wash." Wagons were run through the nearby river to wash the mud off the wheels: Kolomyja. Yet another story was that the origin of the town name was a corruption of the Latin word *columba*, meaning "dove" or "pigeon." Thousands of wood pigeons, a staple of the local diet during medieval times, once frequented forests of the region.

It was hard to comprehend the terrors, the sheer cruelty unleashed on the population here. In the early thirties, thanks to Stalin's paranoia, millions of Ukrainians died in what historian Timothy Snyder calls "the greatest artificial famine in the history of the world." After 1941 German Einsatzgruppen (literally, Intervention Group)—trained assassins—perpetrated massacre after massacre of Ukrainian Jews.

In Kiev my Steinman cousins barely escaped the bullet. In September 1941, my cousin Rita was a nineteen-year-old radio dispatcher in the Soviet Army, stationed in Kharkov, Ukraine. Alerted by Morse

code to news of the massacres of Jews by the Germans, she immediately caught a convoy heading to Kiev and begged her father, her
aunts to get on a train, any train, as long as it was heading east.

Her father remembered how the German soldiers had treated the
civilian populace in World War I. The Germans were "civilized."
They'd simply "wait it out."

Rita persuaded her family to board a coal train commandeered by
the Soviets to evacuate citizens to Tashkent. Two days later the Nazis
rounded up the Jews of Kiev and herded them to a ravine called Babi
Yar where they executed as many as 150,000 Jews and 50,000 others.

Cheryl queried our guide from the back seat. "Alex, what do
you think is a typical Ukrainian characteristic?" Alex thought awhile.
"Jealousy, meaning . . . the envy of another's good fortune. I think
that is the basis for anti-Semitism here. People feel betrayed when
someone else takes initiative." Cheryl settled back in her seat to brood.

In small villages we passed open-air markets, tables laden with
mounds of onions, potatoes, bundled stalks of bright green dill. Pale
blue and chartreuse stucco huts were stenciled with folk designs.
Red-billed storks—*bozok* in Ukrainian—flapped their wings from
enormous nests astride the multistoried lighting fixtures that lined the
highway. "Everyone thinks they're good luck," Alex told us.

We were nearing the sizable town of Ivano-Frankivsk (formerly
Stanisławów). Most tourists visiting small towns in this area stay in
this provincial capital, some thirty miles from Kolomyja, and Alex had
politely suggested we do the same. Accommodations in Kolomyja, he
warned us, were likely to be Spartan. Cheryl was adamant. We would
stay in Kolomyja.

Alex parked his car in front of the synagogue. He often turned
to the Stanisławów rabbi for advice when he conducted genealogical
research for his Jewish clients. When Cheryl had learned we would
visit a rabbi en route to Kolomyja, she fretted about not knowing the
rabbi's measurements. "If I'd known, I would have had a new suit
made for him in France," she said.

Alex banged on the door. No answer. He called the rabbi on his
cell phone. In moments, a young man in his twenties wearing a yarmulke—the rabbi's assistant—unlatched the deadbolts and escorted
us through the drafty building into the cluttered office of the rabbi.

Moshe-Lieb, the rabbi, was from Zhitomir, my father's birthplace. His pale blue eyes were Zhitomir blue, like my father's. He had bad teeth, a stringy beard, fingers yellowed from nicotine, and a ready laugh.

Stacks of books and an ancient dial-up computer obscured Moshe-Lieb's desk. With Jack Nicholson–like panache, he pulled a pack of unfiltered cigarettes from the pocket of his musty, black suit jacket and lit up. His acolyte offered us hot instant coffee. While we added sugar and nondairy creamer, the rabbi answered his cell phone in rapid Ukrainian.

Moshe-Lieb was one of the few rabbis in Ukraine. With Alex translating, he explained the difficulty of becoming a rabbi in Russia in the 1970s. He studied Torah with a few others in a small Moscow apartment. One person always stayed out on the street to make sure the KGB wasn't coming. Not only did Moshe-Lieb have to watch out for the authorities, he'd had to defy his Communist father as well.

In the nineties, after the fall of Communism, when citizens of Ivano-Frankivsk destroyed the town's Lenin statue, they discovered that the base had been constructed from Jewish tombstones. Moshe-Lieb devoted himself to making sure the stones were reused for a Holocaust memorial.

The rebbe opened his desk and pulled out a broadside, a recent anti-Semitic tract that had been circulating around town. "Ask him why he stays here," I instructed Alex. "Because my congregation would be lonely without me," the rebbe replied with a sad smile. His congregation was just a remnant, fifty elderly Jews. Because there were so few rabbis in Ukraine, Moshe-Lieb ministered to a large area, including Kolomyja.

Cheryl wanted to know whether it would be dangerous to say the name Blitz on the streets of Kolomyja. I was confident that if Cheryl stood in the middle of the town square and shouted, "I am Max Blitz's daughter and I have come *back* to Kolomyja! Blitz! Blitz! Blitz!" no one would care. But I didn't say that. Moshe-Lieb was noncommittal on the subject. He did, however, show us his universal precaution. He opened his desk drawer again and this time extracted a handgun.

He tapped it with his fingers. "To protect myself from crazy people," he said with a shrug. I thought of Cheryl's lion dream. It wasn't good to be a lion—or a Jew—in a lawless town.

We couldn't shake the rebbe's hand in parting, but he agreed to pose for a photograph standing between the two American women. Alex snapped the photo. Three pairs of blue eyes looking at the camera.

THE ROAD INTO KOLOMYJA was broad for a reason. The Soviets widened it in 1968, after the upheaval in Czechoslovakia. The Soviet leadership was worried that the spirit of the Czech uprising would spread to other parts of the Soviet bloc, and Kolomyja is near the border with Romania. "Wide enough for a tank column to cross the Carpathians," Alex said.

On the outskirts of town, we stopped the car and I took a photo of Cheryl standing under the giant Cyrillic letters on the road sign that said Kolomyja. She looked like she was hanging on to the sign for ballast. Soon we were driving into Kolomyja, past Max Blitz's elementary school, down quaint streets lined with small shops that looked exactly like the images on old Kolomyja postcards.

Cheryl did not intend to waste a minute. "We must find my aunt's house on Walova Street," she proclaimed as soon as Alex had pulled over to the curb. We walked into the center of town, found the Walova street sign and walked several blocks down a lane of rickety old brick row houses. A drunken gentleman with a bad crew cut in a tattered black suit followed us. "I LOVE MY BROTHER!" he bellowed in English, as if practicing his limited vocabulary. And then again: "I LOVE MY BROTHER!" He switched to Ukrainian, screaming something at Alex. "He tells me he's mayor of Kolomyja, that he'll arrest me," Alex laughed. He steered the drunk in the other direction.

No sooner had he done that than three young schoolboys, with close-cropped skulls, fell in behind us. We were a novel sight, to be sure. Strangers speaking English. The kids were giggling. Alex turned and with a stern look on his face, yelled at them in Ukrainian, "Why do you follow us like cars on a train?" They vanished.

Twenty-eight Walova Street was missing. A hulk of a building sat forlorn and empty on the even-numbered side of the street. The beautiful brick house Cheryl's great-grandfather built in 1934, with the big ballroom upstairs, wasn't there. Cheryl's shoulders slumped.

Maybe there was another Walova Street? Alex led us to a building that housed various bureaucracies, including one he translated as "the

Office of Living Exploitation Section." While Alex explained our search for the fate of 28 Walova to a harried young woman, I studied a 1950s hand-painted civil defense poster illustrating the proper way to don a gas mask.

The woman pulled a few dusty cardboard boxes of property records from a closet and distractedly thumbed through them. Nothing.

On the front steps of a church where parishioners were leaving mass, Alex snagged a woman and asked a few questions. She confirmed that 28 Walova Street had been torn down because it was on the side of the street in the Jewish ghetto. "There's a shoe factory there now," she told us. She professed to remember the old Grand Hotel of Kolomyja and gave us the coordinates for finding it.

There was no house on Walova. Aunt Jean's dowry was long lost. Chunks of information were flying fast, landing hard. Our next pressing goal was to find the Grand Hotel, what had once been the nicest hotel in town.

We followed the woman's directions. It led to a corner building near the center of town. This must be it! I pulled out my camera and began taking lots of pictures until Cheryl concluded, "It doesn't feel right." We continued walking, found ourselves in a little square where vendors hawked used blue jeans, Tupperware made in China. Alex checked his notes. "This was the site of the main synagogue of Kolomyja," he said.

Cheryl blanched. Another brick to the gut. This was spot where her grandfather and her uncle had been burned alive. "I want to take a photo," she said, slowly drawing out the camera she had yet to use on our trip. To remind her later on that this was not just a photo of a sidewalk sale, I walked into the frame of the picture, sat down on the curb, and crossed my legs lotus position, my palms gesturing upward. It would be a signal.

It was getting dark and time, Alex hinted, that we check into Kolomyja's new (and only) hotel. Its single notable feature was its location next door to a museum that was not only dedicated to the folk art of Ukrainian Easter eggs but also constructed in the shape of a giant Easter egg. The taciturn young woman who worked at the front desk sat in a cage. Our room featured sheer, frilled pink curtains, a mirrored vanity with synthetic skirts tied with a bow, and straight-backed, shiny chrome chairs. Nothing about the place was comfortable.

In our hotel room, Cheryl lit five of the ten votives she'd brought and placed a Ukrainian eggcup woman on the television. "We can leave in the morning," I reminded her. "We don't have to stay."

Sleep was impossible to summon. The images of the day and the history they evoked were too specific.

I listened to Cheryl cry, felt her tremble in the sheets. How could I comfort her? In a *New Yorker* I'd brought, there was a Czeslaw Milosz poem—his version of the myth of Orpheus and Eurydice. Cheryl's visit to Kolomyja, like Orpheus's visit to the underworld, was an attempt to reclaim some memory, some version of the dead. One summoned that memory, those spirits, at one's peril. I read to her about the "ashy traces" of a "kingdom that seemed to have no bottom and no end," about the poet-wanderer searching the faces of the shadows that crowded around him, searching for those he knew.

Milosz's melodic verses had a calming effect. The votives had barely flickered out at dawn when Cheryl finally fell asleep, dreaming that the museum outside had been transformed into a United Nations building, not in the shape of a Ukrainian Easter egg but instead in the shape of our protector, the Eggcup Woman, in her polka-dot apron and harem pants, bearing the eggcup of emptiness on her head and spreading goodwill in her dedication to the cause of tolerance and dialogue.

WE ATE BREAKFAST DOWNSTAIRS in silence, downing cups of black coffee against our bleariness. Alex soon returned from the history museum, where he'd been "making inquiries." Now he knew for certain that the spot where we had taken all the pictures was not the Grand Hotel. What had been the Grand Hotel was now the chief prosecutor's office, next to the town hall. We hurried down there. The clock tower was visible across from the hotel, just as Cheryl's father had described. Cheryl was inside the building in a flash. I dashed behind her.

Two somber men in dark suits with walkie-talkies stood at the top of the stairs. They were not pleased we'd entered unannounced and were taking pictures. They were not pleased that Cheryl was bounding up the stairs into the hallways. Alex followed close behind, trying to smooth things over. But Cheryl moved too fast, swinging through doors with the two hulks lunging behind her like a Marx Brothers' routine.

Alex talked his way into the chief prosecutor's office and explained to him that Cheryl's family once owned the building. He sent one of the hulks to welcome us inside, but Cheryl had already darted ahead; indeed, she was practically in the bewildered chief prosecutor's lap.

She acted as if she owned the place. "Take our picture!" she demanded. The chief prosecutor smiled wanly. "For my father," she said without apology. Then she walked out.

We sat down to collect ourselves on benches across from the hotel. Cheryl was giddy. "This must be how commedia dell'arte evolved," she mused. "You turn to slapstick when the pain is too much to bear." She pulled out the cell phone that worked in Poland and Ukraine and dialed Max Blitz in New York.

"Papa, can you believe I'm standing right here, in Kolomyja, in front of the Grand Hotel?"

"Why are you in Kolomyja?" he said. "Why did you go?" He couldn't really believe she'd followed through with the trip. The news was still a shock to him.

"Because I love you, Papa."

"So that's nice, you're having a good time."

"I don't know if I'm having a good time," she faltered. "I came here because I love you."

The satellite connection wasn't strong. A surfeit of emotions shorted out the conversation. She put the phone away.

IT WAS MARKET DAY in Kolomyja. The streets exploded with commerce, small stalls piled with everything from mackerel to tobacco, cornmeal, vests, peonies, mushrooms, dahlia bulbs, and fresh dill.

One market vendor grinned at us from behind her piles of seeds and tobacco. She was matronly but not old. Her wiry hair was flecked with silver, her face ruddy. She wore a polka-dot apron over her cotton dress.

"Come here!" she gestured with wind-chapped hands. Her wide smile, revealing glinting gold teeth, was irresistible. "Tell her my family is from this town," Cheryl entreated Alex.

The vendor, Maria, was excited to hear this. Alex filled in more details. I made out the words "Grand Hotel." Maria considered this information with nods, smiles, eyes widening. She hugged Cheryl to her bosom. The word spread fast. Other market women gathered around Maria. I caught the word for "Jews." What did she say? "She said, 'If the Jews were here, they'd buy my peaches,'" said Alex.

"Wait!" Maria gestured. She dashed off through the maze of stalls, disappearing for several minutes, returning with a gift for Cheryl: a *pysanky*, a delicate painted Easter egg. Alex explained that in Ukraine, the Easter egg symbolized new hope, prosperity, new life. This one was maroon with delicate geometric patterns dotted on the surface. Alex told us that dots used to represent stars or cuckoo eggs, a symbol of spring—or the tears of the blessed Virgin. Maria placed it gently on Cheryl's open palm.

Maria filled bag after bag of beet seeds for me, enough to make cauldrons of Ukrainian borscht, enough seeds—as it turned out—to plant six seasons worth of backyard beet crop in Los Angeles.

Cheryl pulled the equivalent of a forty dollar bill out of her bag and stuffed it into the pocket of Maria's apron. Maria shook her head. "She doesn't want it," explained Alex. Now Maria was crying as she thrust the money back at Cheryl. "For your children, for your children," Cheryl insisted. Maria both grinned and wept. She wrapped her arms around Cheryl, pulling her once again to her generous bosom.

We made our final farewells to ebullient Maria and walked back through Kolomyja to Alex's car. The town that had seemed mean and gray the night before was considerably brightened, even pretty. We hadn't been able to find the house on Walova Street nor anyone who knew anything about the Blitz family. But meeting Maria had lifted our spirits.

Cheryl settled herself into the back seat. As she reached out to close the door, Maria's Easter egg slipped out of her grasp onto the asphalt with a soft but sickening crunch.

Cheryl stared at the broken shards, shrugged her shoulders, and asked in a nearly inaudible voice, "How could anything be whole again anyway?"

CHAPTER 13

In the Uniform of the Perpetrator

Before the war, the Blitz family summered in Yaremche, a resort town nestled in the foothills of the Carpathian Mountains forty-five kilometers from Kolomyja.

"Yaremche . . . the most beautiful town," Cheryl's father Max raved when she told him we were going there. It was the first time Max Blitz ever admitted he loved anything about his life in Poland/ Ukraine. During the last two summers before the war, Max's sister Jean rented a pensione with a dance hall in Yaremche. Max bused tables while his sister ran the establishment, ordered the food and drink, ejected rowdy patrons.

I imagined the Blitz dance hall in Yaremche on a summer night before the war: Chinese lanterns, a wooden floor, summer breezes through open windows. The men wear vests, white shirts, and Panama hats; women are in patterned rayon dresses, seamed silk stockings, open-toed shoes. Conversation switches back and forth from Polish to Yiddish; couples sit and nuzzle at small round tables in the back of the hall; single men carry glasses of beer or iced lemonade to their dates, coaxing them out on the floor for a tango or a fox-trot, or maybe the kolomyka, the sprightly Carpathian dance particular to Kolomyja. When the klezmer band from Lwów strikes up "Ikh hob dikh tsufil lib" (I love you too much) or "Oygn" (Eyes), with a curvy chanteuse crooning the lines that Molly Picon made famous, the couples pull closer.

Max the busboy kept a sharp eye out for who drank the most. He cleared cigarettes from the drunks' tables, sold them back when they demanded more smokes. He laughed recounting the memory to Cheryl.

Before we could explore Yaremche and its convivial memories, however, we were sworn to carry out a more difficult pilgrimage. Max Blitz had instructed Cheryl: "Go to the place in the forest outside the town where my mother and my sister were shot and are buried in a mass grave with other women from Kolomyja."

Alex had tried—through the local historical museum in Kolomyja—to track down some old-timers who might remember Cheryl's family. He'd spoken by phone to two old women who'd long outlived their mates. "One didn't want to talk about Jews. The other seemed to remember the Blitz family," he reported. "She said, 'The same thing happened to them as happened to the others—the Sheparowice Forest.'"

On the side of the highway on the outskirts of Kolomyja, we spotted a stone marker limned by dense forest. A small bricked area and a low metal fence—inset with the design of a menorah, painted in blue and white like the Israeli flag—surrounded it. The monument had been installed by an American descendant of the Kolomyja Jewish community.

Alex parked the car. Cheryl sat glued to her seat, her jaw set. I climbed out, opened the trunk, and pulled out of my pack several *yahrzeit* (memorial) candles in glass jars that I'd brought from Los Angeles. Cheryl emerged from the car, knelt, and lit the candles at the base of the memorial stone.

"Go to the forest," Max said to Cheryl. "Your grandmother is there."

"Come on," I said gently, acting on impulse. I reached for Cheryl's hand. Alex took up a position by the car. We stepped over the low fence that separated us from the forest, walked twenty feet down a spongy dirt path, clambering over rotted logs and downed limbs, avoiding puddles of brown water seeping through the thick humus.

The path may have continued on farther to a clearing, I don't know. Cheryl couldn't, or wouldn't, walk any farther. We were in a lush, mainly deciduous grove. Spring sun, slanted between canopies of ash and beech, cast a honeyed light like some mockery of Eden.

Cacophony of birdsong: hoots, trills, arpeggios. Industrial-level thrum of insect chatter. Wind through branches. Creak of shifting tree trunks.

On this spot, thousands of people were murdered. Young people like Cheryl's aunt. Old people like her grandmother. "Digging the graves took a whole day," it says in the Kolomyja Yizkor. Cheryl shivered, her body rigid next to mine.

Pungent scents wafted up from the moss stewing in rainwater. In the distant canopy an unfamiliar two-note cry—a European cuckoo. Iridescent dragonflies took flight from lichen-padded rocks. Fifteen minutes? Thirty? We clung to each other in a trance. Then it broke and we walked back without a word. Alex started the car.

We drove south toward the mountains, past small churches, open pastures, a woman who sat reading a book while grazing her milk cow. Storks alighted in ungainly nests on light poles along the highway.

In one village we slowed for a funeral procession. The villagers walked somberly alongside the horse-drawn hearse. The mourner in the front of the group carried a framed photo of the deceased, a lovely young woman. I wondered how she'd died.

The crowd passed and we drove on as the road rose toward the Carpathians. Alex pointed out the remains of a collective farm.

"Stop the car!" Cheryl urgently demanded. I thought she was sick.

Alex swerved onto the shoulder. Cheryl jumped out and began running away in the opposite direction we were headed on the highway. From the rearview mirror I watched her lurch to a halt, then bend over. I closed my eyes.

It began with a guttural groan—like an animal pierced by an arrow. As breath unknotted from her gut, it rose in volume and pitch, a jagged succession of vowels.

Alex and I sat frozen, staring forward as the sound lodged in our viscera. The crunch of Cheryl's footsteps on the gravel grew louder. She opened the door, flung herself onto the seat, slammed the door shut.

"*That's* what I can leave here."

WE DID NOT FIND a dance hall in Yaremche. The once-charming resort was now cluttered with the concrete shells of behemoth tourist hotels built in the Soviet reign. There were few tourists there. We ate shashlik in a gabled wooden restaurant decorated with sheepskins and wandered listlessly through a crafts market where locals sold trinkets.

When we walked back to our car, two men astride patient, shaggy ponies awaited us. They were dressed in the black embroidered vests of the local mountain people, seminomadic shepherds called Hutsuls. "Ancient and noble people of the mountains unspoiled by Western civilization," boasted the tourist brochure, which also alleged that "stork's beak soup" was a Hutsul culinary delicacy.

The older of the two horsemen asked Alex if we wanted to take their photo for a fee. Alex pressed some money into his hand with a grunt and waved them away. They trotted off.

The drive back to L'viv was long. We climbed into our beds after midnight, exhausted, and slept a long sleep.

IT TOOK ALL OUR energy the next morning to gather ourselves for the noon train to Krakow. The scream had emptied Cheryl out.

Guarding the portals of the L'viv train station, an Art Nouveau masterpiece, were two marble statues. One of them is Hypnos, the god of sleep, son of Night, father of the Oneiroi, the guardians of dreams.

"A dream which is not interpreted is like a letter which is not read," says the Talmud. In the little shtetlach of Eastern Europe—in towns like Kolomyja and Zhitomir and Radomsk—traveling book-sellers once plied their routes. Dream books were among the most popular items they offered for sale. In those books you could learn the meaning of any dream: the baby born with the head of a carp; the midwife dancing in the beet field; the miller's daughter with the extra eye.

To Cheryl, dream logic was the obvious portal for this part of the world. Military sabotage by itchy coats. A lion with concealed weapons. You could lose your mind trying to comprehend why humans would burn other human beings alive, or shoot thousands of them in a lush forest of ash and oak. It made sense that the Oneiroi were watching over us on this journey.

We purchased our tickets from a pale young woman who calculated the tariff on a well-worn abacus. In the high-ceilinged waiting room, we said our final good-byes to Alex.

He'd been such a patient guide, though at times we baffled him with our reactions, our decisions. That morning, for example, we'd stopped at the main post office as our last errand. Cheryl wanted to mail a gift package to her father: a roll of Ukrainian toilet paper, snapshots from Kolomyja, a package of coffee, a map of the Kolomyja ghetto plus a copy of the anti-Semitic tract that the Stanisławów rabbi had given us.

"Why do you send that to your father?" asked Alex, appalled.

"Because these things still go on in Ukraine," she answered grimly.

WE WEREN'T ON THE train for long when two unsmiling Ukrainian border officers—a tall burly man and a heavyset buxom woman— entered our car. The woman barked at us to produce our passports.

They wore knee-high leather boots and peaked military hats. The tall officer scrutinized our photos, glancing from passport to face and back down again. His partner made a desultory survey of the contents of my backpack. The two pounds of Ukrainian beet seeds, my gift from Maria in the Kolomyja market, were safely stashed in my suitcase overhead.

I eyed the massive epaulettes on their olive green jackets. They reminded me of the characters in a series of portraits Cheryl had painted. "When I began," she told me, "I had no idea what or whom I would paint."

In one of them, her uncle Junek (the diminutive for Andrzej)— that same dreamy older brother of her father's who had survived the war in Soviet Russia with him—sits in profile in a columned room. He wears a military jacket with high collar and stiff epaulettes. The painting was in the dusty, muted colors Cheryl associated with the old country: maroons, sap green, cerise.

In Cheryl's painting, Uncle Junek is finally able to sit and drink his wine in that once-elegant, now war-damaged dance hall. But to be safe, Uncle Junek is disguised "in the uniform of the perpetrator."

The officer returned with our passports. An hour later, we crossed the border from Ukraine back into Matka Polska—"Mother Poland"—as the colors of the old country blurred past our windows.

CHAPTER 14

Polonia on Trial

Tomek, beaming, greeted our train from L'viv at the Krakow train station. In the eighteen months since we'd last seen him, he'd been certified as an official guide at the Auschwitz-Birkenau State Museum. He was studying for his exams as an official Krakow city guide, as well as courting beautiful vivacious Sylwia, a fellow student at Jagiellonian who came, he explained, from a "very proper Krakow Catholic family."

For the next few days—before we drove to Radomsko—he'd planned an ambitious agenda. As well as showing us historic sites in Krakow, he'd responded to our desire to have a dialogue with a group of Poles by rounding up a posse of his university friends and setting a date.

Our home base was a fourth floor flat in a medieval building near the main square. From the open window of our aerie I gazed out at the copper-roofed building opposite ours. Under its eaves, a Polish Romantic paradigm was rendered in bas-relief: a bare-breasted maiden in the grip of a bearded man thrust toward a throned king flanked by a crowned eagle. Polonia—the captive nation—was historically represented by a heroic suffering woman.

Cheryl declined to accompany us on a walking tour that first afternoon. I wasn't surprised. Her scream had accompanied us back to Poland from Ukraine. She'd been monosyllabic for most of our train ride, immersed in Eva Hoffman's book *After Such Knowledge*. Toward the end of the trip, she'd set the book down and stared out the window. "I guess you can get used to anything," she said, "like standing in front of a synagogue where your grandfather was burned alive."

Hoffman's book was Cheryl's anchor, her talisman on this journey. Hoffman probed the responsibility and challenge of the second generation, whose parents had survived the Holocaust. She used a vocabulary of metaphors like "needles, shards, pinpricks" to describe the psychological discomfort passed from survivor parents to their children. Hoffman points out that the children of survivors took in the first "incoherent utterances" of their parents' speech "broken under the pressure of pain."

These utterances, these images of familial humiliation and destruction were "indigestible"—like Cheryl's dream of swallowing fishing line, or her dream of the "big cinderblock gallstone" lodged in her gut, or her reference to "calcified feelings of love" she stored in her body—for Kolomyja, for Poland, for the lost family she'd kept vigil for since early childhood, when she listened to her parents crying in the middle of the night.

Hoffman and her sister made a trip to the town in Poland, now Ukraine, where their parents survived in hiding. They were astounded to find people there who knew their parents as a young couple. It was the kind of reunion Cheryl had longed for in Kolomyja.

That our visit had yielded nothing of the kind was an intense disappointment.

TOMEK AND I WALKED up the cobblestones of the Royal Way to Wawel Castle. I was buoyed by Tomek's enthusiasm for his city, his country, its history. Nothing gave him more pleasure than sharing what he knew, fielding questions, opening up new areas of inquiry about Poland's past. As opposed to English, he pointed out, if you say "it's history" in Polish, it means it's *very* important.

We climbed the interminable winding stairs of Wawel Cathedral's fourteenth-century belfry to see the eighteen-ton Zygmunt Bell. It takes twelve strong people to ring the bell. You can hear it as far away as the small town of Wieliczka, thirteen kilometers from Krakow.

"People say, when Zygmunt is rung at Easter it can be heard until Christmas," said Tomek. Touching the bell is said to bring good luck. New brides climb the steep steps to touch the bell and wish for children.

In a small crypt under the castle, I watched reverent Poles file slowly around the tomb of their great poet, Adam Mickiewicz. I tried to imagine Americans paying similar homage to Walt Whitman, Carl Sandburg, Emily Dickinson.

In another large crypt, separated from the others by a heavy iron gate with two Polish white eagles, was the tomb of Marshal Józef Piłsudski, a tireless fighter for Poland's independence.

Piłsudski often appears in photos as a dashing figure in a long over-coat, peaked cap, and handlebar moustache. He was a radical socialist, an ardent Polish nationalist, and a supporter of Poland's tradition of religious tolerance. He presided over one of the great triumphs of Pol-ish military history, the 1920 battle for Warsaw against the Soviets. He ruled Poland from 1926 to 1935 after seizing power in a coup.

Piłsudski may have unified the country, but his own body was not quite whole. The general's corpse was buried here, but his heart was buried in Vilnius near his mother.

The only time Rafael Scharf ever saw his father cry was when Pil-sudski's hearse rolled past their house during the funeral procession in Krakow. He was not the only Jew who wept at Piłsudski's death. The general had been a bulwark against the anti-Semitic nationalists. His demise marked the beginning of boycotts against Jewish businesses and quotas on Jews attending university that intensified in the years leading up to the war.

The next morning a thin, shy Polish woman brought Cheryl and me our breakfast: kaiser rolls with butter and jam, a pot of coffee, and hot milk in tiny majolica pitchers. We exchanged *zhen dobrys*, "good mornings," and she slipped away. Cheryl and I sipped coffee, our talk wandering off into personal histories.

For good friends, there was so much about each other we didn't know. Our time together, for the most part, had been in unusual cir-cumstances. "I don't travel to mass grave sites with anyone but you," she noted dryly.

We talked about our relationships with husbands and ex-husbands, our early struggles for autonomy, and the bonds of shared wounds.

We talked about our first young marriages: what brought us together and what thrust us apart. Her ex, a Dutchman, had subsequently become a friend and had mentored Cheryl and Henry's daughter in her studies in Amsterdam. I told her it had taken me years to realize I'd never apologized to my ex for the pain I'd caused him, and what relief it brought us both when I finally did.

We talked about Henry and Lloyd, the pleasures and quirks of long marriages. It was a relief to take a break from talking about Poland, even though we faced bare-breasted Polonia's dilemma right out our window.

AS THE VENUE FOR our dialogue group, Tomek picked the Galicia Jewish Museum, new since our last trip to Krakow in 2002. The handsome converted brick factory was located in Kazimierz, now the Bohemian quarter of town, a constellation of "Jewish-style" cafés, bookstores, museums. "It is good to show your face in Kazimierz," Tomek quipped. There were Israeli and American Jewish tourists here as well as hip young Poles, all drawn to the ambience.

With a cozy café and a bookshop well stocked with titles on Jewish history and culture, the museum was inviting to both residents and tourists who mingled over espresso and cakes.

The museum was founded and run by a former photojournalist named Christopher Schwartz, a red-bearded Welshman whose father was a Polish Jew from Krakow.

Schwartz, a genial host, told me how he'd originally come to Poland in the early eighties to photograph the Solidarity movement. He was struck by the lack of documentation of former Jewish sites in Poland, how "an eight-hundred-year-old culture had been destroyed in six years." In 1990 he set himself the challenge of "photographing absence." A permanent exhibition of Schwartz's large format photographs was on display in the main gallery.

One photo in particular captured my attention. It was a very simple image taken outside a small village called Stary Dzików: a large field with a stand of tall pines in the center of spiraling plowed furrows. To understand what you were looking at you had to read the caption: "This clump of trees is the site of the Jewish cemetery here.

It is unmarked. There is no boundary fence, nor are there any tombstones. But the local peasants remember that it is a Jewish cemetery and have left it as it is." The presence of the past is kept alive by the *observance of absence* in the plowed field.

Our little group consisted of me, Cheryl, Tomek, and three of his Jagiellonian friends. They all had experience living abroad. Skinny Marcin, "100 percent intellectual," was an Asian studies major. Sylwia, Tomek's lovely girlfriend, was a student of international relations and had studied in Sweden. Jerzy, also a native of Oswiecim, was majoring in Jewish studies.

At Wannsee two years earlier, Cheryl and I had imagined convening some grand international conference where Jews and Poles would hammer out all the problematic topics in Polish-Jewish relations. Now, here we were—two fiftysomething American Jewish women with four sincere Polish university students. It was a start.

Sylwia began by bringing up Krakow's wildly popular annual Jewish Culture Festival, often criticized by Jews because it is staged and attended primarily by non-Jewish Poles. It didn't matter, she insisted, whether someone attended because they had a longstanding interest in Jewish history or just wanted to hear some cool music. Their initial motives were irrelevant as long as the festival ignited their interest in Jewish culture.

I admitted to my own bewilderment and suspicion of a Jewish festival presented by non-Jews. Weren't the Poles merely exploiting the vanished Jewish heritage for tourist dollars? Wasn't this patronizing?

"Like a theme park," Cheryl chimed in. Maybe this approach wasn't so inappropriate in our homogenized global culture, Marcin countered. Since everyone all over the world lived in such a similar manner now—Starbucks in Kyoto, McDonald's in Prague—in order to define differences, you need to explore traditional cultures.

Tomek once told me that when he first got interested in Jewish culture, his parents worried it might estrange him from family and friends. I wondered if he thought their concern was warranted.

Tomek thought no; Sylwia begged to differ, recalling his return from a long stay in Israel. Tomek had been so deeply immersed in his study of Jewish culture that Sylwia feared his Catholic identity might be subsumed.

I understood how a passion could become an obsession. In my own family, I'd had to overcome a certain resistance. Why was I going to Poland of all places? Now, after several visits, it irritated me to hear stereotypes about Poles and Polish history.

Holocaust education was radically changing in Poland now, Tomek said. New textbooks were being published, there were new efforts to teach a more complete history and to commemorate Poland's Jewish citizens. There were more and more commemorative plaques to mark places of Jewish historical memory. In his opinion, the problem in Polish-Jewish relations rested more heavily with how Jews judged all Poles.

Tomek and his friends were aggrieved that neither American nor Israeli Jews were able to fathom the risks and stresses of Poles under German occupation. "There is the ongoing question, 'Why didn't you help? Why were you only onlookers?'"

A number of my American Jewish friends who'd seen Roman Polanski's film *The Pianist* asked me why Polanski (himself a Polish Jewish survivor) had shown the Poles in such a good light. As if that was inconceivable. Eva Hoffman writes of this "permitted prejudice" among Jews in the postwar decades, a prejudice that "one needn't examine or bother to conceal." She usefully points out that the varied tonalities of feeling and opinion that must have existed in the long centuries of Polish-Jewish coexistence have been lost in the absence of actual contact.

Sylwia recalled how the Israeli teens who came to her high school when she was a student brought their own (kosher) food and wouldn't touch any refreshments offered by the Polish students. The Poles experienced this as an insult. The Israelis saw the Polish students as the inheritors of a legacy of anti-Semitism. The Poles saw the Jews as arrogant and standoffish. Instead of allowing the students to experience each other in an unguarded way, the visit perpetuated the stereotype on both sides.

What most troubled the Polish students was how the Israeli teens clung to their preconceived idea that the Holocaust took place in Poland because the Nazis counted on the Poles' help in exterminating the Jews. Before my first trip to Poland, I also shared those erroneous ideas about Poland. The camps were most probably constructed in

Poland because it was convenient. The Germans, after all, were big on efficiency. Poland was a fully conquered country and the overwhelming majority of European Jews lived there.

"We tried to tell the Israeli students that during the war, Poland was considered German territory," said Sylwia. "They didn't want to hear *anything* we said."

The Israeli teens who visited Sylwia's high school were part of the March of Living, arranged by the Israeli government annually since the early 1990s. The teenagers tour Poland by chartered bus, with Israeli guides, visiting places connected with the Holocaust. They visit Maidanek, Treblinka, Auschwitz-Birkenau, the remains of the Warsaw Ghetto. Then they fly by charter plane back to Israel. "It's like forcing someone to get to know each other in a cemetery," observed Jerzy.

Cheryl observed how survivors like her parents got stuck in the trauma and suppressed the memory of everything else that was good. Her parents hated Poland because they felt so betrayed. But they still spoke the language. They cooked the food. They kept the cultural ways of their Polishness. "Because it was in them," she said, "it rubbed off on me."

Sylwia jumped back in. "I don't think that it is possible that Jewish culture won't exist in Poland. Too much has happened here."

"We share this enormous history together," Cheryl said. "Even if we weren't speaking for a while, an intimacy still exists. Like a long marriage—or a divorce. An uneasy intimacy."

Before we left, we asked someone in the gallery to take a picture of the six of us. We huddled together and smiled for the camera, feeling closer than when we'd begun. Sylwia had said in conclusion that, for her, the most important thing in counteracting stereotypes came not from studying books, rather from "meeting real people with real bones." We had to allow time and space for our misconceptions and mutual attractions to collide.

As the others gathered coats, I went back to the gallery to take one last look at Christopher Schwartz's photo of the field outside the village of Stary Dzików. I stared at that expanse of plowed earth surrounding what had been the centuries-old cemetery of Stary Dzików's Jewish community.

There was nothing tangible at the center of the field, but the older Polish inhabitants remembered what had been there. They honored that memory in their own way.

Would their children and their children's children honor that memory as well? How long could you feel an absence?

CHAPTER 15

A Chink in the Wall

I'd hoped for a reciprocal symmetry on this trip with Cheryl. She would find Aunt Jean's dowry house on Walova Street in Kolomyja and I would locate 27 Rolna Street, the last known address for my great-aunt Fayga Konarska Wilhelm and her family in Radomsko.

But there was no house on Walova Street. It would have been wiser, I belatedly realized, to have gone to Kolomyja at the end of our trip. The anticipation would have carried Cheryl through her second visit to my bleak ancestral hometown.

Radomsko did look slightly more attractive on the sunny April afternoon we arrived than on the chilly November afternoon eighteen months earlier when we departed in a downpour. ("Every eighteen months, time to go to Radomsko!" Cheryl teased.) I didn't need bad weather, however, to feel that mantle of gloom and unease settling on my shoulders. I couldn't shake a sense of responsibility for bringing Cheryl and Tomek here. In Krakow there had been elegant tearooms, cabarets, castles. Radomsko was a quiet, private place.

We checked into the Hotel Zameczek, our Radomsko home away from home. Until our one scheduled appointment with the mayor's assistant the next morning, we were without plans.

Tomek drove slowly down a side street past a lovely park we hadn't noticed the last time. A pair of swans floated under the boughs of a yellow-green willow. We sat down on cement steps near the water's edge. A bevy of mallards slowly paddled toward us, hoping for a handout.

We followed a path through the park to a concrete block building—the Radomsko Cultural Center—adorned with spray-painted graffiti that would have looked at home in Los Angeles. Once inside, we heard clapping, some celebration in progress. "Mother's Day," whispered Tomek. We slipped into the darkened auditorium.

Onstage, a cherubic girl with pigtails and straight-cut bangs recited a poem, to the enthusiastic applause of the assembled families. I looked over at Tomek and Cheryl—they were charmed. I felt suffocated. I couldn't explain. We didn't know anyone. We didn't belong here. I had to leave.

It had started to drizzle. We took shelter in an empty pizza parlor down the street. My stomach was in a knot. The sour proprietor glared at us. None of us was hungry. Cheryl leaned closer: "I don't know what you're looking for here," she said quietly. "It's all gone." Her words stung.

Retreating to the Zamaczek was unappealing. I suggested a walk through the neighborhood around the hotel. We noticed a group of people at a crossroads, in front of a statue of the Virgin Mary. They were singing religious songs in the drizzle. The priest gestured for us to join. Tomek had no hesitation, but I didn't know their songs. We stood near the back listening to the soft voices. The priest's cell phone rang and he stepped away from his congregation.

On this street of modest houses, gardens were coming to life. Rust-colored bearded iris. Purple azaleas. Peonies. I love the word for peony in French, *pivoine*. In Polish, we say *piwonia,* said Tomek. Lovely. My judging mind took a break. Relief.

NO ONE SLEPT WELL that night: a combination of a pervasive smell of ammonia and the rough-textured sheets.

Andrzej, the Zameczek owner, was wheeling and dealing on his cell phone in a corner of the breakfast room. Tomek attempted to make arrangements for us to visit the Jewish cemetery. There was a map of the gravestones, Andrzej said, but he couldn't give it to us because of some proprietary arrangement with the mapmaker whom he declined to name. He finally scribbled a Warsaw phone number after admonishing Tomek not to tell this person how he'd learned of his existence. Unfathomable intrigue. Eventually, we got our hands on the map that listed my great-grandmother Golda Zylberman Wajskopf's stone as number 2,306.

At the city hall, the mayor's assistant received us warmly. Marlena was around thirty, stylish in a dark pantsuit with a blue silk blouse. She wanted to know why we were here. What was our interest in Radomsko? My family lived here for generations. I hoped that was answer enough.

"You must meet Maciej Ziembinski!" Marlena exclaimed. Maciej was a newspaper editor in town. He'd published more than sixty articles on the Jewish history of Radomsko in his paper. Marlena would call him for us. She also arranged for us to have a special tour of the Regional History Museum next door. She walked us there herself and introduced us to the museum curator, a tall, sober young man in a drab black suit, starched shirt, vest, and tie. "Mr. Ziembinski will meet you at the pizza parlor at 2:00 p.m.," she told us as we shook hands good-bye.

The curator—solicitous, attentive—led us through the rooms of the museum, turning on the light in each one as we entered and turning it off when we exited, just as on my earlier visit with Lloyd.

In the last room, the curator paused in front of the glass case of Jewish artifacts. I hadn't been mistaken. This one glass case contained the entirety of the museum's collection of objects from its former Jewish residents, who once made up a quarter of the town. It was disheartening.

We had an hour before meeting Mr. Ziembinski. Tomek suggested we try to find Rolna Street.

The address on Rolna was on the "List of Jewish Residents, 1939" unearthed by the Polish typist employed by Daniel Kazez's Internet research group. There were three Wilhelms on the list, one of them my aunt Fayga's husband, Fayvel. As in all the transcribed lists, the spellings of proper names translated into English from Russian, or in this case German, varied widely.

Wilchelm	Abram	50	Carpenter	Dluga 46
Wilhelm	Aron	53	Tailor	Pilsudskiego 10
Wilhelm	Fajwel	55	Tailor	Rolna 27

We walked past prewar brick buildings within what had been the confines of the ghetto. My pulse quickened when I saw "Rolna" on a street sign. The small houses had well-kept gardens. There were pigeons in cages on some of the roofs. Much of Radomsko had been bombed during the war, so some houses were missing, replaced by two-story concrete block apartments. Would 27 Rolna be among the missing?

No, there it was. A small, solid stucco house. Its four wooden casement windows faced the street, a faded lace curtain behind each one. Sepulcher-like columns framed the red-brown door. Dormer window under the tin roof. I was stunned, a stubborn layer of abstraction punctured.

I had no idea how long Fayga and Fayvel had lived here, nor what terrifying sights they had witnessed from the windows of 27 Rolna Street in 1939, the last recorded year of their existence.

After the German invasion on September 3, 1939, life for Radomsko Jews immediately turned brutal. On October 30, 1939, all Jewish men from fifteen to sixty were ordered to register at the city hall, under threat of death. The German city commander announced all able-bodied men would wear a patch on the left side of the chest.

The Jews of Radomsko were the first in Poland to receive the infamous cloth patches with the large J (Jude). The red patches went to old and weak men, only obliged to work three days a week. A full week's labor was demanded of those who wore the yellow patch. Fajvel Wilhelm would have been fifty-five in 1939. Did he wear a yellow J or a red J?

Cheryl was ready to charge up the steps to the front door. I hesitated. My knock could upend the lives of the inhabitants. That wasn't what I wanted. We had to be elsewhere to meet Mr. Ziembinski in fifteen minutes. The material existence of the house was revelation enough for now.

An old man tended his yard across the street. His peonies were lush, scarlet double blossoms. Did he know who lived in number twenty-seven? No, he hadn't lived here long. No, he didn't know anything about the house across the street.

The house on Rolna retained its secrets.

—⚬—

MACIEJ ZIEMBINSKI WAS HANDSOME, in the battered manner of a former boxer. His face was as creased as an old map. He wore a seventies-era shiny gray suit with padded shoulders over a dress shirt the color of ripe tangerines. He took Cheryl's hand, then mine in his nicotine-stained paw and gave each of us a kiss on the wrist. He treated our presence as a gift, a special occasion.

The proprietor of the pizza parlor gave a satisfied grunt when we ordered lunch for four. Maciej preferred smoking and talking to eating.

He explained, in Polish, how he decided to start a newspaper fifteen years earlier, at the very beginning of the democratic era. Until that time, newspapers were the mouthpiece of the state. Maciej's paper, *Komu i czemu* (For whom and what for?), was Radomsko's first alternative weekly. The aim of his journal was to keep people informed, to make them think. The straightforward name was to remind readers of that objective.

Maciej's father raised his son to keep an open mind. During the Nazi occupation, his father had rescued a young Jewish woman to whom he'd been secretly engaged. With an offer of a pig, his father bribed a policeman to take his fiancée off the transport to Treblinka. She survived the war in a labor camp and now lived in Chicago.

Maciej explained his childhood indoctrination in anti-Semitism. He'd repeat to his father what the priest told him in church, that Passover matzoh was baked from the blood of a Christian child. His father screamed, "Get that idea out of your head!" Later, when Maciej heard official propaganda against Jews, he didn't believe it. "I cannot be deceived so easily."

Over the years, Maciej observed that Jewish descendants of Radomsko were drawn back to the town. They came because of their grandfathers and grandmothers. They came back because of the cemetery, because of the tzaddik. "When they come by coach bus and see the sign for Radomsko for the first time, they cry at the sight."

This made sense to Maciej, who'd grown up in a small nearby village. "When I haven't been there for a few days," he said, "I feel I'm missing something."

The civic authorities recently published a photo album on the town's history that included nothing about Radomsko's Jewish past. Maciej, paging through the album, thought he would explode. He stormed over to the town president. How could they have omitted the Jewish cemetery, the grave of the Rabinowicz rebbe? Not even one page?

It was Maciej's own private war with town hall. He scolded the town officials again and again, reminding them that they could not tell the history of Radomsko without the Jewish history of the town.

AFTER LUNCH, MACIEJ PULLED on his black leather jacket and suggested he accompany the three of us to the cemetery. The sky had cleared.

The old caretaker opened the gate. We walked through the lush grass. The cemetery had been recently cleaned by a group of local teens with materials supplied by local Radomsko businesses. The brambles had been cut low around the matzevot. There wasn't a speck of trash.

We searched for Golda Zylberman Wajskopf's stone according to the register number from the map Andrezj had finally been persuaded to share with us. But the few numbers chalked on the old stones at the ends of the row had faded. The wording on the stones was etched in Hebrew, and Tomek was our best shot at reading that. He didn't look hopeful.

Maciej gestured at the stone wall at the back of the cemetery: "There were witnesses to the massacre here." Maciej had interviewed one of them for his newspaper. This witness, then a young boy, observed the horse-drawn carts under tight guard carrying terrified Radomsker Jews from the ghetto to the cemetery. The carts returned empty. Though Poles were strictly forbidden anywhere near the vicinity of the ghetto or the Jewish cemetery, the boy and his two friends followed one of the wagons.

They took turns watching through a chink in the wall. They saw a table piled with kielbasa and bottles of vodka. They saw the German soldiers drink until they staggered. They saw the Jews, at gunpoint, forced to dig a big pit, undress, and stand at the edge, backs to the soldiers. The soldiers shot each person in the back of the head. One person. One bullet.

The boys were spotted before bolting away. The Germans searched for days. Their parents hid them in bales of hay. If they'd been discovered, their entire families would have been shot. It was a reminder of what the local population risked even by daring to witness what went on within the isolation zones guarded by the occupiers.

Cheryl listened with a tight jaw, relaxing somewhat when Maciej summoned a different story, heard from his father, a memory from before the war.

"Did you know," he said, "that Radomsko Jews made excellent potato kugel?" But this kugel was more than just good-tasting. He explained how they took the cast-iron pan with the burned-on leftovers, placed it in a fishing net, and lowered the net and the pan into the Radomka River. The fish, attracted by the food, swam into the net. From their leftovers, they netted a bounty of fish.

"Only a Radomsko Jew could make such good business," he said, grinning. It was a stereotype, but an affectionate one. Radomsko Jews were smart. They were good at business. The Polish nobility understood that as far back as a thousand years ago. That's why they invited the Jews to live in Poland to begin with.

We gave Maciej a lift to his apartment on the other side of town. He kissed the ladies' wrists once again and tipped his visored Lenin hat at Tomek. He waved good-bye as we started to pull away.

"I wonder if he was in the Communist Party," said Tomek.

"He's the kind of man you could run away with," Cheryl murmured.

I looked out the rear window at the solitary figure in a black leather coat, trudging up the cement walkway toward a cluster of forbidding-looking cement-block high rises.

Our new Radomsker friend.

CHAPTER 16

Saviors of Atlantis

A few days later, in Warsaw, Cheryl and I scanned the floor to ceiling bookshelves in Kostek Gebert's flat. This was the library of a working journalist and scholar. Kostek had been on the front lines of the Solidarity struggle. He'd reported from Bosnia; he'd translated Torah into Polish.

If you could inhale all the knowledge on these shelves, you might understand Polish history, the history of the Jews in Poland, the whole history of Europe over the centuries. There were books in Polish and French and English and Russian and Hebrew. Volumes of history by William Shirer, Norman Davies, Rebecca West. Novels by Joseph Roth, I. B. Singer, Isaac Babel. Poetry by Milosz and Tuwim and Szymborska. Natural science. Atlases. A collection of antique toys graced an end table and a well-worn Persian carpet warmed the floor.

A mutual journalist friend originally put me in touch with Kostek. For the past two years, via e-mail, Kostek was a patient guide to all things Polish. With courtesy and wry humor, he'd faithfully answered all my questions about Poland's difficult history, no matter how naïve, rudimentary, or misguided. This morning he'd set aside deadlines for a history tutorial.

In the late 1970s, Kostek was part of a group of Warsaw intellectuals, Jews and non-Jews, who formed an underground seminar called the Flying Jewish University, so named because it moved its lectures from apartment to apartment, storefront to storefront—to evade the gangs of police-sanctioned toughs who often upended their meetings.

The Flying University, an idea replicated in the eighties during Solidarity, was a resistance strategy dating back to the late 1800s when Poles under Russian rule were forbidden to teach—or study—Polish history, language, or literature. Norman Davies writes: "The typical Polish 'patriot' of the turn of the century was not the revolutionary with a revolver in his pocket, but the young lady of good family with a textbook under her shawl."

There were major emigrations of Jews from Poland after the 1946 Kielce pogrom, mainly to Israel. Most Jews who remained after 1946 left in 1968, when the Communist Party loosed an anti-Semitic purge in the wake of Israel's Six-Day War. By some estimates, some ten to twenty thousand Jews remained in Poland by the late 1970s. Jan Karski once suggested that those Jews who chose to stay in grim Communist Poland when they had both the opportunity and good reason to leave for the West should be considered among Poland's "most patriotic Poles."

The Flying Jewish University was an attempt—partly therapeutic—to help the Jewish generation who came of age in 1968 make sense of their heritage. "It required an effort to learn to be able to say, 'I'm Jewish' in a normal tone of voice," wrote Staszek Krajewski, another of its founders.

All the participants—Jews and their non-Jewish friends—were equally ignorant about Judaism. They viewed their desire to learn about what had been taboo under the Communists as part of the larger struggle for a democratic Poland.

The scheduled December 1981 meeting of the Flying Jewish University never took place because martial law was imposed. Most of the Flying Jewish University students joined the underground. Life was concentrated on strikes, political meetings, protests, and, as Kostek wrote, "the ever-present fear of a crackdown."

Kostek avoided internment during the 1981 coup. Under the pen name Dawid Warszawski, he became well known as the editor and columnist of various underground publications. In 1989 he covered the roundtable Solidarity-government talks on transition to democracy and joined the new independent daily *Gazeta Wyborcza*, where he was a columnist and international reporter for several decades.

Kostek was also the founder of *Midrasz,* Poland's only Jewish monthly magazine. He wears his yarmulke on the streets of Warsaw and finds no contradiction in being both an observant Jew and a patriotic Pole.

He joined us in the library, setting down a tray with glasses of amber tea on an old metal trunk. He is a stocky, bearded, voluble man with a deep rich voice. Settling into a favorite armchair, he lit a cigarillo and smiled. "Now, what would you like to know?"

Did Kostek know about Maciej, our new friend in Radomsko who had published more than sixty articles on the Jewish history of the town?

"I don't know him," said Kostek, "but I know dozens like him."

I was surprised.

"There are dozens," he repeated.

"Do they miss us?" Cheryl, of course, wanted to know.

"They miss the Poland we were part of," said Kostek, exhaling smoke. "They're as unsentimental as can be. They're nuts-and-bolts people. Not *Fiddler on the Roof* people. Which is a very, very good thing." He spoke with convincing authority.

"Communist Poland was built for my generation, born right after the war. The earlier generations, born under capitalism, what did they know? My generation grew up in Communist Poland—we were supposed to appreciate and then endorse the project. This was the general idea.

"We took a hard look. We said, 'This is the last thing we want.'

"The Poland we were seeing was not genuine. It was a fake. People living in East Germany could look to the west for people living in the 'real' Germany, but we didn't have a West Poland. We had to look to the past. The last time we had a 'genuine' Poland was the interwar republic. And it was the Poland of the Jews."

"The Poland *with* the Jews?" I asked.

"Yes. In the paradox of Polish nationalism, a Jewish presence is what makes Poland genuine." He glanced at our expressions of amazement.

"Let's not get too carried away . . . it's not the most important thing, but it was *an* important thing. Since we cannot have this Poland once again, we can at least recreate it mentally. This is what sent people scampering, looking for Jewish remnants, Jewish relics, trying to recreate them in what was really a symbolic act of recreating a genuine Poland.

"There are dozens of people like the gentleman you met in Radomsko. I call them 'the saviors of Atlantis.' They remind me most of the *hasidey umot ha'olam*, the saviors of the Jews in World War II who, in their overwhelming majority, are as unsentimental as can be. They were simply doing the right thing. It wasn't about the Jews, it was about remaining human.

"When you meet those saviors of Atlantis today, they'll indulge in small talk for five minutes and then they'll say, 'Look, there's this cemetery I need to renovate and I need five thousand dollars. Okay? Or two dozen volunteers, or a good connection to some organization abroad. Can you help with that? No? Sorry, well, nice to have met you, but I'm busy.'"

Maciej, I told Kostek, had convened a meeting in Radomsko of other people from all over Poland doing similar reclamation work in cemeteries.

"There's *lots* of that happening. Most of those people invest not only their personal time but as often as not—their personal money. They do this not because they're philo-Semitic (a term going around Poland now) but because they're philo-Polish."

"Or humanists," suggested Cheryl.

"They wouldn't even say that. They won't say much about their deep motivations. 'It's a thing that needs to be done because it's the right thing. Period. Okay? If you don't understand that, you're wasting my time.'"

One of those saviors was named Miroslaw Jedruszczak. He served as a lieutenant in the Home Army during the war. When the Russians invaded, they sent him to Siberia.

In 1956, Jedruszczak returned to his family in Poland. He started tracking down the wartime cemeteries of his comrades in arms. He discovered that they were unmarked, and he used his personal money to mark them. He also discovered that Jewish cemeteries and sites of Jewish executions remained unmarked. "So in a very natural way," Kostek recounted, "he started spending his money on marking those too—for years and years and years.

"Eventually, some distant relative died in Warsaw and willed him her small flat. So he moved to Warsaw and continued nosing around and he discovered this bizarre piece of wall cutting across a courtyard. It didn't make any sense architecturally. He realized it was a piece of the ghetto wall! That is, *the* piece, the only piece left, the one people visit today.

"He paid with his own money for a plaque to be put on the wall. That was 1991. To this day, he hasn't been acknowledged by the Polish government or the Israeli government. His neighbors hate him because, thanks to him, they have those crowds of tourists coming into the yard, leaving their mess or whatever.

"I asked him," Kostek continued, "'Lieutenant, why was this so important?' Jedruszczak looked at me as if I were an idiot and said, 'Look, history is an exact science.' Now, that's a powerful statement in *this* country, where for half a century you always knew that what was going to happen tomorrow was the same as what happened today; but you never knew what was going to happen in the past, because the past kept changing. . . . 'History is an exact science.' It's either *that* wall or *no* wall. That's what makes him tick, that's what makes other guys like him tick.

"And don't confuse this with philo-Semitism. It's not Jew-specific. It's Poland-specific."

"It's such a relief to hear this," sighed Cheryl. "It takes the onus off. It makes us more like *people*, rather than . . ."

"The carved wooden folk figures in the marketplace?" I suggested.

"Right," said Kostek.

"Could you talk about the Poland of Kolomyja?" asked Cheryl.

"Sure," said Kostek. "What would you like to know?"

"Anything you could tell me. I've just been to see it for the first time, and what I found was a provincial city with a lot of Neanderthal-esque types. What was it like in the past? Wherever I go, people say, 'Kolomay . . . it was a pretty place.'"

"It was," said Kostek. "It was. It had its best time a century ago, when it was part of the Austro-Hungarian Empire. It was a provincial town with a relatively calm history. It was very multiethnic.

"Okay, to be more precise, it was mainly a Polish-Jewish town with a strong percentage of Ukrainians and Romanians thrown in," he went on. "People would routinely speak two to three languages, because that was the way you communicated. They all knew German, because that was the language of the empire. And they knew also Hungarian, because that was also the language of the empire, the Crown of St. Stephen. People would dive in and dive out of different languages in different contexts, accepting that as the most normal thing in the world. People would be shocked out of their mind if they traveled to some place like Paris. What a provincial place, people only speak one language!"

"We heard a story in Kolomay," said Cheryl. "Someone travels to Paris from Kolomay and when they come back, they say, 'Paris is nice, but it doesn't compare with Kolomay.'"

"Of course. It's so boring! So uniform. Today, Paris is much better and Kolomay is much worse. But a hundred years ago, it was exactly the other way around.

"After 1919, Kolomay became part of Poland. Now, it was much worse off than when it was part of the Austro-Hungarian Empire because it was a backwater on the borders of nothing. There was an Iron Curtain to the east. Romania, on the southern border, was not a place you looked up to. The rest of the country was elsewhere, west and north of Kolomay.

"World War II killed Kolomay. The Soviet empire that occupied it afterward had no interest in developing it, and especially no interest in developing what had been the strength of Kolomay—this tolerant, liberal, open, pluralistic society. So yes, Kolomay is dead."

The idea of Kolomyja as a liberal, tolerant place was hard to imagine.

"Is that why the Jews went there?" asked Cheryl.

We had it backward, Kostek explained. The Jews were part of what made it that way. "Don't get too carried away," he said. "It was liberal, tolerant, democratic by the standards of the day. It was also horribly provincial, stifling, and boring. In pre-partition time, Kolomay was synonymous with boondocks. There's an expression in Polish, 'An Englishman from Kolomay,' which means a country hick pretending to be better than he is. However, a hundred years ago, Kolomaya was a much better place than today, and this was to a great extent due to the Jews.

"Fifty years before World War II, the Jews of Central Europe had become the first Europeans," he said. "They had one leg in Yiddishkeit, the other leg in whatever local culture they were part of. They had their head in the clouds, mixing identities, ideas, and culture.

"Where do Freud, Mahler, Einstein come from? They made the best of an incredible mix. Suddenly the Europe of nations was confronted by national Europeans. The Europe of nations couldn't stand the logical consequence of a European idea. That's why the Jews were murdered. The Jews were European above all else. The Jews were the yeast of that society."

His sweeping generalization was shocking and perceptive. The Jews in Europe were always pan-nationalistic by virtue of their lingua franca and culture—Yiddish and Yiddishkeit. A Jew in Radomsko considered Jews in other countries his or her brethren.

Yeast in itself is not exactly tasty, Kostek reminded us. "But try baking bread without it. What you get is matzoh, and we only eat matzoh once a year; it's so memorable that we write in our prayer book about it."

I told Kostek about young Tomek growing up in Oswiecim, how his parents were chemists at a factory on the site of the former I. B. Farben plant. "He's getting his degree in Jewish studies. He's a very thoughtful, extremely bright twenty-four-year-old who's very concerned about the kind of Jewish tourist that comes to Poland to look at Auschwitz. He's been studying Hebrew because he wants to be able to lead Israeli groups. But he's learned that those groups really don't want to hear about Polish history."

"I won't even pretend I'm unbiased on this subject," said Kostek. "I have very strong opinions and they're probably ultimately unfair. But let's consider something that has been so terribly unfair to us Polish Jews: the March of the Living."

The March of the Living was the program Sylwia had recalled in our dialogue group in Krakow—those busloads of Israeli students who would not sit and talk with Sylwia and the other Polish high school students.

"It's only been four years since Poles were allowed to participate in the march," Kostek told us. "Before that, there was no Polish participation. Not only was it discouraged, it was forbidden , though Poles would apply."

"Even Polish survivors of the camps?" I asked.

"Poles. Any Poles," said Kostek, heating up. "The same applied to Polish Jews. If you were a Polish Jew from Venezuela, you could join the March of the Living, but not if you were a Polish Jew from Warsaw. We did not fit the pattern.

"The message of the March of the Living is 'Here you come to visit death . . . then you travel back to Israel to see resurrection.' Now, no matter how hard you try to ignore us, we—Polish Jews living in Poland—we're still not dead. We contradict the main message.

"If we'd been willing to play the role of the hapless victim, waiting for the next pogrom to happen, sure they'd have us. But this was simply not our story. We didn't fit, so we were excluded.

"It gets worse. They not only ignore Poland as it was and as it is, which is bad enough, but until a couple of years back, the orientation pamphlet the participants received contained the following quote: 'You shall see the local inhabitants. You shall hate them for their part in the atrocity. But you will pity them for their miserable living conditions.'

"Teaching kids en route from Auschwitz to Birkenau to hate somebody doesn't strike me as the kind of thing I'd like the Jews to do. The organizers finally removed it after the president of Poland complained to Netanyahu in 2001.

"The message of the March of the Living is that the only interesting part of this 'obscure Diaspora history' is the five years of murder. What preceded it and what followed it is of no consequence for Jews. It's more than forgotten, it's denied."

"Perhaps it's threatening?" I asked.

"We're talking about me, my kids, my parents, my grandparents. Okay, so if you don't want me, I'll live with that. *But I'm still here.*"

"This does not mean," said Kostek, softening, "that the intentions are evil, that the organizers are wicked. No, it seems like a real misperception."

That was why I found Tomek's desire to guide Israelis visiting Auschwitz-Birkenau so interesting. "He's so pained at being rejected, yet he remains so optimistic," I said.

"It's a tough country," said Kostek. "When you grow up here, you end up—often as not—more mature than you would elsewhere. Or— you grow up completely confused and wrong. When I was twenty-three, I started doing underground work. It's not exactly *normal*. This country is pulling itself up—I'm very impressed with Poland."

We were nearly out of time, but I wanted to ask Kostek about the Museum of the History of the Polish Jews, the ambitious project intended for central Warsaw. Wouldn't a megamuseum render little museums, like the one in Radomsko, irrelevant? After all, Radomsko had such a small collection of Jewish artifacts. "Only one glass case," I said sadly.

"Believe me," he said, "ten years ago there was *nothing* in Radom-sko. What you saw was *not* just 'a little glass case,'" he said.

He tapped his cigarillo. "Please. You must understand, there's infinity between nothing and a little glass case."

WE SAID OUR GOOD-BYES. Buoyed by Kostek's insights and his generous consideration of our questions, we fairly floated up the Royal Way toward Old Town. Dark skies threatened rain. We ducked into the venerable Bristol Hotel and gravitated to its luxurious bar.

The Bristol's Art Nouveau décor endeared it to the Germans, who made the hotel their headquarters during the occupation. To Poland's Communist rulers, the Bristol's interior was the height of bourgeois folly. After the war, when the state-run Orbis Tourist Agency took over, they allowed the building to deteriorate. Now the Bristol had been restored to its former splendor.

Cheryl and I settled onto velvet loveseats lit by Tiffany lamps. We ordered Polish vodka from a waiter with a blond goatee. American jazz played in the background. This was our last day in Poland for a while. In the morning I'd fly back to the States, Cheryl back to France. We clinked our glasses and downed our shots of clear, cold zubrovka: "*L'chaim.*" "*Na zdrowie.*" Then we pulled out our journals to write. We sat in silence, connected but separate.

I wrote to my great-aunt, whom I'd never met, trying to explain why I could not knock on that door of that house on Rolna Street, now inhabited by strangers. I asked her why she didn't leave, why she didn't join the exodus to the Promised Land. Had she loved

Radomsko too much? The smell of lilacs in the spring? The chestnut trees in the market square? The stars painted on the blue ceiling of the Radomsko synagogue?

Cheryl focused on that same moment on Rolna Street. She was surprised how big and pretty the house was, its tangibility versus those archival copies of names and professions. If only we could have seen how the light came into the house, where the strands of light and shadow fell—at least we could have experienced something of what Fayga and Fayvel knew in their lifetimes. She wrote:

> Walking past crooked tombstones in spring to the tune of Radomsko's aviary chorus, disturbing the grass under foot, shedding our skins a little more this time in the cemetery, leaving a bit of our own dust there to mingle with the ancestors, their friends and neighbors. This we could do.

CHAPTER 17

Liver and Onions, or the Last Jewish Butcher in Radomsko

I'd longed to speak with someone from Radomsko who could tell me firsthand about prewar Jewish life there. Among the hundreds of e-mails I'd received over the years from Dan Kazez, I recalled his mention of a cousin who survived the Radomsko ghetto. I scrolled messages in my archive and, sure enough, there it was. Dan's cousin's name was Berek Ofman, a retired tailor who lived in Sun City, Arizona.

"Berek's story of survival is long, complicated, and fascinating," Dan wrote. "He seems to remember everything about prewar Radomsko."

One of Berek Ofman's ancestors figured in a story in the yizkor titled "This Is How Jewish Radomsk Started." The story begins, "Radomsk was an old city, but it was not an old Jewish city." Until 1780, no Jews were permitted to live in Radomsk. A tailor named Moishe Ofman was the first Jew who lived near the city of Radomsk, in the village of Mlidzew.

According to legend, the Prussian emperor, traveling through Radomsk, had need for a tailor. But there are no tailors living in the city, he was told, only in the village of Mlidzew. The emperor summoned Moishe Ofman the tailor and asked him why he didn't live in the city. The tailor told him it was forbidden.

The emperor issued an order that "the Jew" be permitted to live in one of the old houses at the outskirts of the town. (When a Prussian emperor needs new clothes, he should make sure the tailor does not sew him an itchy coat.) When this area became part of the city proper, Moishe Ofman became the first Jewish resident of Radomsk.

The esteemed tailor Moishe Ofman had two sons. The first son was an oil presser—he extracted cooking oil from flax and sunflower seeds. The second was a butcher. All the Jewish butchers in Radomsk—and there had been fifty-two of them—were his descendants. Berek's father, Pinchas Ofman, was the last Jewish butcher in Radomsko.

In the summer of 2004, I wrote to Berek Ofman. A month passed with no response. Was he worried I'd stir up memories he'd rather not recall? I waited another month, then phoned him.

A man with a Polish accent answered. Yes, he'd received my letter. He was noncommittal about a visit. His wife had suffered a stroke a year earlier and she required his vigilance. He'd "think it over."

I wrote again, explaining how I'd made three trips to Radomsko. "In my family, I never learned anything about life left behind in Poland—what was good, what was difficult."

Perhaps my persistence persuaded him. When I called again, he welcomed me like a landsman. "My wife says she will be waiting outside the house for you. She thinks you are long-lost family."

THE 2004 PRESIDENTIAL ELECTION was weeks away. Lloyd and I joined a contingent of Angelenos headed for Arizona, a swing state, to campaign for John Kerry. Sun City is a suburb of Phoenix and I could interview Berek on the same trip.

The Arizona autumn light was blinding, bouncing off the crushed white rock that substituted for a lawn in the orderly grid of stucco and brick desert homes. Regina Ofman paced on the sidewalk outside the house, wringing her hands like my grandmother Becky used to do. She was a doll-like figure with a mop of gray curls, bright red fingernails, and an enormous welcoming smile. Berek came outside to join her. He was a slim, wiry man with attentive blue eyes, a chiseled nose, and a shock of silver hair. Inexplicably, considering the temperature, he wore a woolen vest over several layers of T-shirts.

Huge barrel cacti and ocotillo occupied the Ofmans' front yard. Stepping inside, we were transported from the American West to the atelier of a Polish tailor. The den featured tools of his trade: three industrial sewing machines on metal stands with fabric stacked neatly beside each one. I counted three refrigerators and two stoves, which were, I thought fair to assume, the legacy of a survivor's impulse to hoard.

Heavy drapes concealed any light from the street. The room was dim, brightening toward the back of the house where a sliding glass door opened onto a small patio shaded by orange trees.

Inside, we were joined by the Ofmans' handsome son Leo, an engineer with the electronics giant Intel. "I haven't heard a lot of Papa's stories myself," he said by way of introduction. Leo was born in a DP (displaced persons) camp in Germany after the war.

We all settled down at the kitchen table. Regina took out her crocheting. Berek proposed making coffee. He heated water on a small propane stove next to the real stove, as if he were camping out. I noticed that the chairs we were sitting on were bentwood. Did Berek remember the Thonet-Mundus furniture factory in Radomsko?

"I swear to you, this chair is from Radomsko!" Berek said excitedly. "I bought it at Sears Roebuck twenty years ago, and when I got it home, I looked at the stamp underneath." He upended the chair. It was stamped "Thonet," but no country of origin.

"How do you know it's from Radomsko, Papa?' asked Leo.

"We can ask Sears Roebuck, they will tell us it was made in Radomsko. They keep the book from where things come," vowed Berek. Lloyd gently pointed out that Sears was unlikely to have kept inventory records that long.

"They know from where comes the chair!" Berek was adamant.

I tried another question. Berek was born in Radomsko in 1925, in the interwar years of the Polish Republic. In 1930s Poland, chauvinist and near-Fascist attitudes were on the rise. As a Jew, did he feel like he was a full-fledged Polish citizen?

There was a long pause.

"When you're young, you don't think about such things. Most of my father's friends were Polish."

He poured the coffee. Did we like hot milk? We nodded. He poured milk into two mugs. Mine had the boiled-milk skin, a word I learned in Yiddish from my grandmother Becky. "I got the *plefka!*" I laughed.

"Your family was from Ukraine!"

How could he tell?

"From your Yiddish!"

Everyone—Lloyd, Leo, Regina—began talking at once. I was loudest: "Berek, have you told your story to many people?" I said that I understood that his past was difficult to talk about.

He sighed. "It is. That's why I don't go for a visit to Poland. When you're young, you can take anything. When you see a soldier chop people to pieces . . . you can take it. But when you're older, you cannot. What I'm trying to say is, I would love to go, but I don't know how I would react."

But he thought about Radomsko constantly. In the States, after all, one could not find "a decent piece of meat, good cheese, real bread."

Did he remember any Wilhelms, the family of my great-aunt Fayga?

The gears whirred in Berek's razor sharp memory. "Regina . . . what was the name of that photo studio? Venus. Foto Venus." The photo studio was owned by a family named Wilhelm. He remembered the photos in a glass display case outside the shop. Everyone—Poles and Jews alike—went there for special occasions, to have a wedding or graduation photo taken. "Wilhelm the photographer," he said with admiration, "he was some kind of guy! Very sharp! I went to school with one of the Wilhelm children."

I was thrilled by this first live corroboration—however slight—of the existence of my aunt's family.

Regina erupted into Polish sentences containing many exclamation marks then switched to English: "HE WANTS THE LITTLE DOG! AND HE WANTS TO KILL HIM!"

"She's telling a story from 1945," explained Berek. With great tenderness, he addressed his wife in Polish. This calmed her. Since her stroke, she was easily agitated.

Berek launched into the convoluted story about the little dog given to them after the war, then dognapped by a "rotten guy," a Jew named Goldberg who came into Radomsko with the liberating Russian Army.

The puzzling details of this tale elicited questions from Lloyd and Leo and then Leo's lovely wife, Ester, who had joined us. Berek's animated narration—with Regina's contributions overlapping fugue-like in Polish and English—lasted almost an hour, at which point Leo suggested ordering Chinese takeout. I still didn't know the first thing about Berek's life before the war or how he had survived.

It was dark out, the table littered with cartons of cashew chicken and broccoli with oyster sauce when I asked Berek to start at "the beginning" . . . as if that were some definable moment. Did one begin with the boycotts of Jewish businesses in the months leading up to the war? Did one begin on that gorgeous September morning in 1939 when the first bombs fell?

He began in April 1942, two and a half years into the occupation. There were rumors that if you signed up to work in one of the factories supplying the German regime, you wouldn't be relocated to the East.

Berek's two older brothers, both master carpenters, signed up to work at a factory, owned by a Jew named Nemerovsky, that produced desks and tables for the military. At his father's suggestion, Berek, just fourteen, signed up at a branch of Thonet-Mundus. "Our factory built wagons . . . those flat wagons with two sides like this," Berek said, placing his hands a few inches apart, palms facing one another, on the table.

In June, according to the yizkor book, a young man of thirty—a messenger from the Warsaw Jewish Underground—appeared on the premises of the ghetto's Jewish Council. He reported that Poles and Jews with an Aryan appearance had followed sealed trains supposedly taking Warsaw Jews to work in the occupied Russian territories and discovered their true destination—an extermination camp called Treblinka.

The news caused shock and panic. As a result, many Radomsker men and women anxiously sought employment in factories or agriculture, hoping to obtain a work card. Berek's father had been prescient; the Ofman sons were already employed in what looked to be vital industries.

On October 9, 1942, the first *akcja*, the Germans ordered all Jews to register at the Sports Platz (the soccer stadium).

"So we gathered," said Berek simply. "We were surrounded mostly by the black-shirts. Ukrainians. The Gestapo also came from military headquarters."

He laid his chopsticks on the table to illustrate: "Here is the place. All the people are there. My brothers—they were in a different column. The leaders from the companies gave to the Gestapo the list of their workers. How many Thonet workers? How many from Nemerovsky? The Gestapo decides which workers stay. The rest go to Treblinka. They come around with the whips, to separate the people."

On the Eastern Front, German forces were nearly within bombing range of Stalingrad. The Gestapo didn't need the beautiful bentwood furniture that Berek's brothers crafted at Nemerovsky's factory. They needed wagons to transfer matériel to the German troops.

"They had such sophisticated machinery, but what they needed were horses and buggies," said Berek, shaking his head.

"Were there Poles watching? Your neighbors?" I asked.

"No. The stadium was surrounded. Nobody could go out or go in."

Berek's group of selected workers was detained three days in a brick house next to the stadium. No one was allowed to look outside. Meanwhile, all the others were marched from the Sports Platz to the *statcja*, the train station, where they were loaded onto the train to Treblinka.

"At that point, did your brothers go?" asked Ester, herself a daughter of Hungarian survivors.

"Yes. They took the young people first. The rest of the people they took to the synagogue. In Radomsko was a beautiful synagogue with a sky painted on the ceiling. From there, they took them to the cemetery or to the trains."

"What were you feeling?" I immediately regretted asking.

"People were . . . confused." His voice quavered. "When you have just lost your father and mother and brothers . . . I really don't know . . . you would have to ask some sophisticated psychiatrist what people really think. It's history you never heard of," he said, without pause for sentiment.

After the final selection in the stadium, those Jews who remained in the brick house were watched over by the Polish police.

"Polish police from Radomsko?" I asked. "Did you recognize them?"

"Oh yes," said Berek, brightening. "Oh yes!"

And then Berek began to tell us how he survived.

—⁓—

PINCHAS OFMAN, BEREK'S FATHER, bred racing pigeons as a hobby. Some of his friends were also pigeon fanciers. Berek's face registered pleasure at the memory. "My father enjoyed the height of the flight. Some of his pigeons were the expensive kind. Viennese pigeons. Persian butterflies. The pigeons had to have special qualities. The eyes, the nose. The whole face. They were doubling, those pigeons, having children."

Pinchas Ofman's other good friends were Polish police who dropped by the butcher shop for men's talk over beer and roasted chickpeas with lots of pepper. Police in Poland were poor. "For the holidays, my father would give them a couple of pounds of meat or a duck. They never paid."

When they patrolled on frosty nights, the policemen stopped outside the Ofmans' butcher shop and rapped their knuckles on the windows: "Hey, Pinchas, open up!" Berek's father woke his son and handed him a big key: "Go to the *yatka* (the storage room) . . . and bring a piece of liver."

"So I brought a chunk of liver. Pure, good liver." Berek's father cooked up the liver with onions, distributed beers, poured glasses of vodka, sat with his police friends while they ate.

It was tough to make a living as a Polish policeman, and tough to make a living as a kosher butcher. "If a poor butcher slaughtered a cow, and the cow was a hundred dollars," explained Berek, "he'd be lucky to make twenty-five dollars."

If Pinchas sold all the parts of the cow, including the hide, he could make another five to eight dollars. But then it cost another fifteen dollars to pay the veterinarian at the slaughterhouse for the state health inspection. A Jewish butcher also had to pay the rabbi to kosher the meat.

Berek's father bypassed these restrictions—he slaughtered the cow at home, which was illegal. The rabbi came to the house so it would be kosher. His Polish police friends looked the other way and Pinchas was able to make fifteen more dollars.

"That is the reason," said Berek triumphantly, "why the Polish police need the kosher butcher—and why the kosher butcher needs the Polish police!" It explained a lot about how Radomsko functioned before the war.

Berek continued working in the wagon factory after the selection, but he knew his days were numbered. He planned an escape from the ghetto and identified a potential safe haven—a house on the outskirts of town belonging to a Polish carpenter named Wladek Bereska, to whom one of Berek's older brothers had been apprenticed before the occupation.

"You had to be very good to work for this guy. The Poles are excellent workers, very precise."

Berek ducked into the latrine and hid when the guards' attention was diverted. Later he'd scale the fence and flee. But there was one big problem: someone else was already hiding in the toilet.

"He was not from our town. They used to chase them from smaller towns to bigger towns. He was from Zarki. And he was smart! He figured I must know where to hide. He said, 'If you don't take me with you, we're both going to the Gestapo.' What would you do?" asked Berek.

"I would hit him with a brick," Lloyd said.

"The guy was twice as big as I am!" said Berek. "So we went together. We threw our overcoats over the fence, then we went over and put them on. While it was still dark, we ran to the house of the carpenter."

It was late at night by the time they arrived at Wladek's house. "I knocked. I said who I am. Janka—Janina—Wladek's wife, opened the door. She didn't hesitate. She wore wooden shoes. She had a nine-year-old boy and a girl four years old. She let me in and then she ran back to her bed. The other bed was empty. 'Where is your husband, Wladek?' She said, 'My husband is not alive anymore.'

"We didn't have any communications. We'd been in the ghetto. She'd been outside the ghetto. She had three children. Now she had two. After her husband was taken to Auschwitz, her sister took the baby."

Berek was shocked to learn that Wladek, Janka's husband, a "big maestro" at the Thonet-Mundus factory, had been arrested in the middle of the night—still wearing his pajamas. He'd died in Auschwitz.

Wladek had been a Home Army officer; he'd attempted to blow up a factory producing military equipment for the Germans.

Berek explained to Janka that "his parents, his brothers . . . that everything was gone."

"She didn't say anything at first. She took me aside and asked why I brought the other guy. She said, 'You're so small. I can hide you anywhere. But I can't hide a guy like this! Take him back to town and let him go. Then I will hide you.'"

Berek told me how Janka walked into town to scope out the situation. On her return, she reported that soldiers were searching everywhere for the runaways. She'd also learned that, in addition to the Jewish workers at the wagon factory, the Germans had left forty Jews to run the gendarmerie. Janka suggested Berek escort his companion back to town and smuggle him into the gendarmerie with the other Jews.

Berek paused in recounting the story and disappeared into the bedroom. He returned to the table with his worn copy of the Radomsk Yizkor, a synagogue in flames embossed on its maroon leather cover. He opened to a map of prewar Radomsko. "Across from the church in the center of town there was a kiosk. Where they used to sell papers. Cigarettes. There, at the police station, was the prison, with the gendarmerie on the lower level." Radomsko was still in his body, in his physical memory.

The guard at the gendarmerie was a Polish policeman, a friend of Berek's father. Janka delivered the message: "Expect a 'delivery' from Pinchas Ofman's son."

Berek and his charge sneaked back to town before the 8:00 p.m. curfew. A group of German soldiers stood forty feet in front of the kiosk they had to pass to get to the gendarmerie. They froze.

"Were you wearing a patch, a Jewish star?" I asked.

An indignant snort. "I talk like a Polack! I didn't look Semitic." Degrees of assimilation—in looks, in speech—had immediate survival value for Radomsko's hunted Jews.

The best tack was to walk straight toward the soldiers. If they stopped them, they would have to run. They'd be shot—but they must not give away other people, must not give away Janka.

He rose from his bentwood chair and mimed with kinesthetic precision. "One of them was over here. I was on this side."

They walked on by. The gendarmes ignored them completely. "Even if you are not a believer, you have to believe—this was a miracle!"

The minute they passed, Berek told his charge: "Cross the street, straight. Go through the entrance in the church wall, then take the path to the gendarmerie. They know you are coming.'"

After the war, Berek learned this man had survived after internment in the Hasag labor camp in Czestochowa.

"You know," remarked Berek, "if the same situation would happen now, and if I would come to my own son, and if he would know that they would kill his whole family, he wouldn't let me in."

Leo was aghast. "Papa, of course I would!"

"No! You would say, 'Look Dad, they would kill my whole family! My children!' I try to analyze these things. The Poles are very heroic people."

"Not all of them," muttered Leo.

"But a lady alone! She was young, in her early thirties. With two children! The cost was so big. No one in my family would do such a thing." He persisted in this thought that so distressed his son.

"The moment I dropped him I was newborn," Berek continued, his face registering relief even now, sixty years later. Because of curfew, he had to stay overnight in town. He made his way to the home of a Polish policeman, another of his father's friends. Though Berek did not know this at the time, this policeman was a leader in the Home Army. His two sons and two daughters all belonged to the Underground. Eight German soldiers were billeted in his house. Nevertheless, the policeman welcomed the hunted young man and showed him where to sleep. "If there is a knock in the night, jump out from the window."

Like the Jewish police in the ghetto, the Polish police were under the orders of their German superiors and subject to fierce discipline.

"A day before, the soldiers brought back some ducks. That policeman asked me to make him the dish that he'd eaten in my father's shop. A duck kishka. In Polish, they call it *shika*."

You sliced the duck's neck lengthwise, then stuffed it with chopped meat, onion, garlic. You roasted it in the pan next to the duck. He chuckled. "In a house full of Germans, he asked a Jew to make him *shika!*"

In the morning, Berek returned to Janka's house. She told him, "I had such a bad dream. We have to watch ourselves." She was right.

The Germans came looking around three in the morning. They knocked off the deadbolt with their rifle butts.

Berek slid under the bed. "It was a cheap bed, very low. But I was so small. If the big guy was there, we'd have been done. It was two gendarmes. Not SS. 'DO YOU HAVE HERE JUDEN?' She says, No. 'WHO YOU HAVE HERE?' 'My two children.' . . . 'SEARCH THE CELLAR! GO ON THE ROOF!' They didn't find anything. And they walked out."

That same night, with the help of Janka's nine-year-old son, Marian, Berek began constructing an elaborate false cellar beneath the kitchen. Eventually, Berek brought four others to Janka's cellar: a schoolmate named Regina Epstein, her parents, and her cousin. They all hid in Janka's cellar for more than two years. There were many close calls.

Berek refused to judge those Poles who lacked Janka's courage. "It's too much to sacrifice. If somebody did hide a Jew, then they are the most heroic people and I cannot explain why they did it."

I wanted to see the bunker. I wanted to meet this angel.

"Janka passed away several years ago," Berek told me. "But her son, Marian, still lives in Radomsko."

CHAPTER 18

Interlude: Poland in Wyoming

Two years would pass before I was able to return to Radomsko. In the meantime, in the late fall of 2004, I took a leave from my job at the Los Angeles Public Library, packed up my laptop and forty pounds of books about Poland, and took off for an artists' retreat in Wyoming.

There were only eight of us on the twelve-seater from Denver to the tiny Sheridan, Wyoming, airport. The other seven were immediately gathered up by friends or kin. I waited a quarter hour and was relieved to see the Best Western van pull up curbside. The lone baggage handler inside the terminal waved at us, then turned off the lights.

I climbed onto the seat beside the driver. In silhouette, I could see his square jaw, his long pony tail. He was friendly. He wanted to know why a woman had traveled alone from LA to remote Wyoming with no one to meet her plane at night.

I explained that the next day I'd be heading twenty miles outside Sheridan to the Ucross Ranch for a writing residency. He knew the place. "What are you writing about?" he asked.

"Poland," I said, realizing I couldn't leave it at that. "I'm writing about the place where my grandparents came from." He nodded in the dark.

He was Lakota Sioux, he told me. His parents, his grandparents, his great-grandparents, all his ancestors had lived in this area for hundreds and hundreds of years. He was particularly close to his grandmother, who told him stories about her father who'd fought Custer at

Little Big Horn, the battleground—now a national monument—sixty miles north of Sheridan.

I tried to take in the idea of one's connection to a place persisting over centuries, longer. My grandparents settled in Los Angeles in 1941. They're buried there, as are both my parents, and even that is unusual for most Angelenos.

"Those hills out at the Ucross ranch," he said quietly, "those were Sioux hunting grounds . . . the best hunting grounds." I took it as a reproach. Where his ancestors once freely hunted buffalo to feed their families was now part of a twenty-thousand-acre cattle ranch belonging to the Apache Oil Corporation. To my surprise, however, he meant it as a benediction: "That's a good place to write about ancestors."

The next day I settled into my writing cabin. Across Clear Creek, black Angus grazed the foothills of the Big Horns. In the uppermost branches of an enormous cottonwood, a bald eagle surveyed its domain. It was an archetypal view of the American West, but my thoughts turned eastward—toward Poland.

How do you nurture a budding relationship—with another human or a place—without actual contact? I thought of all those Polish exiles during Partition, when Poland was simply a "country in one's head." In the early nineteenth century—for Poles living under Czarist or Hapsburg rule—Polish poets were key to keeping Poland's identity alive.

In Wyoming, I read Polish poets for a similar reason—to shore up the Poland in my head. They transported me into the landscape—peonies in village gardens, gray cement-block housing flats, cobblestone streets. I read them to immerse myself in the ironies of Polish history—forced emigrations, deportations, incarcerations and uprisings. I read Polish poets to steep myself in that country's dark humor, forbearance, its well-honed strategies for subversion and survival.

I began each morning in my studio armchair, cup of coffee nearby, reading poems by Adam Zagajewski from his book *Mysticism for Beginners*. I treasured the slim volume, purchased in Krakow and signed by the wry, gentle poet himself when he came to read his work in Los Angeles.

Zagajewski's poems capture that Polish conundrum, where national existence was not a certainty but a wager, where your country had been—and could again be—erased from a map of Europe. "Our dead don't live in this country" he writes in his poem "Postcards," reminding us that not only are the addresses on those brittle old postcards illegible, but the very nations engraved on those old stamps also no longer exist.

If my great-grandparents had left any letters, the stamps would have been issued by Czarist Russia or the empire of Franz Josef. Had my great-aunt Fayga Konarska Wilhelm managed to send any cards after 1939, they would have been postmarked "Generalgouvernement" for the Nazi regime that occupied that part of Poland.

On my work table I arranged the Ukrainian eggcup woman in her harem pants and yellow bib. I laid out photos as if they were tarot cards. For every sorrowful image—the guard towers at Birkenau, the massacre site in Kolomyja—there was a healing, joyful one: Tomek, smiling, wearing a yarmulke in a synagogue in Krakow. Cheryl in the Kolomyja vegetable market alongside grinning, gap-toothed Maria, whose beet seeds I'd sowed in my garden in LA. I unpacked the cardboard box with the messy stack of pages, studded with yellow sticky notes, that constituted my copy of the Radomsk Yizkor.

I'd brought another artifact with me: a small purple velvet bag, the size of an evening clutch. It contained my grandfather Louis's tefillin, which I'd discovered with my mother's possessions after she died in 1990.

Louis Weiskopf died of stomach cancer on May 3, 1945, my mother's twenty-sixth birthday. At the time, my father was a US Army infantryman, fighting the Japanese in the Philippines. My mother wrote to her husband, her faraway comfort:

> I know that no man is immortal. Only—Papa did not deserve to go as he did . . . Oh! He was a stubborn man! He even died a stubborn death. He was a simple man—he asked and received very little in life. How he loved children. How he adored his grandchildren. Until the very last, he prayed for your homecoming. He did so want to see you again. I'll always remember the relationship between my father and mother. Theirs was a love of years—a love of toil and constant struggle . . .

In the sixteen years since my mother's death, I'd never opened the velvet bag to examine its contents. Now I caressed the faded purple cloth and ran my hands over the Hebrew letters embroidered in gold that spelled out the word *tefillin*. Stitched around the gold characters was a garland of melon-green leaves. The bag was secured with blue cotton drawstrings and neatly lined with white muslin, yellowed with time. The hand stitches were tiny, even.

I took the tefillin out of the pouch. Since his bar mitzvah in Nowo-Radomsk, around 1894, until 1945 when he died, my grandfather handled these quarter-inch-wide leather bindings every day for his morning prayers. ("The width of the straps should be equal to the length of a grain of oats," I read somewhere.) They were soft, pliable.

Each of the two little wooden boxes contained a parchment on which a scribe had carefully written a biblical passage. The boxes were lacquered in bright red and yellow, with black borders. I'd thought of these devotional objects as foreboding and somber; I didn't expect bright colors. I lifted the lid of one box. The interior was patterned with irregular red dots against a background of Prussian blue—a merger of Paul Klee and Polish folk art.

Holding the little box in the palm of my right hand, I tentatively wound the leather strap around my forearm. The New Testament refers to tefillin as phylacteries, from the ancient Greek meaning "to guard, protect." The tension of the well-worn straps was a protective embrace from my grandfather, whom I'd never known.

No doubt, there were those among the observant who would consider my handling of my grandfather Louis's tefillin a blasphemy. First of all, I'm a woman. There are myriad rules and commentary on precisely how you bind the boxes to your body with the straps.

There were sure to be those among the secular who would have been dismayed as well. I didn't care. The strap spiraling around my arm linked me to my grandparents, their parents, and beyond, to Radomsko, a place, a tradition, a culture, a sense of humor, a code of ethics, a respect for words, a love of stories.

I danced spirals in my studio—a private communion. From the corner of my eye, I caught movement out the window on the other side of Clear Creek. A herd of pronghorn antelope bounded across the dun-colored hills.

—ɯ—

WHEN I COULDN'T REMEMBER details about travels with Cheryl in Kolomyja and L'viv, Krakow and Warsaw, I jumped onto my bicycle and careened down dirt roads, across a cow pasture and over a bridge to a cabin with Internet hookup to fire off questions to Cheryl in France. What did she recall of the concert in the synagogue in Krakow? How had she realized that the building we initially identified as the Grand Hotel in Kolomyja was not the one? She was usually reliable about responding quickly. But days passed and she didn't answer.

There had been other warning signs. The first was her response, soon after we returned from our last trip, to my proposition that we travel together to Krakow for Tomek and Sylwia's wedding. "I can't face going to Poland again," she wrote. "My reasons for going may be over. My fascination with the things there that remind me of home— now remind me of grief."

I'd last seen Cheryl when I was in New York months earlier. She and Henry were in town from France to see family and invited me for supper at their apartment on the Upper West Side. Their daughter Anna joined us.

After dinner, I was excited to show them a short film by a French Jewish artist named Frédéric Brenner, whose vast enterprise, *The Jewish Journey: Fréderic Brenner's Photographic Odyssey*, was touring US museums. Brenner, trained as a social anthropologist, spent twenty-five years photographing Jews in more than forty countries on five continents: Jewish motorcyclists in Miami. Jewish barbers in Tajikistan. A Soviet general with his uniform full of medals. Marranos celebrating a hidden Passover in Lisbon. Henry Kissinger. Ruth Bader Ginsburg. There was a soulful portrait of Monika and Staszek Krajewski, friends of Rabbi Singer's whom I had twice visited in Warsaw.

The photo that stopped me in my tracks, however, showed Polish Catholics performing a Purimshpiel, a Purim play. I remembered our annual Purim carnival at Temple Akiba, when I'd dress up as Queen Esther and shake my rattle at mention of evil Haman, advisor to the Assyrian king Ahasuerus, who plotted the destruction of the Persian Jews.

Brenner had filmed the Purim play in a Polish village called Tykocin. I'd procured a DVD of the film to show Cheryl, Henry, and Anna.

It was startling. The town's priest wrapped himself in tallit, the Jewish prayer shawl, and pressed a fake beard onto his chin. A young Polish woman with long, dark hair wore the robes of Queen Esther, the Jewish heroine, who saves the lives of her Jewish countrymen. The whole cohort then proceeded to Tykocin's medieval town square, where in a final tableau, Esther alerts the Persian king of Haman's wicked plot, and an effigy of the villain is strung up on a gallows.

What was the story behind this spectacle? Jews celebrate the festival of Purim to commemorate the survival of an ancient Jewish community. The Jews of Tykocin, no doubt, were all dead. What gave these Catholic villagers the idea? Who had organized the play? Why did they perform it? I thought Cheryl and I should go and investigate.

She watched the film silently, said nothing when it was over. She did not share my enthusiasm about Poles honoring their towns' former Jewish inhabitants by performing a Jewish play. She mistrusted their motives.

For Anna, watching the film brought up unanswered questions. "Mom," she said, "when you came back from Kolomyja, why didn't you want to talk about it?"

"No one asked me any questions," Cheryl protested.

"Don't you remember?" Anna prodded gently. "I *did* ask you questions. You said you didn't want to talk about it." An uncomfortable silence followed. We didn't talk about Poland for the rest of the night.

EVERY EVENING DURING MY Wyoming interlude, I checked for Cheryl's e-mail messages. Nothing. When my residency was over, I reluctantly packed up notes and photos, my grandfather's tefillin, the Ukrainian eggcup and flew back to Los Angeles from Sheridan.

It would be another whole month until I heard from Cheryl. By then the discomfort implied by her silence was glaringly evident. Finally, her message in my inbox:

> I haven't been able to write to you because it has been impossible to share my feelings, for two reasons. The first because then I have to make them clear to myself and feel them and second, I don't want to burden you with what I myself don't want to feel—namely "rage."

When I think about any part of our trip in order to recall a story—my mind always ends up with Kolomay. My grandfather burned alive in the synagogue, my female relatives marched out of town, shot and buried in a mass grave.

I wanted to find a different story in Kolomay. I wanted to find the beautiful house and the Grand Hotel and the lilacs. I could never understand why I couldn't persuade my father to come back there with me. I can now see how he couldn't deal with my feelings, which set off his feelings. Just as I can't deal with Anna's feelings which set off my feelings of not wanting to have passed such a legacy on to such a sweet being, as my father never wanted to pass this information along to me.

There was a time when I thought about all of this with my whole mind and my whole heart. Now it is hard to think about these things without frightening feelings of rage.

Cheryl's message, not totally unexpected, was still a shock. These forays to bleak Polish towns, this inquiry into the Polish Jewish past and present would be so lonely without her companionship, her humor, insight, support, without—what you call in Yiddish—her *sechel*, her common sense.

I understood Cheryl's need for distance, but I grieved the loss of our partnership, our intimate dialogue.

When I received a fellowship from a foundation for further travel and research in Poland the following spring, it was strange not to include Cheryl in the planning. The silence between us was an ache.

AROUND CHRISTMASTIME, I FLEW to Phoenix and drove out to see Berek Ofman in Sun City once again. In the yards of the Ofman's subdivision, the cacti were adorned with sparkling lights and Christmas ornaments. When Berek came to the door, I could see that his full-time job as Regina's caretaker was wearing him down. Berek looked decidedly older and more tired than on my visit nine months earlier. He welcomed me inside. I remembered the front room as dim but now it struck me as pitch black.

We joined Regina, absorbed in her crocheting, on the back patio. An awning warded off the intense midday heat. Regina smiled at me, though I wasn't sure if she remembered me or not. "Where's your boyfriend?" she asked, obviously thinking of Lloyd.

I turned on my tape recorder as Berek began to talk about his childhood, his Polish schoolmates, how he would go out to the barn to eat ham so his father wouldn't know. Regina interjected comments in Polish, which amazed Berek. "It's coming back to her!" he said.

"She makes you a *pamiatka*, a souvenir," he said, gesturing to her yarn and needles.

He returned to his story, telling me about dangerous night forays from Janka's to seek food at the homes of Polish friends, Polish policemen. Marian Bereska, Janka's young son, also risked his life, bartering table linens for food to feed the five fugitives. A larger network of people helped, but they didn't know about each other. It was best not to know.

From their hiding place, Berek and Regina heard the Russian bombardment day and night coming closer. He knew the Germans had been routed when Russians came to the house, banged on the door, asking for vodka. He laughed. "We didn't have *anything*. They also asked for perfume, with alcohol. So they could drink."

I asked about his contact with Janka's family after the war. Her grandson Witold had once visited Berek and his family when they lived in Cleveland. He had since moved to Germany from Poland to work. "But his father, Marian, still lives there," Berek said.

I resolved on the spot to visit Marian Bereska in Radomsko on my pending visit, but Berek shook his head. "It's risky," he said.

Surely Berek was mistaken; he didn't understand how the climate had changed in Poland.

"It will be risky forever," he said emphatically. "Very risky." Then he added, in a phrasing all his own: "You would open a can with worms."

"But Marian's mother was a hero!" I protested.

"The greatest hero in the world!" Berek said, slapping his hand on his chair. "She was an angel! To do what she did you have to be a saint!"

I tried to reassure him. My translator Tomek was smart, discrete, and diplomatic. He could write to Marian and ask him to meet us somewhere—not at his house. He would tell him that I would just like to talk to him.

"Yes, you probably would," Berek conceded. "But . . . you cannot comprehend this history." His voice rose with emotion. "It's something that I won't touch," he said flatly.

He wasn't even sure if Marian had ever told his own children what his mother had done during the war, or that he himself had been involved in the rescue effort. "You don't know how they would react," Berek told me. "Because this was the greatest secret in the world!"

It was ungracious to press him anymore. Berek was right. I could not begin to comprehend what had happened in Poland during the war.

Regina wanted me to try on the bright red scarf she'd crocheted for me. It barely fit around my neck, but nevertheless, she was pleased. "*Pamiatka,*" she said with her gorgeous smile.

BEFORE I LEFT, BEREK offered to make coffee. I sat at the little table in the kitchen while he fussed with the propane stove. While water boiled, he pointed to Christmas cards heaped in a bowl on the sideboard. He picked up an envelope addressed in a feathery European-style handwriting. "This is a card from Marian Bereska in Radomsko. You see, he remembers me every year."

He set the envelope upside down on the table right in front of me. The return address in Radomsko inscribed in the corner was clearly visible. He did not try to conceal it. He was possessed of opposing desires.

We both sipped our coffee. Berek watched as I carefully transposed the upside-down address in Radomsko into my little black notebook.

He did not give it to me; but he did not prevent me from taking it.

CHAPTER 19

"It Costs You Nothing"

There were still patches of snow on the streets of Vilnius, Lithuania's capital city. It was early spring, 2007. My solitary two days—before Tomek arrived from Krakow—were a welcome transition from my workday frazzle to the contemplative state of mind I'd need for this challenging journey.

The window in my room at the B&B faced a round brick wall and roofline of a building that had been a Jewish prayer house. Vilnius was once full of Jewish prayer houses. Until the war, the city was so renowned a seat of Jewish learning, it was called the "Jerusalem of the North."

I spent hours in my room, watching snowflakes fall and melt on that roof, thinking what I'd ask Marian Bereska, son of Berek Ofman's rescuer, when Tomek and I reached him in Radomsko.

Berek's reluctance to reveal the address of his rescuer's son hadn't surprised Tomek. But he assured me that times had changed. There was no longer any reason to avoid revealing such acts of heroism during the war. At my request, Tomek wrote to Mr. Bereska and, after some encouragement, Mr. Bereska agreed to meet with us. Perhaps Berek's fears were unwarranted after all.

I ventured out to walk around Vilnius. It took just an hour and a half to circumambulate the city. On a cobblestone street, I entered a tiny Russian Orthodox chapel. In the darkened interior, illuminated by beeswax tapers, the dark, passionate eyes of saints stared out from silver frames. The wooden naves and plaster columns were painted with barber-pole stripes of primary colors, now faded.

A banner hung aloft announced a performance by the Belarus Free Theater from Minsk. The image was of a woman muzzled by a horrific leather contraption, a reference to the recent volatile protests in Belarus against the dictator Lukashenko and his government's savage response. At the Vilnius Contemporary Art Center, graffiti near the cloakroom reads, "It is easy to infiltrate public libraries. Try to make the book look as much like books that are already in the system."

I planned to end my walking tour at what my guidebook noted was the last functioning synagogue in Vilnius, but the gates were padlocked and no one answered even when I shouted.

Back in my room, I crawled under the covers and watched sleet fall from the iron gray sky. I'd already finished the novel I brought; that left my only other selection—an advance galley of Jan T. Gross's new book, *Fear: Anti-Semitism in Poland after Auschwitz*. I dreaded reading it.

Gross had caused a sensation in Poland years earlier with *Neighbors*, his study of the massacre at Jedwabne, exposing how it had been Poles—not Germans—who had committed a horrific act of violence against the town's Jews.

In his new book, Gross tackled head-on the subject that was arguably most sensitive to Polish-Jewish relations: why Jews returning to their homes from the death camps and from the Soviet labor camps were received with such hostility by their one-time Polish neighbors. The shots fired at Max Blitz from the Grand Hotel in Kolomyja still echoed in his daughter's life sixty-plus years after the fact.

Betrayal was the archetypal theme in Gross's narrative. The Poles were betrayed by the Soviets—who arrested and deported thousands of Poles during the war, and in the aftermath of the war executed Poland's Home Army heroes. The Jews returning from the camps were betrayed by Polish neighbors who appropriated their homes, property, and jobs. It was a combination of greed and guilt, Gross concluded, that made the sight of the returning Jews so threatening to their Polish neighbors.

One had to bear in mind that it was a traumatized and upside-down world to which the camp and Gulag survivors returned. The Germans had been skillful in blaming the Jews for the cruelty of the Soviet occupiers who preceded them. Thousands of Poles had been deported or shot by the NKVD. Civil war raged in Poland until 1947; the Partisans were still active against the Communists. The Communists were imprisoning and executing those who'd fought with the Polish Resistance. There were scores to be settled; the country's infrastructure was ruined.

In his introduction, Gross warns that readers will experience "a sense of discomfort." For me, it induced gut-wrenching distress. What to do with Gross's accusations in the here and now? The Poles defined themselves as resistors to Nazism. Of all states under the Nazi heel, they had not produced a quisling. There were thousands of Poles who risked everything to aid their Jewish neighbors, many more who did nothing, and plenty who had aided in their neighbors' humiliation and capture.

If I believed Gross, must it tar my feelings toward all Poles? Would this mean rounds of defensiveness, of accusation and counter-accusation with my Polish friends and acquaintances? When had I assumed the weight of Polish-Jewish relations on my shoulders? I wasn't even sure I could bear to be in Poland after reading Gross. What did that mean?

The next afternoon on one of my walks, I saw a cleaning lady scrubbing the steps in the courtyard of the locked synagogue. I waved at her, but she gestured for me to go away. I persisted and she set down her bucket, put her hands on her hips, and went inside to fetch someone. An older gentleman in baggy pants and a cardigan appeared with a set of keys. He looked at me through the gate and shrugged. His face was lined and melancholy. He spoke no English; I spoke no Lithuanian.

"Shalom" turned out to be Ali Babi's password. The melancholy gentleman opened the gate and gestured for me to follow him into the ornate but empty sanctuary.

"Minyan," my host said, pointing upstairs toward the sounds of a few men praying in Hebrew. The minyan is the minimum number of observant male Jews required for a prayer service. This in what was once the heart of a thriving Jewish community.

THE DESK CLERK KNOCKED on my door that evening to let me know "my Polish friend" had arrived. There was Tomek, beaming even though he was tired from his two-day-long journey north from Krakow. Over dinner we caught up on each other's lives. Tomek was now "the happiest man on earth." He and Sylwia had married in a big church wedding in Krakow.

My delight in seeing Tomek was tempered by disappointing news. En route Tomek had phoned Mr. Bereska in Radomsko to confirm our get-together. He'd changed his mind and now refused to meet with us. Tomek spent half an hour on the phone with him trying to understand why.

Mr. Bereska said he was old, he was diabetic, that he knew too many people in Radomsko, and—most crucially—he knew exactly what they had done during the war. There were some, he said, who walked around town "bent over so low, their noses cut a line in the pavement."

Tomek tried to persuade him otherwise, but Mr. Bereska would not budge. "Call me in twenty-five years," he said, "maybe then this reality will be different."

"It's a long process to reassure these rescuers," Tomek conceded. They'd lived most of their lives under Communism, when it wasn't safe to talk about the past. How, I asked, was it *political* to meet with us?

"Nothing is not political in Poland in the last fifty years," Tomek sighed. He used a word, *lustration*, that I'd never heard before and that does not appear in English dictionaries. It comes from the Latin *lustrum*, a Roman ceremony of purification. In Polish the word *lustro*, Tomek explained, means "mirror." In the post-Communist era, lustration was supposed to mean self-examination and reckoning. But it had been corrupted and misused to cast blame and ruin careers.

Tomek also brought other unexpected news. Our friend Maciej, the newspaper editor in Radomsko, had called to tell Tomek we were invited to a special cultural ceremony in Radomsko. There would be a representative of the Polish Parliament there as well as many townspeople from Radomsko. Maciej wanted me to make a speech at the ceremony.

Now that I'd read Jan Gross, I'd have to think carefully about what I wanted to say to the people of Radomsko.

—〰—

WE LEFT VILNIUS MIDDAY, traveling through a landscape of forests and farms. Our destination was the tiny medieval church town of Sejny, on the Polish side of the border. A visionary artist and feckless cultural activist named Krzysztof Czyzewski had located his Borderland Foundation in this remote corner of Poland. It was Czyzewski who first published Jan Gross's *Neighbors* in Polish; I was eager to meet him and learn about his work.

Stalks of tawny rye and wheat emerged from a blanket of snow. Storks were returning from Africa, and some had already built their ungainly nests on chimneys and eaves. "Everyone hopes for one to build a nest on their house," newly married Tomek informed me.

Every so often we passed a sign with an arrow: "Site of Jewish Massacre." We'd drive a short distance past a farmhouse or two, park the car on the side of the road, and then walk the inevitable path of trampled leaves and melting snow into the forest of oak and ash to a clearing. We stood in silence, staring at the simple granite marker exhorting the mourners to remember those murdered on this spot.

It was quiet except for breezes stirring the linden, pines, and ash. Who would have heard the volley of rifle shots? We never saw anyone at these sites, though there was evidence of recent visits: flowers, *yahrzeit* candles, small pebbles on solitary granite markers. There are at least two hundred of these massacre sites in present-day Lithuania.

Just a few miles from the border crossing in Ogrodniki, we paid a visit to Stalin World, a theme park built by one of Lithuania's wealthiest entrepreneurs, a canned-mushroom baron. His enterprise—which many Lithuanians consider a travesty—was an attempt to lure tourists with souvenir stands, picnic tables, and petting zoos and then to engage them in a history lesson about those hundreds of thousands of Lithuanians exiled to Siberia by Stalin. Disneyland meets the Gulag.

The proprietor had rounded up all the mothballed statues of Lenin, Stalin, and local Communist apparatchiks from around Lithuania and installed them on several acres of a reclaimed swamp circled by razor wire. Guard towers blared recorded slogans and patriotic Communist songs.

On this cold, gray day, we were the park's only visitors. We strolled wooden walkways raised above the marshy ground, passing Lenin and Stalin in various heroic poses. "That's *my* Lenin!" Tomek said excitedly, thinking he recognized the statue that had towered over gatherings in Nowa Huta, the eastern district of Krakow where he'd lived as a student. But all these statues were the Lithuanian versions of the same dictators.

WE JOINED A LINE of cars idling at the drab border crossing. Half an hour and five vehicles later, it was finally our turn. The Lithuanian border guard checked our passports on his computer, handed them back, and motioned us forward with a grunt. We inched forward and handed our documents to the Polish border guard, who glanced over to match photos with faces, then checked our names on his own computer. The two guards—literally back to back—were not on a first-name basis.

With the last rays of sun slanting across the fields and forest, we drove into Poland. A gray fox darted across the road in front of us— according to Tomek, that was a good-luck sign.

Now we were in the fabled borderlands, once part of a single country that stretched from the Baltic to the Black Sea, a country that came into being in the fourteenth century, when Poland's Queen Jadwiga, a Catholic, married Lithuania's Jagiello, hunter king of Europe's last pagan nation. In the wake of this union, Lithuanians became Christian. There were mass baptisms and, according to one historian, "the ritual fellings of sacred oak groves." God's son on the cross replaced the pagan god of thunder with his lightning bolt.

For Poles, Lithuania represents what the historian Simon Schama calls a "semipaternal homeland." Every child in Poland memorizes the national poem, Adam Mickiewicz's epic *Pan Tadeusz*. It opens with the lines:

Oh, Lithuania, my fatherland
You are like health—so valued when lost
Beyond recovery; let these words now stand
Restoring you, redeeming exile's cost.

Imagine how strange it would be, Tomek suggested, if American schoolchildren recited odes to Canada as a way of being patriotic.

After Poland was partitioned in the late eighteenth century, much of Lithuania—including Vilnius—became Russian. Poland's great patriot leader Marshal Józef Pilsudski, who was born in Vilnius (then Wilno) under Russian rule, was forbidden to speak his native Polish as a boy. Language became a political issue. Pilsudski's mother read him Polish literature outlawed by Russian censors.

Czeslaw Milosz, Poland's Nobel Prize–winning poet, was born to a Polonized Lithuanian family in Russian-ruled Lithuania in 1911. Even in his later years, when living and teaching in Berkeley, he wryly referred to himself as the "last resident of the Grand Duchy of Lithuania." In his beautiful memoir, *Native Realm*, Milosz describes—in stories specific to his own family—how in the days of the Grand Duchy, the Lithuanian language became the peasant idiom, Polish the language of the educated. After the First World War, he points out, when Lithuania was established as an independent state, matters about language and ethnic identity often "severed even the closest ties and set brother against brother."

I was about to see these matters in action. Before we'd left Vilnius, Tomek and I had visited the city's Holocaust museum, a small green-shingled bungalow set back from a main road. Witness testimonies and original documents told the story of the Jewish community of Vilnius, its rise to prominence and its destruction by the Nazis. The museum was not old; it opened in 1991 after Lithuania became independent. One room was dedicated to the Talmudic scholar Eliyahu ben Solomon Zalman, the famous Gaon of Vilna, and his influence on Jewish learning. The rooms describing the occupation featured a model of the Vilna Ghetto and its escape routes.

There were lists of those executed by the Einsatzgruppen at Ponary, the grim massacre site on the outskirts of Vilnius. One hundred thousand dead, the sign read, "consisting of Jews, Poles, Lithuanians and Gypsies." The Nazis were intent on killing Jews and also bent on wiping out Vilnius's sizable population of Polish intelligentsia.

I already missed Cheryl, though she would have likely remained in the car while Tomek and I studied the room's sober displays. "You could get used to anything," she'd have said with a grim laugh. "Now let's go have a beautiful lunch." That prospect was unlikely; skinny Tomek—usually a hearty eater—was on a Lenten diet and only indulged in one meal a day.

"Can I help you?" A museum curator, a sixtysomething woman wearing a pleated skirt, emerged from the administration offices. "I can answer any questions you might have," she offered in crisp English. Tomek took her up on the offer, posing questions about the massacre at Ponary.

She had already gauged him for a Pole by his accent. "Why are you so much interested in Jewish culture?" she demanded. Her tone was not friendly. Tomek explained he was indeed Polish—from Krakow—a historian by profession and an official guide at Auschwitz.

"In Lithuania, before 1991, it was impossible to have any discussion about Jewish history," the curator informed us.

"Yes . . .," said Tomek, "it was exactly the same in Poland."

"It was different in Poland," she said curtly. "In Warsaw, you had the Jewish Historical Institute."

"But the institute could do little under Communism," Tomek protested. "It would have been shut down."

"Now you have that big Jewish festival," she said, "and you have so much money for the festival." She was referring to the popular annual Jewish Culture Festival in Krakow, which attracted thousands of tourists. "You take money from the European Union. And it costs you nothing," she said bitterly. "What is the point? Reconciliation? Nostalgia?"

"It *does* cost us something," contradicted Tomek without raising his voice. "It costs us a discussion about Jedwabne. At the festival, when we talk about Hasids, we are also obliged to talk about what happened to them. Many people who go to the festival also go to Auschwitz-Birkenau."

The curator claimed the last word, almost spitting out her accusation: "It costs you nothing! I wish to talk more, but I have not another minute." She turned on her heel and left.

"Now you have a firsthand view of old tensions with our neighbor," Tomek told me with a sigh in the car afterward. "In Vilnius, it is better for me to speak English than Polish."

What I knew about Polish–Lithuanian tensions before this trip would have fit into a thimble. I didn't know that there had been a civil war between the two states. I didn't know there was competition for money from the European Union for history museums and massacre sites.

What *is* the price of talking about the past? That phrase "it costs you nothing" kept playing in my head. What did it mean for Poles to explore the Jewish history of their country? What uncomfortable truths were part of reclaiming Poland's Jewish past? Jan Gross's book pointed to some of the most painful: collaboration with the Nazis, appropriation of Jewish property.

It was dark when we finally drove into tiny Sejny. Tomek hailed a man on the street to help us find our lodging. We were going to stay at a place called Lithuanian House. The Lithuanian Cultural Center was located there. "It's easy to find," the man said. "There's a police box right in front of the hotel."

"Why the police box?" asked Tomek.

"The policeman is stationed there," he said, "because someone keeps tearing down the Lithuanian flag."

CHAPTER 20

Among the Odd Believers

In the morning, Krzysztof Czyżewski welcomed us into Sejny's old Jewish gymnasium, now the headquarters of the Borderland Foundation. Krzysztof was a short, compact man of copious warmth. With his shaggy hair, corduroy jacket, and black turtleneck, he looked like an affable American college professor from the sixties.

The building's improvised furnishings and relaxed atmosphere recalled nonprofit arts centers in low-rent warehouse districts of various American cities. The stucco walls were painted cobalt blue, the wooden trim burnt orange, and doors were forest green or bright red.

Krzysztof escorted us into a large gallery. At the far end of the room, displayed on a trestle table, was some kind of elaborate scale model. We took a closer look. It was a ceramic version of Sejny, that town, as Krzysztof has written, "of abundant traditions, at the end of the world."

The earthenware houses with red roofs were miniatures of the ones on Sejny's crooked streets. There was the Lithuanian basilica, the twin spires of the Dominican church. There was the diminutive of the old White Synagogue, its portals like those on the real building across the street.

The tiny town, Krzysztof explained, was the set of a play called *The Sejny Chronicles*, written by teens who'd participated in Borderland Foundation workshops. To learn their town's history, the young people interviewed their grandparents and elderly neighbors. They studied old photographs for clues about Sejny's Russian, Jewish, Polish, and Lithuanian past.

Even on video, the performance had the power to move me to tears.

In the play a dozen or so teenage actors—the girls in simple white cotton smocks, like angels, the boys in black pants and white shirts—hover over the miniature town like solicitous relatives over a newborn. They uncover the stories in these houses, one by one becoming their own ancestors who voice memories of the tailor's daughter, Roma caravans, a Jewish child rescued from disaster.

A lantern's glow illuminates the miniature city and the excited, young faces peering down on it. In a dreamlike atmosphere reminiscent of a Chagall painting, the actors pray in Polish, sing Lithuanian wedding songs, and hum wordless Yiddish devotional melodies. The circular patterns of ecstatic Hasidic dancing—palms turned upward—morph into the intersecting lines of a Lithuanian folk dance: different geometries for different cultures.

The children tower over their tiny town. Thanks to the Borderland Foundation, they are intimate with its rich history.

IT ALL STARTED IN 1990, just after the fall of Poland's Communist government, when Krzysztof with his wife, Malgorzata, and their first child, a dozen fellow artists and actors, and one bony old brown horse caravanned into Sejny. "At first," explained Krzysztof, "the local people thought that the Gypsies were back. Then they thought the Jews were back."

The inhabitants of Sejny were wrong. Krzysztof Czyżewski was not a Gypsy nor was he Jewish—nor were any of his fellow artists who accompanied him to this tiny border town in pursuit of their post-Communist artistic destiny.

The locals were at first suspicious of the newcomers. The rules for private property were shifting in the transition from Communist rule. The monastery had been given back to the church. Some manor houses had been given back to the owners. Townspeople were fearful of losing their homes. "It was a cruel time," Krzysztof explained in articulate, accented English.

I wanted to know what had brought Krzysztof to this work. He'd grown up close to Poznan near Poland's border with Germany, in a country devastated by World War II and under the boot of a regime that forbade any honest discussion of the past. He knew nothing, he said, about the Jewish presence in the area where he grew up. He swam regularly at a municipal pool, but it wasn't until he'd graduated from university that he realized that the building that housed the pool used to be a synagogue.

"We lived without the knowledge passed on through generations, without the continuity of tradition," he said, which accounted for his feeling "of being nowhere," his strong need to be "rooted somewhere."

After university, Krzysztof achieved renown as a dissident theater director. His troupe's creative process involved extensive historical, anthropological, and ethnographic research. Yet after the triumph of Solidarity and the fall of Communism in 1989, alternative theater became a questionable concept. Alternative to what? Krzysztof would have to redefine himself as an artist, find a new locus for his art.

What primarily drew Krzysztof and his collaborators to Sejny was its multicultural heritage. Before the war, Lithuanians, Poles, Jews, Gypsies, Tatars, Ukrainians, Byelorussians, and Old Believers (a sect of Russian Orthodox who adhere to strict religious practice) all lived in this border region in relative harmony.

Two world wars severed the borderlands from their tradition of tolerance. The First World War gave national identities to Poland and Lithuania. In Sejny, it ignited a local civil war. Then, during the Nazi occupation in World War II, the Germans rounded up Sejny's Jews—more than 50 percent of the town's population—for annihilation in the camps.

There was no longer any Jewish presence in Sejny. The loss was so devastating that it was never discussed and of course, under Communism, it was never taught. To those born after the war, Sejny's Jewish past was unknown. Now this little town of six thousand—which carried the baggage of all the tragedies, conflicts, and ideologies of the twentieth century—was divided among Poles and Lithuanians and a few Old Believers.

Yet in the memory of the inhabitants, "a space for others" still existed. People in Sejny had *always* lived with others. People rich in cultures tended to be tolerant, attentive to other people. They were known as *lugenda*, "people of the borderlands."

Jews were natural borderlanders. They lived at the margins of the societies in which they dwelled—both of and apart from the mainstream. My grandmother Rebecca—who grew up in Ukraine speaking Russian, Ukrainian, Polish, and Yiddish—was familiar with the world of shifting borders as empires collapsed and new regimes struggled for dominance. She was in her nineties, living in Los Angeles, when she had a heart attack and was transported to a Catholic hospital, where she died that same day. A nun came into her Jewish patient's room to ask, "Mrs. Steinman, may we pray for you?" To which my grandmother answered with a shrug, "Yes, of course. What's the difference?"

The first major blow to the long era of tolerance in the borderlands was the so-called Sejny Uprising, in 1919, when the Polish minority in the ethnically mixed area rebelled against the Lithuanian authorities. "To this day," Krzystof explained, "people in Sejny know who—from which family—killed whom. The Second World War is far away, but the Polish-Lithuanian war is something very fresh here—because they're still living together."

Yet for fifty years, the community had no way to confront this raw wound. Any discussion of this cruel war was taboo.

What happens when ethnic tensions are left to fester was made painfully apparent in the brutal conflict that erupted in the former Yugoslavia after the demise of Communism. "That's why we came here," said Krzysztof, "to help with these kinds of problems from the past."

With a healthy dose of blind faith, the members of his troupe committed themselves to a new phase of creative work in Sejny. They worked hard to win the respect of local bureaucrats, to garner support among the town residents. And, timing being everything, they made one very special friend—the Nobel Prize–winning poet Czeslaw Milosz.

During the Communist era, Milosz's books were banned in Poland. If his name did appear in print, as poet Adam Zagajewski noted, "It was frequently accompanied by the official Byzantine formula 'an enemy of the People's Republic of Poland.'" Young Polish intellectuals could only obtain Milosz's work with great difficulty. He was revered as a great artist and a voice of conscience.

As it happened, the old estate of Milosz's mother's family—called Krasnogruda—was located eight kilometers outside Sejny. Milosz had spent the summers of his childhood there.

One day, in the fall of 1989, Krzysztof and his wife took a long walk in the countryside outside Sejny. On a forest path near the abandoned Milosz estate, they were shocked to encounter the legendary poet himself. Were they witnessing an apparition?

In fact, Milosz—then seventy-eight—had just returned from the United States to Poland for his first sanctioned visit in nearly forty years. The young couple shyly greeted the great man, then hurried on their way. Later that same day Milosz caught up with them in Sejny and asked, "Why are you running away? Could we talk?" It was a fateful meeting. Milosz immediately grasped what Krzysztof and his fellow artists wanted to do. He became their staunchest supporter and mentor.

Two years after their encounter with Milosz and after dogged engagement with the local town authorities, the Centre Borderlands of Arts, Cultures, and Nations was granted an official seat in Sejny, thereby becoming the first nonprofit arts organization in post-Communist Poland. How revolutionary that must have felt to be able to do one's own work!

The Borderlanders focused on Sejny's children, the heirs of the era when Communism suppressed curiosity and enforced conformity. "Psychological latchkey kids," Krzysztof called them. Many of them lived in grim apartments in the concrete high rises at the edge of town, where alcoholism was endemic and eating dinner alone in front of a television was common practice.

"They didn't know that a table is where you gather together to share food and stories," said Krzysztof. In their workshops, the artists used strategies from theater, ethnography, and psychology to focus the children on fundamentals: "What is a table? What do you do at a table? What is a window? Who do you see through a window? What is a neighbor? What do you want to say to your neighbor?"

After two years of working in Sejny, an unknown benefactor bestowed upon them a nickname. Krzysztof recounted the story with evident glee. "We often convened a circle of people to share our stories and songs." Outside in the parking lot, someone wrote on their dirty car the phrase, which translates into English, "Odd believers."

Townspeople assumed it was the work of the same juvenile punks who had spray-painted other graffiti around town, zingers like "Poland for Poles" or "Jude Raus" (literally, Jews Out, a phrase appropriated for rival football teams) or "Lithuanians to the Gas Chambers." Exasperated townspeople scrubbed off that kind of graffiti as soon as it appeared. In this case, the intended targets at the Borderland Foundation were in no hurry to erase it.

"It was very beautiful," said Krzysztof. "We were recognized."

We'd moved from the gallery to Krzysztof's office. We sat around an aged, round oak table. Inside a wooden bookcase with glass windows were antique photographs and some of the books published by Borderland. Upstairs, there was a huge archive devoted to the culture of the borderlands. It had been difficult to pry Tomek out of the stacks.

A young Borderland colleague arrived with a tea service on a wooden tray: an old teapot, delicate china cups and silver spoons, jelly cakes on a hand-painted porcelain plate. The presentation had Old World elegance, a connection to a time before malls and high rises and eating alone in front of the television set. Yes, a table had meaning. What was valuable from the past—artifacts, legends—were all cherished and preserved here.

But equally important, what was problematic from the past was also held up to the light of day. Borderland artists, together with the town's youth, were still in the process of renovating the town's Jewish cemetery, neglected for the past fifty years. The Nazis had torn out many of the old tombstones, and for the last several years, the Borderlanders had been unearthing them in people's yards, under the asphalt of roads, and returning them to the cemetery.

This reclamation work was central to the Borderland's philosophy of "taking responsibility," which meant, according to Krzysztof, "learning what really happened in this place."

In 2001 that credo led the Borderland Foundation to publish Jan Gross's controversial book *Neighbors*, about the massacre of Jews by Poles in the nearby town of Jedwabne. Not everyone in Sejny was pleased with the resulting national uproar, or the major role that the Foundation played in exposing such painful history. But to Krzysztof's mind, since the old regime had offered only falsehoods about history, pursuit of the truth was a "fundamental act of opposition" against that old system.

I confessed to Krzysztof that the new Jan Gross book, *Fear*, gave me ethical vertigo. I couldn't reconcile the selfless gestures of Polish rescuers—like Berek's Janka—with stories of Cheryl's father's friends shooting at him when he returned to Kolomyja.

Gross's new book had not yet been published in Polish, but I anticipated an inflammatory round of accusations and defensiveness. I worried such vituperative exchanges would damage efforts by Jews and Poles to reach out to one another.

Krzysztof registered neither alarm nor defensiveness. "Yes, it will be very painful," he agreed. "We have to take this relatively peaceful time to look at what is cruel and painful in the past," he explained. "It is the only way we can build a democracy. We cannot lose this time. We must be honest."

It was such a simple fact: obvious, clarifying, and a deep relief. If you wanted to build a tolerant and democratic society, you *had* to have the confidence to look honestly at what was dark in your country's past. This kind of openness had not been practiced in Poland for a long time—maybe never—until Borderland Foundation published Gross's *Neighbors*.

When the Borderlanders first arrived in Sejny, the whole period of the Holocaust had been erased from the discussion. "It was forgotten here," said Krzysztof, "especially among the young generation."

We stood now in front of the White Synagogue. During the Nazi occupation, the synagogue was used as a stable and, during Communist times, as a fertilizer warehouse. Krzysztof pushed open the heavy wooden doors and we entered a vast space with vaulted ceiling and dazzling white stucco walls. I voiced a few loud "heys!" The acoustics were fabulous. It made sense that a theater director would respond viscerally to the place that was the heart of the spiritual life of Sejny's vanished Jews. Theater space is, after all, sacred space. "Can you feel it?" he asked. Oh yes, I did.

I thought of my friend Allan meditating at Birkenau, how he'd been possessed by the wandering souls crowding into him "like rush hour on the subway." In the White Synagogue in Sejny, Krzysztof Czyżewski also became possessed with the presence of an absence. The first play he staged here, appropriately, was S. Ansky's *The Dybbuk*, which tells the story of a young Jewish bride possessed by the soul of her dead fiancé. Sejny's Jewish dead were calling out for recognition.

During one of these performances of *The Dybbuk* in the White Synagogue, a Jewish survivor from Sejny—a cantor from the United States named Max Furmansky—arrived in Sejny for his first visit since he left after the war. Furmansky ventured into the White Synagogue to pray and heard the spirits of the dead speaking through Polish teenagers performing Ansky's play. He was so intrigued with the Borderlanders that he decided to return for a longer visit, sending Krzysztof and his cohorts into overdrive to prepare a proper reception.

On the first day of Furmansky's return visit, the old cantor held court as a Borderland guest, regaling young people from Sejny about his youth in their town. As a teenager, Furmansky was a star runner. Every day he practiced by running the two kilometers from the synagogue uphill to the cemetery. His athletic talent saved him when he jumped off the German transport and sprinted into the forest with SS soldiers in hot pursuit.

On the second day, the Borderlanders arranged a ceremony for Furmansky in the White Synagogue and invited another Borderland friend, Israel's ambassador to Poland, Shevah Weiss. Weiss had also grown up in Poland and had been rescued by two Polish Catholics. The two survivors sat together in the synagogue.

"All of a sudden," said Krzysztof, "at full attention, they both sang all four parts of the Polish national anthem in Polish!" They surprised themselves. Neither of them had realized the Polish words were deep in their memory. In pre–World War II Poland, everyone learned it by heart.

On the third day, Krzysztof and the town's mayor arranged a welcoming party to help Furmansky find his family's house. "More and more people came to talk with Max about his family—his father who was a famous tailor. He sewed uniforms for Polish soldiers and priests."

On the fourth and final day of Furmansky's visit, the whole town walked with their visitor to the Jewish cemetery for a dignified ceremony of remembrance. While Furmansky recited the kaddish, the Jewish prayer of mourning, Krzysztof noticed the town priest walking to the microphone. "My heart skipped a beat. Then the priest started to pray . . . in Hebrew! Because he remembered, at this moment, that from his education he knew the Lord's Prayer in Hebrew as well. People just started to cry, to kiss each other."

It was heartening to hear what was possible in a returnee's experience. I recounted how Cheryl and I had searched for her family's house in Kolomyja, our visit to the forest on the edge of town, her scream.

Without a considered welcome from the community, Krzysztof cautioned, a returnee could end up feeling "more separated, more distant, with a bigger fear," as had happened to Cheryl, sadly, in Kolomyja.

When descendants of Sejny's Jews returned "even for one day," Krzysztof told me, it was immensely important for the community. "Because someone might ask you a question. Because you were challenged to answer truthfully about the past. Because 'taking responsibility' meant you were also challenged to ask these visitors questions."

The returnees become part of the conscious dialogue that Sejny and its Odd Believers carry on with Sejny's absent Jews, with the history of what happened here.

Cheryl would no doubt conclude, "The Poles miss us!" Perhaps. But what Krzysztof was saying was that the Poles also *needed* us—our stories, our testimony—in order to remember. We need *each other* to reclaim memory from national myths, distortions, and silences.

"BE STRONG . . . YOU ARE always welcome here," said Krzysztof as we departed Sejny. His send-off echoed in my heart as we lurched along a rutted, muddy lane to Krasnogruda. It was late afternoon, a glorious northern European spring day, clouds furling and unfurling in the slate sky. When we could drive no farther, Tomek pulled over and cut the engine. We walked the rest of the way through damp woods, through open fields. Farmers on ladders were repairing barn roofs from the winter's snow and through a dun-colored forest, we could see the pale blue of a frozen lake.

Krasnogruda, like so many old manor houses, had fallen on hard times. The government had appropriated it after the war and divided it up into apartments for forestry workers. Its fruit orchards had been uprooted and the grounds were long uncultivated. We walked through thickets of blackberry and high thistles to reach a weathered old house constructed of now-silvered oak planks.

Odds and ends of wooden furniture were scattered in front of the house. Someone from the Borderland Foundation had cut a rooster silhouette out of a sheet of plywood, painted it blue, and installed it on the peak of the roof.

In his melancholy poem "Elegy for N. N.," Czeslaw Milosz recalls "the house between the lakes." He writes of the "the wooden stairs and the wig of Mama Fliegeltaub," the Jewish innkeeper in the nearby town, no doubt as well known in her day as Jankiel, the Jewish innkeeper was in Mickiewicz's *Pan Tadeusz.* It was probably a manor house quite similar to Krasnogruda where Jankiel strummed his dulcimer in front of rapt Polish gentry.

It had been six months since the great poet had been honored with a huge funeral in Krakow. Before he died, Milosz, together with his brother Andrzej, renounced title to Krasnogruda and deeded it to the Borderland Foundation.

We crunched across a carpet of frozen leaves to the edge of the icy lake, looking back at Krasnogruda through the scrim of oaks. Before we'd left Sejny, Krzysztof had shown us drawings for the International Dialogue Center he envisioned for this site.

The foundation will train future teachers here to spread the message of tolerance far beyond this tiny town. The center will be "spiritually linked" with the thought and work of Czeslaw Milosz, a man of the borderlands.

THIS DAY WAS MY fifty-fifth birthday. Tomek took a birthday photo of me in front of the house, on what was left of the wooden verandah. I wanted to document this moment to show to Cheryl on my return. I wanted her to know that Krasnogruda—with as many magical syllables as Kolomyja—existed. I wanted her to feel hope that the dialogue center to be built here could help heal the hatreds that destroyed her family.

I stood with arms outstretched, the exuberant blue rooster on the slanted roof above my head. New spring grass poked through the patches of white snow glistening at my feet.

At that moment, there was nowhere else I wanted to be.

CHAPTER 21

We Were the Neighbors

JEDWABNE. My shoulders tensed at the sight of the roadway sign. This little town near Bialystok in Poland's northeast corner had become synonymous with Polish shame.

Tomek pulled over to ask directions. I don't remember if he asked the man walking his dachshund for directions to "the barn," or for directions to "the massacre site." I do remember clearly, though, the look of dismay and disappointment on the man's face when he registered Tomek's request.

We were just minutes from the simple stone monument. Blocks of granite marked off the footprint of what was once Bronislaw Szilezinski's barn, where the unthinkable—neighbors burning neighbors alive—took place on July 10, 1941. Tomek and I stood silently in the center of the memorial site. Overhead a pair of storks glided lazily toward their nest on the chimney of a nearby farmhouse. An animal squealed in the distance. Probably a pig. We both shuddered.

The marker was dedicated in July 2001 at the ceremony commemorating the sixtieth anniversary of the massacre, when notables gathered from around the world and Poland's then-president Aleksander Kwaśniewski offered an unflinching apology, carried live on Polish TV:

> We express our pain and shame. We express our determination in seeking to learn the truth, our courage in overcoming an evil past. We have an unbending will for understanding and harmony. Because

of this crime we should beg the shades of the dead and their families for forgiveness. Therefore, today, as a citizen and as the president of the Polish Republic, I apologize. I apologize in the name of those Poles whose conscience is moved by that crime.

It was Jan Gross's book *Neighbors*, of course, that had set off the anguished debate across Poland. At the time of its publication in Poland, Gross was applauded as a truth seeker by some and assailed as a traitor and a liar by others. Some revisionist historians and members of the Polish clergy went so far as to claim that the attack in Jedwabne was revenge for the Jewish collaboration with the invading Soviets, a persistent calumny Gross's book proves false.

Crucial to note was that the debate about Jedwabne was carried out in full public view among Poles. It involved Catholic prelates, former Solidarity leader Adam Michnik (himself of Jewish descent), Polish writers and academicians, and Jewish Poles.

The story of the Jedwabne controversy has been the subject of several books. Scholar Antony Polonsky suggests that the most desirable outcome for this debate would be for both Poles and Jews to "strive for a 'tragic acceptance' of those events that have united, and so often, divided them in the past century."

The day of the dedication it rained heavily. "God is crying," Rabbi Jacob Baker, a native of Jedwabne—who left in 1937—told those assembled. Tomek placed his hand gently against the rough stone of the monument, anchoring himself. He had grown up with a cherished collective self-image of Poles as only victims and heroes. On this particular patch of ground, for the first time, his confident demeanor cracked. I felt no satisfaction in observing my friend's discomfort.

Affixed to one side of the plinth was a weathered door, a visual memento of the original wooden barn. Grieving visitors had placed small stones of varying shapes and colors on the flat top of the monument, as is the custom when Jews pay respects to the dead. They'd piled flowers, now wilted, on the ground at its base.

We stood awhile longer in silence, then retreated to the car. There we sat without talking, both of us staring straight ahead, for several full minutes.

Tomek finally broke the silence. "It's so easy to talk about the crimes of the Germans," he said softly. "When I guide people through Auschwitz-Birkenau, I can talk about that for hours. When I have to talk about our crimes, something sticks in my throat."

Tomek was among newly democratic Poland's most thoughtful and open-minded students of the relations between Poles and Jews during World War II. Still, he struggled with a revision of the national self-image. "This is still such fresh information for us," he said. In his 2004 anthology *The Neighbors Respond*, editor Antony Polonsky notes that Polish responses to the Jedwabne story run the gamut from deeply defensive to painstakingly self-critical. "When the news broke," Tomek continued, "I wanted proof. I didn't believe it at the beginning. I tried to find excuses, to defend the crystal image that I carried. Then there was no way to deny it. We were guilty. When the Polish president was here and apologized for it, then everyone saw, understood. Our history was not so black and white."

There are still townspeople in Jedwabne who don't want to talk about what happened here. But the facts have been established. The prosecutor's report says that some four hundred Jewish Poles were burned alive in the barn, at the hands of local Catholic Poles. And, after what Anna Bikont, one of Poland's leading journalists, termed "a huge national psychotherapy session," the tragic event is now accepted as fact by most—though by no means all—Poles.

When he leads tours through Auschwitz-Birkenau, Tomek approaches the place from a historical, not an emotional, perspective. "Facts. Dates," he says. But at Jedwabne, it was impossible for him not to show his feelings.

"Maybe I'm mad that I can't understand it. I always said I wouldn't judge history from the perspective of a man living in the twenty-first century. I would never guess what my own behavior would have been. Here," he said sadly, "I am forced to judge it."

Among the essays I found most useful about Jedwabne was one written by Zygmunt Bauman, a Polish Jewish sociologist. "The issue," he wrote, "is not whether the Poles should feel ashamed or whether they should feel proud of themselves. The choice is not between shame and pride. The choice is between the pride of morally purifying shame, and the shame of morally devastating pride."

That the shame one feels over atrocities committed by one's countrymen—whether Polish townspeople in Jedwabne or American soldiers in My Lai—can be "morally purifying," even liberating, is an idea worth pondering. Perhaps a sense of shame is a useful, even necessary part of a community's self-reflection, a prerequisite to restoring a sense of self-respect. The philosopher Anthony Appiah includes both pride *and* shame in his definition of patriotism, a concern for the honor of your country.

We know that *some* American soldiers behaved atrociously in Vietnam. Yet we do not generalize about all American soldiers from this incident. We know that *some* Poles participated in this sorrowful crime, but we must be careful, as the wise historian Norman Davies notes, not to use Jedwabne to "fuel stereotypical misconceptions about all Poles being incipient Nazi collaborators or, still worse, eager participants in the Holocaust."

NOT MANY MILES LIE between the Jedwabne and the village of Tykocin, but there was a huge gulf in how the citizens of each of these towns responded to their respective war tragedies.

Tykocin was a postcard perfect shtetl. No billboards, no fast food restaurants, no boxy Soviet high rises. Slanting wooden houses hugged the market square. Young mothers in blue jeans pushed babies in carriages, calling out salutations to shopkeepers and neighbors.

Frédéric Brenner's film about the Tykocin Purim play fascinated and puzzled me. I was struck by the sense of sobriety and purposefulness the Tykociners exhibited in their performance, but I had no real sense of what lay underneath their decision to perform as Jews. There was a ritual elegance to the procession of villagers costumed as Jews walking through the cobblestoned streets of Tykocin to the simple stage set on the town square: a chair for the king's throne and a gallows for the villain.

In Brenner's film we hear the voices of several Tykocin villagers, witnesses to the 1941 Nazi roundup and massacre of their neighbors, chanting as the camera pans slowly over the town:

They are gone.
They went away.
They went to the forest.

They are gone, they went away.
They went to the forest.

Noonday bells chimed from the tower cathedral at one end of the square, calling parishioners to mass for Palm Sunday. Tomek and I walked the few blocks to the silent Tykocin synagogue.

Inside the synagogue—now a historical museum—daylight streamed through high windows, casting soft shadows on the thick plaster walls. Eighteen generations of Tykocin Jews had prayed in this synagogue, which dates from 1642. Every Friday night, men, women, and children gathered in this building, community gossip intermingling with Sabbath prayers, the rise and fall of the cantor's blessings.

Up until the Second World War, everyone in the Tykocin Jewish community owned a place in the synagogue. You either bought or inherited your seat. If you were poor and couldn't afford a prayer book, you could glance up and read the prayers painted directly on the walls.

The frescoes on the walls of the Tykocin synagogue had been restored. Hebrew characters formed prayers for the dead, prayers thanking God for the gift of dreaming. There was an admonition from the Talmud to "be strong as a tiger, light as an eagle, fast as a deer and brave as a lion." Parrots painted in shades of ochre and rust red peered out from complicated tangles of vines. Eagles perched on thick bunches of grapes. Gazelles bounded over stalks of wheat. A twisted stork's beak slanted toward heaven.

Church bells across the square chimed on the half hour, summoning Tomek and me for our appointment with Ewa Wroczyńska, who originated the Tykocin Purim play. Moments after we sat down in her office, Ewa burst in. She clutched a basket of dried flowers. Her cheeks were ruddy from her dash across the town square from Palm Sunday mass. She was a diminutive, round woman in her fifties, and her lively blue eyes invited conversation. "You came from so far!" she said warmly.

When she pulled off her crocheted hat and ran her fingers through her short red bob, I realized I'd mistaken this middle-aged woman for the young boy in Brenner's film, the one dancing and clanging on pot lids at the head of the Purim procession. The performance was emblematic of Ewa's energy and enthusiasm.

My main question for Ewa—one the Brenner film did not attempt to answer—was simple. Why, I wanted to know, did Polish Catholic villagers dress up as Jews and perform a Purim play?

Before I could ask, Ewa began firing away in Polish. Over the next few hours, I tried to glean from the way she waved her hands, the rising pitch of her voice what Tomek attempted to render into understandable English.

Ewa urgently wanted us to know what had happened to the Jews of Tykocin. It was sixty-five years ago, August 25 and 26, 1941, that a special German army unit murdered almost the entire Jewish population of Tykocin: more than 500 Jewish families, about 2,500 people altogether.

German soldiers with machine guns, she said, loaded Jewish women and children on a truck from the central market square and forced the men to line up in columns with three klezmer musicians—a trumpeter, a drummer, and a violinist—in the front. The Gestapo ordered the musicians to play "Hatikva," the Zionist anthem, as they marched out of town to the nearby Lopuchowo Forest. There, waiting Einsatzgruppen soldiers executed the Jews of Tykocin over three huge ditches their Polish neighbors had been forced to dig at gunpoint.

Tykocin suffered more horrors in 1944, just before the war was over. Local partisans killed a German officer and the Germans exacted collective punishment from the town. "They took all the young people in their twenties and thirties to the concentration camps," Ewa said. "They took young mothers. Only small children and elderly people were left."

Many small children escaped to the surrounding forests where they attempted to survive on their own. Many of them died without their mothers. The majority of people over forty living in the forest died. Very few Poles from Tykocin who'd been incarcerated in the camps survived. After the war, Ewa said, "Tykocin was an empty city, almost without any people."

Ewa hadn't grown up in Tykocin. Her father had been a pharmacist there, but in the 1920s he'd moved his family away to start his own business in a town where the new rail line was going in. The railway bypassed Tykocin, one of the reasons it appeared stuck back in time.

One of Ewa's aunts did live in Tykocin during the war, and she remembered the day the Jews were murdered. "It was the most horrible day in her life, in all the villagers' life," Ewa said. "In the town of Tykocin you could hear the shots, the sounds of execution." Any protest, and you'd join the victims. How could one have heard the sounds of one's neighbors' anguish and not have been traumatized for life?

The Germans used the Tykocin synagogue as a warehouse to store plunder from the murdered Jews. In the late sixties, the Communist government decided to restore the synagogue as a "monument to culture"; by the early seventies, they were searching for a museum director.

Ewa had just graduated in history from university in Warsaw. She wasn't interested in working in a museum, nor was she particularly interested in Jewish history. But her mother started to tell her stories about Tykocin. "She was always saying that without the Jews, Tykocin was no longer the same as it used to be."

She took the job and has worked at the museum ever since, with a notable interlude in December 1981, when martial law was instituted, when—after a colleague denounced her—she was briefly jailed for displaying a portrait of Poland's prewar leader Marshal Pilsudski on the wall of her office.

Not long after Ewa became director of the museum, she learned there were Tykocin families who could document their roots back to the sixteenth century. In 1985, in the aftermath of martial law, she began visiting these families in their homes and from these intimate meetings, Ewa learned of Tykocin's long tradition of amateur theater. Many of the older residents of the town had performed in plays before the war; there had been both Polish Catholic and Polish Jewish theater troupes.

Martial law had virtually killed cultural and community life in Poland. People hardly went out of their houses. "Everything was abandoned, artificial. An entire world disappeared. This country was reconstructed, but it was a totally different reality without life interwoven with Jews," she said, her eyes tearing.

Ewa decided to put the resources of the museum toward the goal of reawakening Tykocin. The key would be bringing people together to make theater. A young priest—who'd grown up with a longing to be an actor—went house to house, coaxing people to join. Then the library director in town proclaimed her theatrical passion. "And so . . ." said Ewa with a triumphant smile, "the theater was created!"

Ewa, who had been writing and performing plays for her family since childhood, wrote her first historical play based on the Polish uprising of 1830. The Tykocin Jews made their first appearance in this play, welcoming the Polish Army into the town as the Russians withdrew. There was a scene in this same play where two women quarreled over a piece of land. She'd found the argument documented in the city chronicles. Descendants of those two families told her the argument continued to the present day.

The overlap between history and present-day Tykocin life fascinated the incipient playwright. In the town archives, she learned that the local noble family, the Branickis, owned distilleries and appointed the town's Jews to collect the tax on vodka. This "privilege" accounted for much of the conflict between Polish Catholics and Polish Jews. And yet, despite this friction, Catholics and Jews traded, they joked. They were used to each other. They lived this way, together, for hundreds of years.

It became Ewa's quest to bring the memory of Jewish life in Tykocin back into the consciousness of the town's present-day Polish inhabitants. Some of the citizen-actors began performing in Ewa's plays as children, progressing to more substantial roles as they grew into adulthood. Roles were now handed down through generations.

Just as Polish Jews would have been familiar with their neighbors' Easter rituals, their Polish Catholic neighbors would have known about Purim. In small Polish towns, Purimshpielers in colorful costumes traveled around the Jewish neighborhood performing skits in private homes, where they were feted with vodka, wine, and pastries.

Jews celebrate Purim to commemorate the triumph of good over evil—a massacre averted. The Tykociners perform the play on the very spot where evil triumphed over good—where the massacre began. Their performance is not intended for visiting foreigners. It is a healing ritual for their community—a salvaging of an essential part of their own history.

Not long after I visited Tykocin, I heard Frédéric Brenner speak at a conference in Los Angeles. He showed his photos from the Tykocin Purim play with a dismissive comment: "We don't have the intellectual capacity to process this." I buttonholed him afterward, explaining how his photos and film motivated me to visit Tykocin, to seek out

Ewa. He shuddered at my mention of the town. Ewa, he said sternly, was "possessed" by her town's history. He was not interested in further discussion.

Brenner meant this as accusation, but it made perfect sense. Theater is an act of possession. You wear the skin of the lion to feel the lion's power. You dress as threatened Jews to relive their terror at history's darkest moment. By evoking the lives and stories of their lost neighbors through the medium of community theater, Ewa nudged the Tykociners to face the cataclysmic crime that had devastated their community.

In Christianity it is possible to atone vicariously for the sins of others. The Tykocin Purim play, which puts the endangered Jews front and center, is an opportunity for the villagers to mourn the loss of their Jewish brethren. "We do not perform these plays out of generosity," Ewa told me. "It is our obligation to the memory of what was here. This is a kind of compensation that we perform here, as we were the neighbors . . ."

Ewa's explanation brought to mind an incident from the Bearing Witness Retreat years earlier. It happened at dusk at Birkenau, at the settling ponds filled with the ashes from the crematoria. Cattails and tall reeds surrounded the murky soup. Red-winged blackbirds and swallows flitted over the surface, eating their fill of evening's insects.

The entire contingent had convened for a kaddish service. The kaddish praises God, celebrates the gift of life and peace, and never mentions the word *death*. The translation we chanted in English was a recent one by Rabbi Singer and poet Peter Levitt and contains these lines:

> Though we bless, we praise, we beautify
> We offer up your name,
> Name that is Holy, Blessed One,
> Still you remain beyond the reach of our praise, our song,
> Beyond the reach of all consolation. Beyond! Beyond!

The words "beyond . . . consolation" carried entirely new meaning as I peered into the terrible ash pits at Birkenau.

Some people lit memorial candles for grandparents, aunts, uncles. The light was fading. People recited the kaddish in their respective languages—German, English, Hebrew, Spanish, Polish, Japanese, French—each translation with its own somber rhythm.

The young rabbi who was officiating invited people to speak. My roommate, Debra, stepped up to the portable microphone to evoke the name of her father, a Dachau survivor. She was visibly shaken after speaking; I moved forward to comfort her. I didn't notice when a priest from Warsaw, Father Michal Czajkowski, stepped forward to address the gathering.

"Brothers and sisters," he began, "only the Shoah made us realize how much we Poles share with the Jewish people. Post-Holocaust thinkers, like Rabbi Heschel, stressed that interfaith dialogue takes place when a belief meets a belief. Only then such dialogue becomes fruitful."

He continued, "Our faith is getting greater by our consciousness of the great suffering that took place in this land. But it also makes us repent. So in the spirit of this faith, I would like to suggest to Christians here to share the prayer that Jesus gave us."

He began the Lord's Prayer:

> Our Father, who art in heaven, hallowed be thy name. Thy kingdom come, thy will be done, on earth as it is in heaven. Give us this day our daily bread and forgive us our trespasses, as we forgive those who trespass against us.

I'd mumbled those words every morning in the chapel of the girls' school I'd attended in Los Angeles, but I'd never seriously considered them until I heard Father Czajkowski utter them in Birkenau. He concluded, addressing the Jews present, "We ask your forgiveness not for our passivity, which would have been understandable, but for our indifference, which is a sin."

There were gasps, including my own, at the priest's contrition. "I have been waiting my whole life to hear a Christian Pole ask for forgiveness," one man murmured. I hadn't known I was waiting for such a thing at all, but at the moment the priest spoke those last words, a weight pressing on my heart began to give way.

CHAPTER 22

A Mensch in Radomsko

Maciej, in his familiar black leather jacket and visored cap, was waiting for us in an empty parking lot of a big hotel in a little town a few miles outside Radomsko. He paced and smoked. When he spotted us, his face expanded with delight. Though two years had passed since we'd seen each other, our easy familiarity resumed in an instant.

He reached through the open car window, took my hand and kissed my wrist, then, before Tomek could turn off the motor, he jumped into the back seat, closed the door, and barked out directions. We drove several miles, parked at the edge of a grassy wetlands where, in the distance, smokestacks belched white plumes into the fair blue sky. No other features on the horizon: no mountains, no buildings, nothing to clutter the view. We walked half a mile across the meadow on a creaking wooden boardwalk.

At the boardwalk's end, Maciej waved his hands toward the vista ahead. "Look!" he exclaimed.

We stood on the edge of a vast abyss. The hellish gash ran at least nine hundred feet into the ground and five miles across. I had to ask myself, why was I always peering into holes in the ground in Poland?

We were looking across at the Belchatów power plant. The rent in the earth was the biggest open-pit brown coal mine in the European Union. "This will provide power for Poland, for the EU for the next sixty years!" Maciej exclaimed with evident pride. The brown coal deposit was the reason, we learned, for this small town's clean streets, big new houses, business park, and gargantuan new hotel, where Maciej's son was manager.

We returned to the hotel and followed Maciej down empty corridors. There were no other guests. He'd mentioned dinner, but I detected no aromas of cooking. We went upstairs and walked down more empty corridors. It dawned on me that the hotel was not yet open. Finally, Maciej stopped in front of number fourteen, fished a key from his pocket, and ushered us into a furnished suite. It felt like a secret meeting of the Polish Underground.

"Sit, sit," Maciej told us, lighting a cigarette. A rap on the door. A waiter divested himself of a tray laden with plates of smoked salmon and blini. Hot borscht. Mugs of tea. He served us, then vanished.

Maciej ate nothing. He just smoked and lectured—among many topics—on the state of journalism in small-town Poland and his relationship with the town's former Communist Party leaders ("I told them, 'Kiss my ass.'").

As background to the impending ceremony in Radomsko, he wanted us to know about the town's strong tradition of drama and culture, how even in the ghetto, the Jewish drama society performed plays to support orphans. He told us about his founding of the Polish-Israel Friendship Society in 2000, the same year the pope went to Jerusalem.

The poet Adam Zagajewski must have had Maciej in mind when he wrote of those Poles imbued with "the ecstasy of the provinces." Bull-headed Maciej was determined to make Jewish history in Radomsko accessible to the townspeople. Publishing study guides for local schools was one project; tonight's cultural award ceremony was another. "If my experiment succeeds," he said with a wink, "then my little town will not suffer from small-town way of thinking."

I scribbled notes as Tomek translated and we both attempted to make a dent in the onslaught of Polish delicacies Maciej had arranged to be cooked specially for us in the big, empty hotel.

Maciej looked at his watch, startled. We couldn't be late to the ceremony! Within minutes, he peeled out of the parking lot while we followed at a safe distance on the winding road to Radomsko.

"He drives as fast as he talks," laughed Tomek. Sure enough, just as we entered the town limits, a police car with flashing lights pulled Maciej over. We watched from our car as he tried to talk his way out of it, but tonight the young policemen were granting no favors to the irrepressible editor of *Komu i czemu.*

—m—

TUCKED AWAY INSIDE THE concrete hulk of the Radomsko Cultural Center was a cabaret theater, a jewel box with red velvet curtains framing a small proscenium. Sixty or so people were already seated, sipping red wine and chatting while waiting for the evening's festivities to begin.

There was another honoree that evening, a twelve-year-old prodigy named Kasia Kabzinka. Her paintings were displayed on the wood-paneled walls of the theater: darkly sentimental landscapes, village houses covered with snow, babushka-wearing peasants harvesting fall wheat. Her still lifes featured clusters of bruised purple grapes and gleaming brass pitchers of wilting tulips and peonies.

Kasia was also fascinated by Judaica. She'd painted the tilting graves of the Radomsko Jewish cemetery illuminated by a silvery moon; a bearded rabbi studying Torah; a man wrapping tefillin around his arm for devotions.

These figures were stiff, generic. No wonder. Young Kasia had grown up in a city without Jewish life, without "the yeast," as Kostek would say. She'd never met a kosher butcher who cooked liver and onions for his Polish police friends. She hadn't immortalized her first Holy Communion by sitting for her portrait at the atelier of a re-nowned Jewish photographer. Kasia found real tulips and grapes for her still lifes, but she couldn't find Jews.

We were ready to begin. The Polish Parliament representative from Radomsko handed me an oversized pair of scissors and gestured toward a ceremonial banner made from three taped-together paper flags—Polish, Israeli, American—stretched across the stage. I made the cut and sat back down, realizing—to my embarrassment—that I'd sliced through the Stars and Stripes. I took a worried glance around; no one appeared offended by my cultural faux pas.

Maciej, spiffy in his pinstripe suit, shiny red shirt, and tie, was MC. He held up the large framed citation I was to receive, featuring my name plus the bolded phrase CZLECZYSKO 2006. "What's a *czleczysko*? I whispered to Tomek. "A mensch," he whispered back.

A mensch! German for "human being." Yiddish for a "stand-up kind of person." A simple word bestowed a big compliment. "Be a mensch!" my grandmother might admonish a difficult grandchild.

Later, a Polish friend saw this same poster in my office in Los Angeles and broke out in giggles. "*Czleczysko* is a word Lewis Carroll would invent!" *Czlowiek* in Polish means "human," something decent, good, reliable. The suffix *czysko* multiples the force of a word several times. "So we're talking big mensch, huge mensch," my friend told me, laughing. "It's a word made up specially for your ceremony!"

My title was not the only fanciful concoction of the evening. To piano accompaniment, three teenaged girls sang "Sunrise, Sunset" from *Fiddler on the Roof* as they performed a Hasidic circle dance. One dancer wore a miniskirt, high heels, and textured black hose. Her bare midriff peeked out under her sweater. The dance was earnest, unintentionally wacky. I'd slipstreamed into Cheryl's "Do You Miss Us?" Cabaret.

A willowy young violinist—Kasia's older sister—swept on stage in a shiny, floor-length gown of midnight blue with faux-fur collar and announced she would play "a memory song for Jewish villages." The audience listened, rapt. She followed her lyrical ballad with two preludes, her own compositions, performed with great verve. Deep bows, applause.

A big-bosomed woman in a black fringed shawl, her black hair pulled back into an elegant chignon, now took her turn on the stage. "An opera singer from Lodz," Tomek whispered. She launched with deep emotion into Yiddish cabaret songs, sung in a soaring soprano to piano accompaniment.

The crowd clapped wildly. I broke out in a sweat. Maciej nodded at me: It was my turn to address the crowd.

I stood in front of the assembly and opened the little notebook to find the speech I'd written the previous night. My throat was dry. My heart pounded.

"Who am I?" I heard myself saying. "I am an American writer. I live in Los Angeles, California." I paused after each sentence so Tomek could echo in Polish.

I told them that more significantly—for this gathering—I was the great-granddaughter of Kopel Konarski and Dvojra Libeskind Konarska; the great-granddaughter of Abram Wajskopf, and of Golda Zylberman Wajskopf, who was buried somewhere in the beautiful, melancholy Radomsko Jewish cemetery. I was the granddaughter of Sura and Layzor Wajskopf, who strolled Reymonta together arm in arm.

I hadn't anticipated how emotional it would be to speak out loud the Yiddish names of my great-grandparents in a roomful of Poles. Nor had I anticipated how those names would make a new kind of sense here, the lovely syllables of De-voj-ra, the *w* for Wajskopf pronounced as a *v*.

I told them they wouldn't know these names, and that for almost all my life, I hadn't either. But my ancestors lived and loved and died here. They were Radomskers. When my grandparents left Radomsko in 1906, they left behind parents, siblings, many other relatives and friends. Like so many other emigrants, they never saw their families again. My great-aunt Fayga Wilhelm stayed behind; she and her family were deported to Treblinka.

I told them about the Radomsk Yizkor, the Memorial Book of the Community of Radomsk. The book told not only of the tragedy and suffering of the Holocaust but also of the friendliness and beauty of this town, where a Catholic painter painted the zodiac on the ceiling of the Great Synagogue and a Jewish tinsmith designed the spires of the cathedral.

I wanted them to know that this night was the second night of Passover. "The words we repeat each year on this holiday as part of the seder take on new meaning in Radomsko: 'Since you were once a stranger in the land of Egypt, thou shalt love the stranger as thyself.'"

I was their honored guest—not a stranger. I was eager to hear *their* stories. Faces in the audience were flushed and smiling.

Kasia rose from her seat in the midst of the applause and held out another gift—a portrait she'd painted—of me. She'd based her painting on a photo she'd found online. I had trouble recognizing the image of a pale, bespectacled woman, her mouth set in a grim line. No doubt those generic old Jews from Radomsko, framed on the wall, would recognize her as kin.

I accepted the painting from Kasia to robust applause. We smiled at each other through the crooked mirror. It was the gesture that counted.

There was more clapping and laughter as the formalities ceased. People crowded around to talk. Maciej embraced Kasia, her sisters, and me. We posed for the camera together with her parents. The mood in the room was jubilant.

A tall, lanky fellow sidled up, speaking to me via Tomek's translation. "You mentioned the name Wilhelm. We all remember Foto Venus. Very important, very famous all over Poland."

A woman named Elzbieta, a representative of the local Poland-Israel Friendship Society, moved closer. "Wilhelm, Wilhelm," she repeated excitedly. "You should know—there are two Wilhelm sisters." She meant the daughters of Aron Wilhelm, the photographer and proprietor of the famed Foto Venus. "The son of Aron Wilhelm was shot by the Germans," Elzbieta told me. The Wilhelm sisters, she insisted, were still alive. One lived in Israel, the other in Beverly Hills, California. I jotted down the name: Ester Wilhelm Tepper.

IN THE MORNING WE drove slowly by the house on Rolna Street, though Maciej and Tomek had counseled against knocking on the door today. After all, it was a major religious holiday and privacy should be respected. I could see the logic. I also noted my residual paranoia: Jews had best lay low on Good Friday.

I asked Tomek to take me to the Radomsko train station. I wanted to see the place where Fayga Wilhelm and her family would have glimpsed their town for the last time before the doors on the cattle cars were bolted shut. Those cars would have finally come to a stop fifty miles northeast of Warsaw, disgorging their human cargo at Treblinka.

Tomek and I had made our pilgrimage there a few days earlier. That afternoon we were the only visitors to the former death camp.

There are no buildings at Treblinka now; they were all dynamited by the departing Germans. For several hundred feet we walked and stumbled over the stone blocks built to simulate the rail spur into the camp. At the crest of the hill a field of jagged stone shards ringed a black granite obelisk gashed from top to bottom. There are seventeen thousand of them, from Polish quarries, representing the villages, towns, and countries of the one million who died at the camp. One thousand were Gypsies, the rest were Polish Jews.

For a long, silent hour the two of us did walking meditation among the mute shards, hundreds of which are incised with the names of the destroyed shtetls of Poland. Tomek called out when he'd found the stone etched with the word RADOMSKO.

Only local trains now stop at the sleepy Radomsko train station. It has retained not a vestige of its original Art Nouveau elegance. There are no amenities; it's not possible to buy even a bottle of water or a bag of chips.

Late at night on this same platform in the fall of 1914, a group of young people from Radomsko waited excitedly for the Vienna-Warsaw express. They hoped to catch a glimpse of their literary hero, the great Yiddish writer Sholem Aleichem, en route to Warsaw. It began to rain, sending them scurrying for scant cover under the roof by the tracks.

The locomotive finally huffed into the station and the express train screeched to a halt. The Radomsko stopover was mere minutes. The bedraggled fans ran up to the window of the first wagon. Where was he? A sympathetic passenger put down his newspaper long enough to gesture toward the right compartment. Just as the train began to pull out, they spied the writer and his wife. Sholem Aleichem wore a coarse, white Russian peasant shirt and a wide Panama hat on his head. Seeing the young people standing in the heavy rain waving with their handkerchiefs, he broke into a smile.

Sholem Aleichem took off his Panama hat and waved it at his cheering young admirers. He waved for as long as he could see them. The yizkor entry: "Our good luck was indescribable. Our best clothes were soaked, but it was worth it to us. We had the privilege of seeing Sholem Aleichem and to be saluted by him."

Fayga Konarska Wilhelm was still young in 1914. She might have been one of those ecstatic young fans who glimpsed the great writer as he passed through their little town.

There were few traces of this great-aunt of mine—all the more reason to imagine the exuberance of her possible life, as well as her probable death, summed up by a stone at Treblinka.

TOMEK WANTED TO BE home with his family for the Easter holiday and we had a long drive back to Krakow. But Maciej wanted to show us one more thing in Radomsko while it was still light.

On a quiet side street, Maciej instructed Tomek to stop in front of a substantial two-story brick house surrounded by an ornate iron fence. Maciej pointed to the fence: "There is a story here," he said.

I'd understood from reading the yizkor book that the beautiful old Radomsko synagogue—the one with the zodiac painted on the ceiling—had been destroyed during the aerial bombardment at the beginning of the German invasion. After my first visit here, nine years earlier, I'd dreamed of wandering through the streets of Radomsko searching for the Great Synagogue. To my amazement, in the dream, I'd found it solid and unscathed. I entered through its portals to discover the building lacked an interior. It was just a façade. Behind it was a beautiful neighborhood where children played, artists worked in their studios, bakers lifted fragrant loaves from their ovens.

According to Maciej, my dream resonated with the historical truth. The German bombs did not completely destroy the Great Synagogue. The wrecked shell, including the façade, *had* survived the attack. The hair on my arm stood on end.

In the early fifties, Maciej told us, the Communist government decided the façade should be torn down. There were local protests. But as Maciej put it drily, "The Party knew better what they wanted." Bulldozers knocked down what was left of the grand building that could accommodate over a thousand people. The synagogue's ornate iron gate and fence, the work of local craftsmen, were relegated to an ironworks to be melted down for scrap.

"It was kept in the storage place of one of the metalworkers," Maciej said. "He was a simple guy, but he realized what he had." Did this metalworker understand that he had a piece of the history of the Jewish community of Radomsko? Or did he see something of purely monetary value? Had his family hidden Jews? Did he touch that wrought iron with reverence and wonder? I pictured him as Wajda's Man of Steel. Burly, thick biceps, not given to long speeches. Before the war, the synagogue would have been part of his Radomsko world.

Maciej had interviewed the director of the ironworks and observed the documents of sale. The director vouched that the purchase of the gate and fence from the iron yard was above board, perfectly legal. "The metal worker saved these monuments," Maciej confirmed. "Now his son is the mayor of our city. And now his son lives in this house."

In 1947, according to the yizkor book, a small group of Radomsko survivors returned to their town from the camps and the forests to see what was left. They stood together in the rubble of the destroyed shul "bent by a great sorrow and pain." While they looked over the ruins, remembering where the rabbi sat, where their fathers and their neighbors once prayed, one of the men spied a copper fragment poking out of the detritus. It was a piece of the Eternal Lamp, which hung over the Holy Ark that housed the Torah. They dug it out. "Even in the midst of their sorrow, they took comfort that something survived."

Maciej grinned. The creases on his weathered face shifted like the complicated borders of Poland. "Strange things happen in this town," he said.

CHAPTER 23

Venus in LA

In the wake of my return from Poland, I discovered a strategy for jet lag. Late at night, sleep elusive, I flew to Radomsko via Google Earth, sipping tea as the glowing globe rotated on its axis and the image on my screen zoomed in on the little town between Czesto-chowa and Lodz.

Had I just imagined the pit mine where Maciej took us? No, there it was—a gash in the landscape. With a click of the mouse I was on Rolna Street, at the Hotel Zameczek, in front of the reclaimed syna-gogue gate.

How could I maintain a connection to a place so many miles and realities away, so far removed from my day-to-day life? Sorting through notes from the ceremony in Radomsko, I found the name I'd scribbled down: Ester Wilhelm Tepper.

Over the next months I called all the Teppers in the bulky Los Angeles area phonebook, with no success. I abandoned the quest, then started up again. In midsummer, a Google search unearthed an Ester Tepper at a medical transportation company in Beverly Hills. I dropped a note in the mail: "If you are Ester Wilhelm Tepper whose family is from Radomsko, I'd love to speak with you. If not, I'm sorry for disturbing you."

Two days later, I received a call from a woman whose voice had a musical Polish accent: "How did you find me?" Then, more cautious, "Who are you?"

I explained as best I could. "Yes," she owned, "my father was the photographer Aron Wilhelm. Foto Venus in Radomsko." The next day she called again, casting suspicions aside: "I can't stop thinking about this since we spoke. That we should meet is *beshert* [fated]. How soon can you come?"

That was how I found myself in a sunny kitchen in a gracious house in Beverly Hills just miles from where I live, looking at prewar photographs from Radomsko taken by the famous father of a woman into whose family my lost great-aunt had married. You go looking for history; history turns up practically in your own backyard.

The woman who met me at the door with a smile and open arms was a svelte seventy-four-year-old with tousled blonde hair, animated blue eyes. She introduced her husband, Nathan ("my lover," she called him), a tall, handsome man in tennis shorts. They'd met in Palestine as teenagers after the war.

Nathan made us coffee, set out sesame bagels, and wisely left us alone in the kitchen. Ester and I talked as if we've known each other for years, our stories spilling out over each other's sentences. Ester had four grown children, eleven grandkids.

I had many specific questions for Ester about her prewar memories. "I can't believe you know so much about Radomsko!" she murmured.

Ester was seven years old on the morning of September 1, 1939— when German bombs rained down on the center of Radomsko. Up until that morning, she'd lived a privileged life as the youngest daughter of one of the town's most prominent citizens. Her father built their big house on Third of May Street, facing the town square. On the second floor, upstairs from the family's living quarters, was the Foto Venus atelier. Their house was filled with impromptu musical performances, boisterous family gatherings of the extended Wilhelm clan. There were matinee films at the Radomsko cinema, trips to Lodz and Warsaw for beautiful clothes.

Aron Wilhelm was an inventor and bon vivant, a polymath who played the violin and loved "schnapps, women, and really good life." Ester's mother was from a traditional Hasidic family; Ester's father's family was highly assimilated. The Wilhelms were Jewish, but saw no contradiction in considering themselves patriotic Poles. The children went to Hebrew school and to Polish school. Ester learned Yiddish only later, in Israel. "I survived because the language we spoke at home was only Polish."

The story of how Ester survived disguised as a Catholic child, first in Czestochowa and later in a convent, pieced together from conversations on subsequent visits and from listening to Ester's recorded testimony for Steven Spielberg's Shoah Archives, was long and harrowing. How could it have been otherwise? "You have to know from A to Z to understand what really happened," she said.

Ester beckoned me into the dining room. Above a sideboard was an entire wall hung with framed family photos: scenes from Radomsko in the teens, twenties, taken by her father. In one, her mother, Gucia, bathed her sister Chana, her brother Maniek, and Ester—the baby—in a claw-foot bathtub. In another, the extended family gathered to celebrate the wedding of an aunt, each member raising a champagne flute. There was a photo of little Ester in her frilly Purim costume, the namesake dressed as her regal heroine. "They used to call me Shirley Temple," she laughed. "I had the curly hair; I sang and danced."

I thought of Cheryl, who possessed no pictures of her family in Kolomyja. She'd painted portraits of them from somber tones in the palette of her imagination. They were never far from her mind.

Ester's family photographs survived the war because Ester's mother regularly mailed photographs to her sisters in Palestine. "My mom used to always tell us, whatever happened, we had family in Palestine."

Radomsko was close to what was then Poland's border with Germany; the Nazi occupiers arrived soon after the bombs. "They came with a truck and took everything—the Persian carpets, the furniture, my dolls and games. They said we had to move into the ghetto. They shot a lot of Jews that first day. It all happened in twenty-four hours. I was seven. I remember it was very cold. I remember thinking, 'We never did anything wrong. What happened?'"

Ester's mother was taken away in a subsequent roundup—destination Treblinka. There was no one to care for the children. Her father was devastated with grief. There was neither food nor fuel in the ghetto. Fifteen-year-old Maniek ventured out nightly to forage, accompanied by Bronka, the Polish orphan who had joined the Wilhelm household. One night the family heard shots outside. They peered out: Maniek and Bronka lay "in a heap" next to each other on the sidewalk. "He was lying there with his eyes open, my brother . . ." Ester's voice faltered. "I see it as if right now."

"The German who killed my brother said to my father, 'Hey, Venus! I knew it's your son. After I gave him one bullet, I gave him two more so he wouldn't suffer.'" Ester groaned. "Such a comfort!"

On New Year's Eve, 1943, several days after the shooting, a few survivors gathered in the Wilhelm flat to mourn the dead. Ester's father played a sad melody on his violin, then "smashed the violin to pieces. People took each a little splinter to remember Maniek."

Aron Wilhelm paid a number of people to spread the word that they'd seen "Venus and his children all dead." He then smuggled his daughters out of the ghetto, entrusting Ester—his youngest—to his mistress, Krystyna, in Czestochowa. "She taught me to be Catholic, how to pray, what to say. She took me to Jasna Góra to see the Black Madonna," Ester said.

I remembered staring up at the jagged scars on the dark brown face of the Black Madonna. To the faithful, those scars were Poland's scars.

Ester became a Polish girl, Regina Kozerowska, her age amended by five years. "I really believed in Jesus and Mary. My story was that my father was in the Polish Army, my mother had passed away. Krystyna was a very nice lady, very patriotic. She believed I will be a Catholic girl forever."

Unfortunately for the false Regina, the mother of the little girl next door had a German boyfriend. Ester and Krystyna were both arrested. "The SS put me in a cell. 'Where are the Jews?' they demanded."

Ester insisted she was Regina Kozerowska, that she wasn't Jewish. The German interrogator put a revolver to her head. "They killed another man right in front of me. They put me in a cell full of blood."

Ester fell on her knees and prayed to Jesus and Mary. One of the SS men looked into the cell and saw her praying. "I did not *pretend* to pray to the mother Mary," she said, "I really believed." She was brought back to her interrogators. "Where are the Jews?" they again demanded.

Ester/Regina feigned indignation. "You will not kill me, a Catholic girl, because of those dirty Jews," she told the police, who released her. She had faith that Krystyna, interrogated separately, would not give her away. "She was very strong, smart. She was released too. She was already home," Ester said.

She paused in front of each photo, as if formally introducing a friend. Her syntax was a charming mélange of Old World and New.

"This is mine father, Aron. He got three brothers and two sisters." Another photo. "This one was my uncle who mostly liked to drink a good vodka. He was making excellent men's suits."

Ester assured me that all the Wilhelms in Radomsko were one family. "My father used to tell me this all the time," she said, adding proudly, "Don't think you come from *schnorrers*!"

I'd wondered why my great-aunt Fayga had not left Radomsko for New York along with her three sisters. She was the youngest. When her siblings emigrated in 1906, her parents were still alive. I'd speculated that she had probably stayed to be close to them. Then she married into the Wilhelm clan.

Ester saw no mystery. "They were Wilhelms and they were successful and why would you want to leave?" She shrugged. "Who thought such a thing would happen?"

Ester illuminated some historical footnotes about Herschel Grynszpan, the Jewish youth, whose parents came from Radomsko, who in November 1939 assassinated the Nazi diplomat Ernst vom Rath. Ester was related to the Grynszpans through her mother. After the vom Rath assassination, the Germans searched far and wide for Grynszpan's kin. Their search led them to Radomsko. Ester's father hid Herschel Grynszpan's grandparents in one of his specially prepared bunkers and helped smuggle the family out of the ghetto so they could flee to Russia, where they survived the war.

We walked through the house, past glass cases displaying Aron Wilhelm's cameras, lenses, glass negatives, special lenses—remnants of Radomsko's famed Foto Venus Artystyczna Fotografia right here in Los Angeles. I paused to look at the Leica in one of the cases. Hundreds of Radomsko citizens—Polish Catholics and Polish Jews— had posed for Aron Wilhelm's camera for their weddings, first communions, graduations, bar mitzvahs, christenings. Everyone loved a photo, even the occupying Nazi soldiers, who sent photo souvenirs of their "heroic deeds" back to their families in the Reich.

"When the Germans killed a lot of people, they made my father take photos to show what a good job they did." Aron Wilhelm photographed old Jewish men scrubbing the sidewalk with toothbrushes, Jews hanging from a lamppost as punishment for some infraction. Those photos vanished into the Nazi propaganda juggernaut.

At war's end, sixteen-year-old Ester and her sister Chana were both working as Polish slave laborers in Austria. They reunited in Vienna, then walked together from Vienna to Bratislava, from there to Radomsko. They hadn't heard news of their father for more than a year.

On May 28, 1945, the sisters finally entered their hometown. They ran through the streets to their house, kissed the threshold. There was a miracle: "Father was inside—alive!" Aron Wilhelm had lived under disguise for part of the war as an Aryan photographer in Warsaw. He survived incarceration in Auschwitz, Mauthausen, Bergen-Belsen, Dachau. Six members of the Wilhelm clan were now alive—the two sisters, their father, an uncle, and two cousins. Six out of a family of sixty-eight.

The survivors' stay in their comfortable Radomsko home was brief. Ester put it bluntly: "After six months came the blackmailers: 'We give you six hours and if you don't leave you will all be killed right here.' So we took whatever we could, and we run away. We left most behind."

After an interlude in a DP camp, they finally emigrated to Israel in 1946. Ester, too young to join the Israeli Army, lied about her age. A photo showed Ester as a winsome teenager, leaning against an Israeli Army jeep.

Her father pleaded for Ester to attend school, but she had no interest after so many years of suffering. "I should have a PhD from what I went through!"

Ester embodied all the dizzying polarities and contradictions of the historical debate between Jews and Poles. She'd been rescued by brave Christian Poles who risked their lives—and the lives of their families—to hide her. At war's end, she'd been chased out of her home at gunpoint by venal profiteers.

She abruptly turned the questions on me. Why was I so interested in Radomsko? Why was I interested in Polish people there today? Why did I care? I was startled. I took a breath and started to tell her about Tomek, who had immersed himself in Jewish history, about Maciej, who had written more than sixty articles about the Jewish history of Radomsko in his newspaper, I was just warming up.

But Ester had scant patience for my attempted explanation. "A lot of them now want to find out more. It's helping, but still—the ordinary normal Polish people hate the Jews," she said matter-of-factly. At her utterance of this broad stereotype, I deflated.

I thought of the children in Sejny hovering like angels over the clay model of their town, telling the stories of their grandparents' lost Jewish neighbors. I thought of the Purim play in Tykocin and young Tomek's anguish standing at the plinth in Jedwabne.

"I don't hate the Germans," said Ester softly. "I don't hate the Poles." Another shrug and a deep sigh: "Where do we go with hate?"

THAT NIGHT I WROTE to Cheryl in France. I was eager to tell her about finding Ester and her house full of photographs, to let her know that even if I could not bring myself to knock on the door of the house on Rolna Street, I'd found a living remnant of my Radomsko family just miles from my home in Los Angeles. A few days later Cheryl responded, in true form:

> Fell asleep on the beach. First swim of the year. Dreamed I found an old book that I'd been looking for maybe all of my life. A book of important facts I needed to know. The book was difficult to open. Like a sealed box. I finally got it open but the wind made the pages fly. Sound of the flapping . . . ffffffffffffttt . . . ffffffttttttt . . . it all happened so fast. The pages were dry and brittle and flew away. The old heartbreak feeling overwhelmed me. I had it and I lost it.
>
> What was left on the spine were just jagged edges from the pages—but I could see through to the binding, and there was—to my shock and surprise—some live flesh. It was glistening. There was still some life left.
>
> Upon awakening—the first thing I thought of was Kolomay. The not so empty place where the whole family came from with no remnants of them that I could see. What knowledge would I have come by, had the house still been there?

CHAPTER 24

The Rosetta Stone

An unexpected invitation from a theater colleague allowed me to return to Poland in the spring of 2009. The occasion was an international theater festival commemorating the tenth anniversary of the death of the Polish director Jerzy Grotowski, one of the world's great theater innovators.

Grotowski disciples—actors, critics, directors, producers from Bucharest to Tokyo, from Palermo to Manhattan—assembled in Wroclaw. Breslau had been the name for this beautiful formerly German city on the Oder River. At the end of the war, when those old men in Yalta carved off a chunk of eastern Poland to give to the Soviet Union, they gave part of eastern Germany to Poland in recompense, and Breslau became Wroclaw—a Polish town.

From morning to night we talked, watched, inhaled theater: in an abandoned piano factory, in the renovated refectory of a fifteenth-century Polish church, and up the worn wooden stairs of the prewar building in Wroclaw's Old Town where Grotowski created his masterpieces. In that hallowed, brick-walled studio, a Polish troupe called Teatr ZAR performed *The Gospels of Childhood*.

Polyphonic chants and lamentations underscored tableaux of work, love, and prayer reminiscent of a Brueghel peasant pageant. Ancient devotional melodies swelled and ebbed. Lithe figures collided and embraced. Beeswax candles dripped onto a wooden table where a man in a white shirt sliced a large loaf of bread. A woman kicked over the table, revealing a heap of rich, black earth and a shovel. In the semidarkness, dirt clods thudded onto a rising mound, the shovel rasped the wooden floor. I choked back a sob. Where was I? In a studio in Wroclaw. At a cemetery in LA, shoveling soil onto my friend Johanna's grave. In the forest outside Kolomyja where Cheryl's grandmother and aunts shivered in the cold.

The actors flung open the shuttered studio windows, replacing the still air and the audience's hushed silence with the epiphany of an evening spring breeze and exuberant voices from the square below. They exited. We remained on our wooden benches for several minutes, staring at the mound of dirt, the shadows cast by the candles, the overturned table. Bells in the clock tower chimed nine times, resonating in my bones.

That night in my hotel room I slept soundly. In my dream, I wandered some Polish city by a river, searching for an overcoat. In a department store, I found one made of heavy gray wool, soft to the touch. I tried it on. I liked what I saw in the mirror. The seams lined up. The weight and cut suited me.

My delight at finding the right overcoat persisted upon waking. The overcoat Cheryl had commissioned in her dream was made from stiff, itchy fabric. It was a strategy to discomfort the menacing invaders. My Polish overcoat was forgiving, pliant.

I RODE THE TRAIN east from Wroclaw across the plowed fields of Silesia to Krakow to rendezvous with Tomek, my indispensable guide and translator. After so many trips and so many years of correspondence, he had become a trusted friend. For this return trip to Radomsko and a first visit—for both of us—to Lublin in Poland's east, he'd offered to serve as my translator pro bono. It would be our second journey together during Lent; I knew enough now not to bring him gifts of his favorite chocolate.

Our drive to Radomsko took us past Poland's only sand dunes, where troops trained for combat in Afghanistan; through softly contoured farmlands, to the small shtetl towns of Gidle and Zarki. In the village of Plawno—where my grandparents were married—a dapple-gray draft horse sporting a red ribbon on his bridle clip-clopped past Tomek's car. The wagon driver tipped his hat in greeting.

Just outside Radomsko, the bright fluttering streamers of a Maypole caught my eye. Tomek pulled over for a photo. Behind gnarled apple trees, I glimpsed a dilapidated manor house, a For Sale sign. Lloyd and I could buy it, fix it up, build a studio! Tomek laughed, "Heating alone will bankrupt you." But he was beginning to take more seriously my growing affinity for Poland. Had I ever considered applying for a Polish passport? I was entitled to one, he explained, since two of my grandparents were from Poland.

I found the idea immediately intriguing, though subsequent inquiries revealed Polish ironies, or Polish Jewish ironies. Or both. When Sarah and Louis left Nowo-Radomsk in 1906, they didn't leave as Polish citizens. There was no nation-state of Poland in 1906. They were citizens of the Czarist empire, an affinity neither possible nor desirable to reclaim.

White storks—Poland's springtime guests—perched atop the occasional church steeple and the chimneys of thatched-roof houses. They fed their young, preened, clacked their beaks in huge nests. Did I know, asked Tomek, that their route here from Africa was not direct?

The direct route from Africa to Poland is over the Mediterranean, but the storks depend on air thermals formed over land masses for their long migration. They glide for hours without flapping their wings. So storks migrating from Africa to Central Europe take the long way around, crossing at the Strait of Gibraltar.

I'd seen three spring migrations of storks to Poland over the past decade. I myself had become a seasonal migrant of sorts. Every two years, time to fly eastward across the Atlantic, change planes in Munich or Frankfurt, a half-day drive from Krakow or Warsaw to this little town. On each return, Radomsko revealed some new aspect of itself, of its past.

Maciej was waiting in the dining room of the Zameczek, my Radomsko home away from home. He wore his familiar shiny suit and the tangerine-colored shirt. He plucked a long-stemmed rose from a vase and handed it to me with a flourish, a kiss on the wrist. (I can never emphasize enough, when offered with love and respect, the potential of this gesture to delight.) He and Tomek exchanged warm handshakes.

On an earlier visit I'd expressed to Maciej my desire for some public monument to commemorate the Jewish community of Radomsko.

He'd pursued the idea with unflagging determination. Now he was eager to show us the big changes in his town. Within half an hour of our arrival we stood in front of a black granite monument, installed on the site of the Great Synagogue. Maciej beamed with pride. The simple inscription was in Hebrew and Polish: "On the 65th anniversary of the Jewish ghetto liquidation in Radomsko. We remember. Citizens of the town. Radomsko 2008."

A few hundred townspeople, city dignitaries, visitors from Israel had attended the ceremony a few months earlier. I'd wanted to attend along with Ester Wilhelm, but Ester's health at the time and my job demands could not be ignored. I proposed that Ester write a statement for the dedication. Ester dictated it to me, Tomek translated, Maciej read it aloud at the ceremony, then published it in his newspaper:

> I remember the day the synagogue was bombed. My father came inside, crying like a baby. I remember this more than something that happened ten years ago. None of us believed something so terrible could happen to Poland. None of us believed something so terrible could happen to the Jewish people. I survived the war as a child hidden by a brave Polish woman from Radomsko. Today I wish to honor her memory and to everyone else who helped me to survive.

I was thrilled that the voice of a Wilhelm survivor had been heard in her hometown. Across the road from the monument, a large signboard detailed the history of the Radomsko ghetto, the fate of its occupants, and displayed a map of its exact location in the city. The monument honoring the dead and the sign showing where they were incarcerated were impossible to miss on one's daily route across the town.

En route to the cemetery, we drove down Rolna Street. A man on the sidewalk in front of his house recognized Maciej and gave us a friendly wave. We pulled over and the two of them chatted, nodding in my direction. This gentleman, named Marek, remembered my talk two years before at the cultural center as well as my connection with the Wilhelm family.

Marek was a law professor in Krakow. His family home was at 57 Rolna. He invited us inside, ushered us into a comfortable dining room furnished with a big wooden sideboard, a table covered with a lace tablecloth, a gilt-framed mirror, bric-a-brac, oil paintings, family photographs. He pointed out a portrait of his parents. It was a photograph by Aron Wilhelm. He rummaged in the sideboard and brought out a vintage photo box, proudly showing me the label Foto Venus.

This part of Rolna Street was outside the boundaries of the ghetto. During the occupation, Marek's grandfather had hidden a Jewish child here. After the war, the grandfather took the child to Warsaw and reunited her with her parents. Marek passed around a cut-glass dish brimming with almonds and raisins. Would I like some?

We walked the few blocks down to 27 Rolna, which *had* been within the boundaries of the ghetto. The house—with drawn curtains—looked uninhabited, as on past visits. Maciej sensed otherwise. "There's someone here," he said, opening the side gate without hesitation. Tomek and I followed him up the driveway.

Behind the house, a small old woman was bent over, weeding her overgrown garden. She wore a threadbare sweater, frayed support hose, rubber boots. Dark soil stained her hands. I backed up to take in the whole picture: a rotting greenhouse with several broken windows, an apple tree badly in need of pruning, overturned lawn furniture.

Maciej and Tomek waited patiently, not wanting to startle her, and then said, "Dzien dobry, pani . . ." (Good morning, ma'am . . .) The woman must have been hard of hearing. "Pani, pani . . ." She finally looked up, eyebrows raised. What did they want with her? She wiped her hands on her apron, scrutinized Maciej. He introduced himself. "Ah," she said with a nod, "you're that journalist." Maciej questioned her gently, urgently. I heard the name *Wilhelm* and the words for "Jew. Occupation. Germans." To each question, the old woman gestured with her weeding claw, like a defensive bird. Neither Tomek nor Maciej paused to translate.

While they talked, I glanced inside an open side door to the house. How did the light fall, Cheryl would want to know. Sunlight illuminated the shiny, plaid plastic tablecloth covering the kitchen table and mottled the bare wood floor. A sink stacked with dishes was in shadow as was a small cot with rumpled blankets. From a radio on the sill of the open window wafted unmistakably patriotic music and intermittent speeches.

After the impromptu interview, Tomek and Maciej thanked the old woman, who waved them off and bent down again to resume weeding. In the car, they repeated the little they'd learned. This house, which was the last known address of Fayga and Fayvel Wilhelm, had been built by this old woman's grandfather. When the borders of the ghetto were established, the house was requisitioned by the Germans, and this woman—then a young girl—and her entire family were forced to move. The Wilhelms had been one of at least three Jewish families billeted in the house.

It troubled both Tomek and Maciej that the old woman was listening to a broadcast of the infamous Radio Maryja, a nationalist, anti-Semitic station. The station, run by a radical priest in the city of Torun, draws its audience primarily from Poland's rural, elderly poor. Though Polish and Jewish human rights groups—as well as the Vatican—have repeatedly condemned the station, no one yet has been able to put Radio Maryja out of business. "After all we went through during the war," the old woman told Tomek and Maciej, "I don't understand why the Jews got so cozy with the Germans."

This was the kind of paranoid falsehood that Radio Maryja constantly reinforced, sighed Tomek. "Poland as the Christ of Nations, everyone else as outsider. And that," he said, "includes gays and lesbians, Jews, and Germans."

The xenophobic pensioner who listened to anti-Semitic broadcasts was on the same block just a few houses down from the urbane law professor who spoke proudly of his grandfather rescuing a Jewish child. During the Nazi occupation, if a Radomsker Jew—like Berek, like Ester Wilhelm's father—fled to a neighbor's house, he had better be damn sure he knew whose door he was knocking on.

THE AFTERNOON LIGHT WAS fading by the time we reached the cemetery. The ruddy-cheeked caretaker again welcomed us in. For this visit my landsman, Dan Kazez, had provided me with a photo of my great-grandmother's headstone. With copies in hand, we began wandering rows of graves in the dimming light, comparing Hebrew inscriptions to the one in the photo, trying not to stumble over exposed tree roots, until Tomek shouted, "I found it!"

I was dumbstruck. Wonder, relief, pleasure, sadness all at once. I ran my hands over the rough, weathered limestone that marked the grave of Golda Zylberman Wajskopf, my grandfather Louis's mother.

I never knew my great-grandmother. My mother had not known her grandmother either. Golda died at age sixty-eight, fourteen years before the Nazis invaded Radomsko and turned life into hell on earth.

Her weathered stone was adorned with a scroll of grape vines and incised with barely legible Hebrew characters that spelled her name and a blessing: "Let her soul be merged in the eternal circle of living."

In the morning, we returned. Once again Maciej banged on the gate and, once again, Janek opened up. It was a glorious spring day, crisp air with bright sun. The forsythia glowed. Yellow butterflies flitted among the moss-covered headstones.

I now knew the way to Golda's grave, and this knowledge pleased me. I lit a candle and settled down, my spine supported by the stone. The others moved away to allow me a private moment. I closed my eyes, followed my breath. In the background were the sounds of a conversation in Polish, birds singing, oak leaves rustling. I felt a light breeze on my cheeks. *Sit down, great-granddaughter. You've come from so far!* I sat for half an hour; a century vanished. It was the first time in all my years traveling in Poland that I'd felt the presence of the dead as comforting.

We spent the rest of that morning walking slowly among the lanes of stones. Though he'd been the cemetery caretaker for close to two decades, Janek had never learned what the carved images meant. Now he listened intently as Tomek, his fellow Catholic, explained the symbolism: a hand pouring water from a pitcher for the Levites; broken candlesticks for a child; stacks of books for a scholar; coins above an alms box a sign of charity; and from the biblical bestiary—a serpent swallowing its tail, crouching lions, and leaping stags.

Janek was himself a witness. "I was seven years old when they shot the Jews, when the shooting happened," he volunteered. "I will never forget."

Maciej paused from time to time in front of a particular grave, lit another cigarette, launched into a story about this or that person he'd known among those few Jews who survived the war and decided to remain in Radomsko. He was like the narrator in *Our Town*. There was his friend Borkowski, who died in 1991. He'd had an affair with the wife of Sandomierski, who died in 1982. But they all wanted to be buried near each other anyway.

When Maciej tired of walking, he seated himself on the flat lid of one of the tombs. He shuffled through a folder he'd brought, removing a charcoal sketch of a beaming young girl in the embrace of a beautiful woman. He'd saved this big story for last.

The child's name was Ania Poniemunska, he told us. She was born in Radomsko in 1937. The previous summer Ania returned to Radomsko for the first time since emigrating to Israel with her parents. "She did not want to step foot in Poland again," Maciej told us, "but her son was anxious to see where his mother came from."

In 1939, just before the Nazi invasion, Ania's parents fled to the Soviet Union. They left two-year-old Ania in the care of her maternal grandmother, a Radomsko midwife named Chava Borys. When the Germans forced the Radomsko Jews into the ghetto, Chava hid with her son Haim and her granddaughter Ania and several others in a bunker. They managed to escape the ghetto to a nearby village where a farmer named Jaguszczyk and his wife sheltered them in his granary. Several other households in that same village were also concealing Jews.

Soon after, the son of the village headman denounced these Polish rescuers, and German soldiers surrounded the entire village at night. They searched every house, every shed, every barn. All those in hiding were taken out at gunpoint. Jaguszczyk and several other Poles were sent to Auschwitz.

In the morning, all the Jews were marched to the nearby forest and forced to dig their own mass grave. Chava's son escaped, but was shot dead on the run. In the melee, Chava handed Ania to Jaguszczyk's wife, who pretended Ania was her own daughter.

Young Ania knew not to cry out when—at the crack of a rifle—her grandmother Chava crumpled into the pit.

Of the twenty-three Jews hidden in the village, only Ania survived. After liberation her parents returned to Radomsko with the Soviet Army and reclaimed their daughter. In 1959 the family moved to Israel. When it was time to choose a profession, Ania chose nursing in homage to her grandmother.

When she arrived in Radomsko the past summer, Ania quickly found her way to Maciej. After all, he knew more about the Jewish history of the area than anyone else around. Ania was in great conflict about whether or not she could bear to visit the site of the massacre in the forest. Maciej encouraged her to make the pilgrimage.

He told her, "Go. It is important to your son. It is the big story of your life. It made you who you are."

I looked at the sepia drawing of Ania in the maternal embrace of her grandmother Chava. Maciej commissioned the drawing from Kasia, the young artist who'd painted my portrait three years ago. She was now a star student at the Czestochowa Art Academy. The drawing was based on a photo recently recovered from a house in the former Radomsko ghetto and Maciej had a copy of that too. Kasia had skillfully captured the likeness.

Ania, deeply touched by the drawing, asked Maciej how she might reciprocate. He knew right away what he wanted. He asked her to translate the Radomsk Yizkor Book from Yiddish into Polish. To Maciej, the Radomsk Yizkor was the Rosetta stone of Radomsko Jewish history.

My own generation of postwar descendants of Polish Jews was cut off from the history of our parents' and grandparents' pasts because we hadn't learned Yiddish, the language in which the yizkor books were written. It had never occurred to me that this same language barrier also prohibited Poles from accessing the Jewish history of their towns.

After their return to Israel, Ania and her husband began the huge task of translation. Last fall, Maciej published in his newspaper the first installment of the Polish translation of the Radomsk Yizkor. He continued to publish a chapter a week. The response was phenomenal. Circulation surged. Readers couldn't get enough. Some readers recognized names of Jewish neighbors.

When the paper stopped publishing for the Christmas holidays, people were frantic. "We got many calls, letters. I had to reassure them this was just a temporary lull."

For twelve years Maciej had insisted there could never be a complete history of Radomsko without the history of its Jewish community. He'd worked doggedly to break the silence on the subject.

The current citizens of Radomsko have forgotten much about their former Jewish neighbors. Those of us descended from Jewish Radomsk have also forgotten—or most likely never learned—about our former Polish co-citizens. We need each other in order to remember the past.

"Nothing can bring back what was lost," writer Eva Hoffman wisely reminds us. "After the Holocaust, we live in an era of symbolic actions."

Ruptures. Breaches. Breaks. Ania's translation of the yizkor into Polish was a healing gesture in memory of her grandmother. Publishing the translated yizkor book in his newspaper and gifting Ania with the drawing of her grandmother were Maciej's gestures in kind.

CHAPTER 25

The Seer

We stood on the hillside down the slope and under the brow of the medieval Lublin Castle, staring down on a vast parking lot. Our guide, Witek, was trying to help us see what was missing, where Jewish Lublin once existed.

"Over there," he said, pointing, "was Szeroka Street, the Jewish Broadway." An old well on Szeroka was at the exact center of what Witek called a "magical triangle"—equidistant from the Old Synagogue (destroyed), the Greek Orthodox church (also destroyed), and the Catholic church (still standing). The Jewish quarter of Lublin once encircled the entire Castle Hill. All that was left was the well on Szeroka Street.

Until 1939 Lublin was two towns—a Christian Lublin and a Jewish Lublin. The Royal Way traversed the city—from the gate on the Christian side (the Krakow Gate) through the Old Town to the Grodzka Gate, which opened to the Jewish section and the Castle Hill. Then came, as Witek called it, "the devil's plan to destroy every trace of Jewish life."

Witek Dabrowski, our new friend, was one of the founders of an artists' collective, Grodzka Gate, whose work addresses the reclamation of Jewish memory in Lublin. In Radomsko, the symbolic gestures of reconciliation were intimate—a family gravestone discovered, a hand-drawn portrait as a gift, a memory book translated from Yiddish to Polish. In Lublin, I'd long heard, the Grodzka Gate artists created gestures on an epic scale.

A native Lubliner in his mid-forties, Witek was the father of a college-age daughter, though he seemed as youthful as a college student himself.

Witek, who considered himself a "typical child of Communism," credited the Grodzka Gate with opening his world—his eyes and his ears. During his years of university, Witek "heard not one word" about the Jewish history of Lublin. His interest grew slowly, he said. Nowadays he wants to scream, "Yes, there is Majdanek; but there is also Lublin—the place where Jews and Poles lived together for five hundred years!"

Lublin's Jewish community dates to the 1500s. Throughout the eighteenth and nineteenth centuries, Lublin's scholars and rabbis were renowned through Eastern Europe. Dubbed "the Jewish Oxford" for the excellence of its yeshivas, Lublin was also a center for Jewish printing and publishing.

The Nazis captured Lublin, in eastern Poland, on September 18, 1939. They incarcerated the Jewish population in two ghettos and blew up the Jewish quarter. After the Wannsee Conference, in January 1942, the Reich designated Lublin as headquarters for Operation Reinhard, the main German effort to exterminate Jews in occupied Poland. Most of the Lublin ghetto's inhabitants—about twenty-six thousand people—were murdered at the Belzec camp, in nearby forests, or at Majdanek, the death camp the Nazis constructed on the outskirts of Lublin.

The Communist authorities completed the Nazis' destruction of Jewish Lublin. In 1953 they paved over the entire area and turned it into a car park. "Their aim," said Witek, "was to create a new world without any connection to the past." The work was so shoddy that the basements and foundations of the former Jewish houses were still there, underneath the asphalt.

Witek pointed to a spot halfway down the hill. It was the site of the house of Yaakov Yitzchak Horowitz, born in 1745, the great Hasidic teacher known as the Seer of Lublin.

The Seer was known as a wise man and a miracle maker; it was said he could see directly into people's souls. In his book of Hasidic legends, Elie Wiesel noted that what most struck people about the master's appearance "were his eyes—one larger than the other—which often took on a disquieting fixity when looking at someone." His community of followers lived together, sharing their material possessions and their dreams.

I imagined black-hatted Hasids at breakfast after a night of dancing, schnapps and prayer with the Seer, arguing over their dreams while noshing on herring and chickpeas.

The Germans destroyed the Seer's house in 1943. "But there is a secret here," said Witek mischievously. "Look at the shape of the parking lot."

Tomek and I stared. The parking lot bowed outward at its north and south borders, tapered at its western and eastern sides. "Like an eye . . . the eye of the Seer!" Witek announced. "That's how we know the spirit of the holy man is still here."

He asked us to count the number of old multistoried buildings that wrapped around the upper curve of the parking lot. There were ten.

"Exactly," he said, with an impish grin. "It's a minyan. Like ten old Jews. They are praying kaddish permanently."

We descended the stairs from the castle and walked across a stone bridge toward the Grodzka Gate. Students chatting on cell phones crossed paths with strolling priests and nuns.

Beside the bridge an old streetlamp shone brightly, though it was mid-morning. One of the last prewar street lamps in Lublin, it was rescued and restored by the Grodzka Gate artists and lit for the first time in 2004, during one of the company's artistic events, or Mysteries. It shines night and day. "This is a symbolic eternal lamp," Witek said, "to help us remember what is missing."

Workmen in white overalls on scaffolding were busy scraping and plastering the four-story Grodzka Gate. The city of Lublin and the European Union were now pitching in to help with major renovations. Witek opened a door tucked under the arch of the gate. We followed him up a narrow stone staircase to the first floor of the massive building. I'd anticipated a tiny office staffed with two or three employees. Wrong. There were thirty artists on staff here, all in their twenties and thirties—Web designers, art restorers, editors, writers, photographers, archivists, fund-raisers. The place hummed.

Tomasz Pietrasiewicz, the organization's mastermind and artistic director, was waiting to greet us. He gestured at the stacked boxes, the plastic tarps, the accumulated plaster dust. "You will have to use some imagination," he said with a smile.

Tomasz, in his early fifties, had a lithe, powerful body. His head was shaved, his inquisitive gaze framed by wire-rimmed glasses. During the days of martial law in Poland, Tomasz had been a leading dissident voice in Lublin, running an underground press and publishing Lublin writers not approved by the Communist authorities. From Witek, I learned that Tomasz ate but one meal a day and slept little, arriving at the offices at 3:00 a.m. so he could meditate and think in private before his staff arrived. He breathed and dreamed the Grodzka Gate.

His academic background was in theoretical physics. After graduate study at university in Lublin, he joined an avant-garde theater group influenced by the teaching of Jerzy Grotowski. Grotowski's own work emphasized the importance of *process*, long days, weeks of physical improvisations in the studio. The master had observed that while most art—including plays and films—was censored by the Communist authorities, no one monitored rehearsals. Process itself could be subversive.

Tomasz's troupe called itself Theater No Name (Teatr NN). For several years, they performed throughout Poland, garnering prizes and reviews. In the early nineties, after the fall of Communism, Tomasz and his collaborators—like many other dissident artists in Poland—began to rethink the mission of their artistic work. Teatr NN also began searching for a permanent home and settled down in the ruined Grodzka Gate.

Though one-third of Lublin's population had been Jewish before the war, most of the company—who'd grown up in Lublin under socialism—knew nothing about Lublin's Jewish past.

Tomasz grew up within shouting distance of Majdanek, but his parents never uttered a word about Jews or the Holocaust. Nor had the topic ever interested him, save for one incident from his childhood. One of his elementary school teachers told her students the story of a nine-year-old Jewish boy who had been dragged out of his house by a German soldier and paraded through the main street of her village "until his hair turned white."

This story made a deep impression at the time, he said, not because the boy was Jewish "but because of the white hair." Years later, when he started researching Jewish Lublin, Tomasz checked with former schoolmates to see if they remembered the story. None of them did. He was the only person left with a memory of that white-haired boy. If he didn't "do something" with that memory, no one would know he had ever existed. "This boy was very patient; he waited for me about twenty years," he said.

In the process of restoring the fourteenth-century building, the troupe began to uncover the symbolic role of the Grodzka Gate. Their excitement about its history grew. Then wonder of wonders, after the deep freeze of the Communist era, they were free to pursue the evolution of their creative work into new territory, as Witek said, "to fly to the moon."

We followed Tomasz up flights of stairs that jutted off at odd angles. He opened the door to a small room that contained a painted cardboard scale model of the vanished Jewish half of Lublin. What had been destroyed had been meticulously recreated in miniature—every house, every alley. The Great Synagogue, the horse market, the well on Szeroka Street.

On another level, in a large open space, a research library was under construction. Thousands of identical notebook binders—containing transcripts of some three thousand hours of recordings about the city's Jewish inhabitants—lined the shelves. Each folder represented one house and everything known about who lived in that house. Some folders were empty; nothing was known about those inhabitants. "The Germans destroyed *everything*. Until the end of the world, they should repent," Tomasz said firmly.

The Grodzka Gate was a memory ark, floating on an ocean of forgetting and ignorance. Remnants of the world before the flood find their way to the gate: matzevot (headstones), pieces of Torah, photo archives, even an old wooden door. "People don't know what to do with these things," Tomasz told us.

The group has also restored—and were already printing broadsides and chapbooks—on a collection of old printing presses and linotype machines from the 1920s. They discovered these massive machines in a rat-infested building slated for demolition. Using an old technical manual, they'd learned how to operate the presses, even pouring molten alloys to create their own type.

In 1891 the Russian Jewish historian Simon Dubnow issued an appeal to Eastern European Jews to collect documents and study their own history. He called this act of collecting by the Yiddish term *zamling* and its practitioners, *zamlers*. Emanuel Ringelblum, the indefatigable chronicler of the Warsaw Ghetto, was a protégé of Dubnow and adhered to this core belief in "collecting everything." His archiving team in the ghetto gathered testimonies and theater tickets, candy wrappers, menus of ghetto restaurants, posters that issued the call to armed insurrection, and much more. They buried their documents in three milk cans before the Ghetto Uprising. Two of the cans were unearthed after the war. Their contents dramatically increased our knowledge of life in the Warsaw Ghetto.

Tomasz was pleased to learn that he was a *zamler*.

He handed me a small booklet. Inside were photos of a charming young boy. His name was Henio Zytomirski. On November 9, 1942, at age nine and with his parents already dead, he walked alone to his death in the gas chamber at Majdanek. Thanks to a few photos salvaged by a relative of Henio's father in Israel, then donated to the Grodzka Gate, Tomasz was able to reconstruct a piece of Henio's brief life.

There was Henio, with huge brown eyes and brown curly hair, age one, in the arms of his father, Szmuel. Henio at his second birthday party, wearing a paper crown and a faux-fur cape, surrounded by laughing boys. Henio with his pretty mother; age three. Henio in 1939, age six, the year he would have begun school. That year, his father wrote to his brother in Palestine, "Henio is a very mischievous little boy but in my eyes, he is the most wonderful child imaginable," adding with unknowing irony, "I am enclosing his last photograph."

In 2005 Tomasz discovered that the last photo of Henio was taken in front of a bank he'd passed every day for years on his walk to work. "It fit like a puzzle," he said.

Tomasz and cohorts installed a life-sized photo of six-year-old Henio at that very spot. Next to the photo they set up a desk, writing implements, a mailbox. Passersby were invited to "write a letter to Henio."

"Dear Henio," wrote a boy named Alek Lewicki, "I don't understand myself why I am writing to a dead child. My childhood was very different from yours, but I think we would have a common language. Your childhood friend, Alek."

The thousands of letters addressed to Henio at 11 Kowalska Street, which inundated the Lublin post office, were of course returned, officially marked "Addressee Unknown" or "Nonexistent Address." Thus the project offered a way for Lubliners to touch the emptiness at the core of their city.

Henio Zytomirski is now known to school children all over the country. His story, rather than an abstraction, is part of the curriculum used to teach the significance of the Holocaust. "You see," Tomasz said, "starting with a small story, we enter a larger story."

Listening to Tomasz, I thought of Cheryl's melancholy dream of that dry, brittle book associated with heartache. The mission of these Lublin artists is to preserve the remnants—those glistening pieces of live flesh—still clinging to the fragile dry pages of Lublin's Jewish past, and, as well, to help present-day Lubliners perceive the Jewish absence in their midst.

For the participatory Mystery (Tomasz's term for the troupe's theatrical spectacles), titled "Poem of the Place," Tomasz talked the Lublin City Council into letting him open up seventy manhole covers that dot the surface of the giant parking lot in the former Jewish quarter. This project was based on his intuition that "memory is stronger than concrete."

The project was a masterpiece of civic engagement. "The city clerks began to like it," he chuckled. "You have to find one person who's at first shocked at the idea, then fascinated." And Tomasz needed the buy-in of the city council, because he proposed to cut off electricity to half the town, as well as bring electrical light to seventy subterranean vaults under the parking lot. Achieving that goal required five hundred kilometers of electrical cable.

On October 12, 2002, the ringing of bells in a church next to the Grodzka Gate signaled the beginning of the Mystery. Tomasz flipped the switch that dimmed all the lights in the area of what had been Jewish Lublin.

The audience of several thousand walked from the brightly lit Christian side of the Old Town through the Grodzka Gate into the darkened area. Light flooded heavenward from each of the seventy wells, as did the amplified recorded voices of Lubliners giving testimony about those who once lived here. Memory broke the concrete. Emptiness was given a voice. The participants followed the illuminated path to the spot where the Great Synagogue stood before the war.

How to end such an experience? The question stymied Tomasz. On a visit to the Chapel of the Holy Trinity at Lublin Castle he found the solution. Viewing the exquisite Byzantine frescoes in the chapel, he noticed how the anonymous medieval artist (or artists) had painted a curtain below the startling images from the life of Christ to separate the sacred from the profane. He decided to hang a vast black curtain at the far end of the car park. The walkers would encounter this billowing barrier after listening to the many voices speaking from under the ground, in the dark. It would be up to each participant to decide where the Mystery ended, when to exit.

"History," Tomasz told me, "is not precise—it has a stronger message." The former Home Army lieutenant who discovered the one remaining piece of the Warsaw Ghetto wall had insisted to Kostek Gebert that history was "an exact science." Tomasz, trained as a scientist, demurred from any such certainty.

"History is bringing you questions that we won't find the answers to," Tomasz said. "The more you deal with this history, the more you realize you do not know, you can never know. "

WITEK MET US THE next morning in the refectory of the Franciscan convent where Tomek and I were both staying, just a few hundred yards from the Grodzka Gate. I was groggy. The nunnery had Wi-Fi and I'd stayed up late e-mailing my husband about Lublin.

Witek drove us to Majdanek, the vast camp on the edge of Lublin. Majdanek was the first camp to be liberated by the Soviets. The Germans had no time to destroy the evidence; the camp was captured intact, with evidence of all its horrors.

The morning we visited some conservators from Warsaw were debating how best to repair some crumbling stone steps to one of the barracks. Whenever repairs were made to the camp, Witek pointed out, they were liable to be photographed and end up on a Holocaust denial site, "as if the whole place is a fabrication." Tomek was familiar with the same phenomenon from his work as a guide at Auschwitz-Birkenau.

In one of the barracks Tomasz and the Grodzka artists had created a permanent installation, *Elementarz* (Primer, in Polish). I'd never heard of artists creating an installation on the grounds of a death camp. It was a sign of the immense trust that Tomasz and the Grodzka Gate artists had earned from the state authorities who operated the camp as a memorial.

Inside the bunker, in dim light, were photos of Henio and a Polish Catholic girl, their schoolbooks, their lesson plans. The first words children learn to write, Witek pointed out, are *house, dog, cat, mother, father.* In the Majdanek primer, the words are *crematorium, transport, selection.*

From a wooden box issued the disembodied voice of a child singing a traditional Polish lullaby:

There used to be a Baba Yaga
She had a hut made out of bones
Many strange things happen in this house
Whoosh, the spark is gone!

Tomek hummed along with the recording. He'd learned the lullaby as a child. The simple, lilting tune lodged in my head. That is what I took away from my visit to Majdanek, along with the cries of the crows, the concrete walls stained with the blue of Zyklon-B, the gargantuan funerary urn that contained the heaped, mingled ashes of more than eighty thousand dead: Jews, Soviet POWs, Polish political prisoners, a variety other nationalities.

In the light breeze, infinitesimal fragments of ash swirled off the pile and joined the wind.

THAT EVENING CLOSE TO sundown with a full moon on the rise, Witek walked with us from the convent to a Passover seder on the other side of Lublin. People were returning to their apartments from work and from school. Shops were open, cooking smells wafted from open windows. Witek was greeted by many friends and acquaintances. He stopped for brief chats, handshakes. I imagined vanished inhabitants strolling through the city to long-ago Passover celebrations, similarly greeting their friends.

This would be the first seder in sixty years at the restored Chachmei Yeshiva Lublin (Yeshiva of the Wise Men in Lublin). The yeshiva was built due to the initiative of a great Polish rabbi, Meir Shapiro. Upstairs in a gallery were enlarged photos of the 1930 dedication ceremony, attended by rabbis, tzaddiks, Polish state officials, and thousands of ordinary people who overflowed the academy's plaza and crowded the nearby streets. In his speech, Rabbi Shapiro, who was also a member of the Polish Parliament, emphasized the long tradition of religious tolerance in Poland.

During the occupation, the Nazis deported the yeshiva's students and faculty to the camps. They threw some twenty-two thousand books out the windows of the yeshiva's famous library, carted them off to the market square, doused them with kerosene, lit the match.

The fire lasted twenty hours. According to an account by a Nazi correspondent, "The Lublin Jews assembled around and wept bitterly, almost silencing us with their cries. We summoned the military band, and with joyful shouts the soldiers drowned out the sounds of the Jewish cries."

During the Communist years, the building housed the State Medical Academy. Now the yeshiva once again belonged to the Jewish community. Just two months earlier the building had been rededicated in a two-day ceremony, which was covered by Poland's leading newspaper and carried live on Polish television.

Leading our Lublin seder were two young, nervous, and adorable Chabadniks, Avi and Szmuel, who'd traveled all the way from Brooklyn with matzoh in their suitcases (enough for me to bring back to the convent for my breakfast the next morning). It was their first trip to Poland, and neither of them spoke a word of Polish. Both their families were originally from Poland. They were astonished that Tomek—a Polish Catholic from Oswiecim, no less!—spoke and read some Hebrew. They drafted him into service as their seder translator.

The service was joyous, all the more so for our having visited Majdanek on the same day. We reclined, we got drunk, we sang "Chad Gadya," the rhythmical song about the stick that beat the goat and the fire that burned the stick . . . all the way to the Angel of Death. Our eyes watered from the horseradish we spread on our Brooklyn matzohs. Children asked the Four Questions with evident pride. Bounteous trays of steaming soup and roast chicken issued nonstop from the kitchen.

When my parents and grandparents were alive, it was not uncommon for two and sometimes three generations of Steinmans to be present at a family seder. As a child, I always loved the moment in the long dinner narration when we opened the front door for the prophet Elijah. At one seder, my ninety-year-old grandmother explained that in Czarist Russia "the reason we left the door open was not for Elijah, but to show the world that we are free people, that we were not afraid to celebrate the seder."

Our sixty or so fellow celebrants included those who had only recently acknowledged their Jewishness or who had one Jewish parent or grandparent. The gentleman to my right informed me he was the "last Yiddish speaker in Lublin." Witek quietly directed my attention to a distinguished middle-aged man with sad brown eyes sitting at the far end of one of the long tables. Father Jakub, as Witek called him, was a professor at Lublin's Catholic University and a good friend to the Grodzka Gate group.

Jakub was born in 1943 to a Jewish couple trapped in the ghetto of a small Polish town near the Lithuanian border. His desperate mother contacted a Catholic acquaintance and begged her to take the infant. The penalties were dire, and the woman, Emilia Waszkinel, hesitated. Knowing that Emilia was a devout Catholic, Jakub's mother pleaded, "Save this Jewish baby for the Jew in whom you believe." Emilia and her husband, Piotr, a metalworker, took the baby and raised him as their own.

At age seventeen Jakub shocked Emilia and Piotr with his decision to enter the priesthood. They'd never imagined this as a path for their son. Young Jakub loved to party, to listen to music with his friends.

In 1978, when Emilia Waszkinel was briefly hospitalized, she decided to tell her son, the priest, the truth. His birth parents had both perished. She knew they had loved him, but she couldn't even tell him their names. She had purposely forgotten for fear of revealing identities under torture. Years later in Israel, among survivors from his parents' town, the priest found his uncle, the brother of his father. He learned that his father was a tailor named Jakub Weksler. His mother was named Batia.

Jakub now uses both family names. He is Father Jakub Weksler-Waszkinel. He refers to the ash heap at Majdanek as "the tomb of my mother."

In the decades since that revelation, Father Jakub has struggled with his religious affiliation, taking counsel at one point from Pope John Paul II himself, who wrote the priest a letter addressed to "My Beloved Brother." Around his neck he wears a Star of David with a crucifix insert. At the dedication of the Chachmei Yeshiva, Father Jakub addressed the gathering: "I carry love for both my Jewish and my Polish parents."

Father Jakub carried that love into "One World—Two Temples," the ambitious Mystery staged by the Grodzka Gate on September 16, 2000. Witek and Tomasz described it to us over potent Bulgarian brandy in their office.

Tomasz assembled two long chains of people on either side of the Grodzka Gate. One chain of people extended from the gate to the reconstructed foundations of the now-vanished St. Michael's Parish Church. This group was composed of Poles distinguished as "Righteous among the Nations" for saving Jews in wartime. On the other side of the gate, a line of Jewish survivors of the Holocaust extended to the site in the Jewish quarter where the Great Synagogue once stood. It was a bold visual conception on a scale worthy of one of Sergei Eisenstein's historical film extravaganzas.

Each of those honored told their stories in a few sentences, their voices amplified by loudspeakers to the more than five thousand participants in the Mystery. One of the Saved: "I owe my life to a Polish foster father who saved me and my mother. I pay homage to him and to all the heroic people who not only saved lives, but raised us and gave us love like my father did."

One of the Righteous: "During the Nazi occupation, me, my brother, and my parents saved a Jewish girl—Sara Zylbersztajn—and my uncles, my mother's brothers, lost their lives because of rescuing Jews."

At the beginning of the Mystery, the Archbishop of Lublin stood on the foundation of the demolished church and the Chief Rabbi of Warsaw stood on the foundation of the ruined synagogue. From their respective locations, each dug a handful of soil and placed that soil in a clay vessel.

After the honorees spoke their stories, the archbishop's clay vessel was handed down the chain of the Righteous and the rabbi's vessel was handed down the chain of Holocaust survivors until they both reached the Grodzka Gate. The soil was then mixed by two children, one Polish and one Israeli, and by Father Jakub Weksler-Waszkinel, who was nurtured by two Polish mothers—Jewish and Catholic.

Two grapevines were planted in this commingled soil—one in Lublin, the other in Rishon Le-Zion in Israel—in memory of the two vanished temples and to symbolize the hope for a better world.

"Such strange but beautiful projects," Witek marveled to me that morning. "Tomasz has a real genius for thinking these up."

OUR LAST MORNING IN LUBLIN, Witek took us to visit the grave of the Seer. He secured the key to the gate from a priest at a nearby church. A sign noted that this was the oldest Jewish cemetery in Poland, established in the early fifteenth century.

The Seer's tomb was behind steel bars, like some exotic bird. The matzevot had been hand-painted—the priestly hands pouring a pitcher of water, flanked by two carved lions painted in gold, as was the Hebrew lettering. The floor in front of the stone was littered with folded pieces of paper, notes of supplication. The Seer was not forgotten. Hasidic faithful still make pilgrimages here.

The Seer was said to inspire joy and ecstasy among his disciples; but he himself suffered bouts of melancholy. After all, every troubled Jew from Bialystok to Lodz came to tell him their sorrows, misfortunes, and doubts. And he listened.

The night before, in my simple room at the convent, the light from the full moon shining in my face woke me in the middle of the night. I sat up; I burst out laughing. How was it possible to feel so full? I thought of Rabbi Singer—hearing his buoyant voice on the phone so long ago, suggesting I attend the retreat at Birkenau, that I take some time to travel in Poland. I thanked him.

I thanked the Seer for keeping his uneven eyes on Lublin, I thanked him for the artists at the Grodzka Gate, the guardians of the passageway between the remembered and the neglected, between the visible and the unseen.

CHAPTER 26

La Bibliothèque Polonaise

I stood in front of the massive doors of La Bibliothèque Polonaise. On a stopover in Paris, on the way home from Poland, this library in exile was on the top of my list of places to visit. It has been in operation at the same building on Île St. Louis since 1838, when it was founded by Poland's intellectual émigrés—poets, historians, musicians, politicians—to preserve Polish culture and to keep alive Poland's struggle for freedom during the years when Poland did not exist on any map.

According to my guidebook, the library was open from 11:00 a.m. to 5:00 p.m., Tuesday through Thursday. Today was Tuesday. I checked my watch. It was 1:00 p.m. The doors at 6, Quai d'Orleans, however, did not budge. I knocked again. No answer.

On the third knock, the doors opened a crack. Staring out at me: a young man with a delicate, pale face surrounded by dark ringlets. *Fermée* (closed), he said sternly.

I protested in my best French. I lived in California. This was my only chance to visit. I was writing a book about Poland. *S'il vous plaît?* He sighed, shrugged his shoulders, relented. "Come inside," he said without enthusiasm. He ushered me into his little guardroom. There was no heat. That perhaps explained why the ascetic young man was wearing a thick woolen scarf on a temperate spring afternoon. "Wait here, I will try to find somebody." He vanished.

I glanced at his cluttered desk: a fountain pen and three sets of a poetry manuscript, in Polish, written in elegant cursive. No wonder our reluctant greeter didn't want to be interrupted . . . it made perfect sense: a moody, young Polish poet guarding the Polish library in Paris.

During the years of partition, Poland's literary patrimony was in dire need of protection. Its fate was never secure. In 1795 the Russian empress Catherine the Great ordered one of the largest book collections in partitioned Poland removed from Warsaw and reinstalled in St. Petersburg.

In 1832, after the failed Polish uprising against the Russians, more books were seized. The biggest disaster was under Nazi occupation. As part of their plan to eradicate Polish culture, the Germans systematically destroyed Polish libraries. The Underground organized a clandestine circulating library, but the loss of books was still devastating. Out of twenty-two million volumes in prewar collections, only seven million are known to have survived the war.

An essay in the brochure of La Bibliothèque Polonaise, written by the chief curator Anna Czarnocka, called the library "a fragment of the free Poland, dependent on the support and the generosity of its countrymen. *Grace à leur sacrifice et à leur dons, elle a surveçu aux aléas de l'histoire jusqu'à aujourd'hui.*" (Thanks to their sacrifice and their gifts, the library has survived the hazards of history intact to this day.)

Paris has long been home to great Polish artists in exile. Among the postwar poets, Milosz as well as Zbigniew Herbert lived here. Adam Zagajewski moved to Paris in the early eighties. "It was a Polish tradition," he explained. "We had it in the genes that once you are in Paris, you don't despair."

The reluctant poet returned with a young woman from the administrative office. The library was closed for renovations, but she could allow me a brief visit to the two main exhibition galleries. I gratefully accepted.

Upstairs, she unlocked the gallery doors and left me alone. I stood in awe in front of the writing desk of poet Adam Mickiewicz. This was the desk where he had written Poland's national epic, *Pan Tadeusz*, which ends with the innkeeper Jankiel—an observant Jew and a patriotic Pole—singing of Poland's fate.

Mickiewicz perceived an analogy between the Jewish and Polish experiences of exile and suffering. At one of his lectures at a Paris university, Mickiewicz told his students, "It was not accidental that this people [the Jews] chose Poland for their fatherland."

There was the poet's feather quill, his inkwell. Another case featured a lock of his hair and a ring given to him by Polish émigrés in Paris on Christmas Day, 1840. In another vitrine were a number of miniscule books—made for elves? During the partition, books of Mickiewicz's poetry were forbidden literature—Polish *samizdat*. Polish patriots carried these matchbook-sized volumes clandestinely, in a pocket, sewn into a coat hem.

Mickiewicz's work was banned by the Czar, by the Nazis, then by the Communists. The first time one of his plays was staged in postwar Poland, shortly after Stalin's death, was intensely emotional. As described by the Polish theater critic Jan Kott, who was in the audience that night: "Government ministers were crying, the hands of the technical crew were shaking, the cloakroom attendants were wiping their eyes . . ."

A day earlier, in Krakow, I discussed Mickiewicz over tea in a café on the main square with Adam Zagajewski. He explained how Mickiewicz was only a poet for the first half of his life. Then he stopped writing and devoted himself to politics, raising an army in Turkey. Adam's wife, Maja, joined us. After decades abroad, the couple now lives in Krakow. The three of us strolled the Rynek at the poet's pace, absorbing beauty, greeting friends in the glancing late-afternoon sunlight.

In the Planty gardens, Adam pointed out a tree with shimmering gold leaves—"the only gingko in Krakow"—as well as a magnificent beech tree and a thrush. Gingko—*milorzab*. Beech—*buk*, like book. Thrush—*drozd*. I loved learning the names in Polish, from a poet. My Polish-language CDs included only prosaic vocabulary.

We stopped at the Wyspianski chapel to admire the stained glass windows. It was Easter weekend; Maja lit a votive and joined others who briefly genuflected in front of a station of the cross. I was touched at the rich coloration of their lives in this ancient Polish city.

I entered the room dedicated to Chopin—another Polish émigré and friend of Mickiewicz's—who longed for Poland but made Paris his home. There was a lock of Chopin's hair, a plaster cast of his delicate hands. After the composer died of tuberculosis in 1849, he was buried in Paris's famed Père Lachaise Cemetery. In accordance with his will, Chopin's heart was removed, pickled in cognac, and transported by his sister to Poland where it was installed in Warsaw's Church of the Holy Cross. Oh, those romantic Poles!

Chopin's *Nocturne in C Sharp Minor* was the last live music broadcast on Radio Poland as German artillery exploded in the streets of Warsaw. At the end of the war, the same pianist, Wladyslaw Szpilman—a Polish Jew who had survived the war in hiding—resumed Poland's broadcasting service by playing that same Chopin nocturne.

In the memoirs of Józef Czapski, one of the few Polish officers to survive the Soviet Gulag, he describes how a Russian stranger on the streets of Tarnopol offered him these words of comfort during his exile: "Excuse me, sir, but why are you so sad? The country that produced Mickiewicz and Chopin cannot perish."

Footsteps on the parquet floor interrupted my reveries about nineteenth-century Polish émigrés. The young woman who'd escorted me upstairs had returned with her boss, the chief curator herself.

Wearing a long purple skirt, black heels, and an amber necklace, with bright red lipstick and bobbed hennaed hair, Anna Czarnocka was a vision of Warsaw-Paris chic. She was curious about this American woman who had wrangled her way into the closed Bibliothèque Polonaise.

What kind of book about Poland was I was writing? Was it *La Pologne de temps passé? La Pologne en present?* Poland in the past? Contemporary Poland?

I thought for a minute. *La Pologne dans ma tête.* The Poland in my head.

"Ah," she responded with a big smile. "J'espère que vous aussi écrivez de la Pologne dans la coeur!" She lightly tapped her chest with her right hand.

I replied without hesitation. "Oui, la Pologne dans ma coeur."

The Poland in my heart.

The Story Continues

More than a half century has passed since hundreds of Radomskers gathered their individual tales and published them as the Radomsk Yizkor. After a decade of visits to Poland, I assumed most stories from the yizkor were frozen in time, unreachable . . . like the lost members of my family.

But some stories demand annotations, new endings. I thought back to Cheryl's dream of finding that big book with brittle pages flapping in the breeze: "I could see through to the binding, and there was—to my shock and surprise—some live flesh. It was glistening." One of those tales that still glistened was the story of Berek Ofman's rescuers.

From time to time, I'd tried to persuade Berek to submit testimony about the Bereska family to Yad Vashem. He was adamant that such exposure could bring harm to the family in Radomsko, and after a few attempts, I'd given up. So I was surprised when, in the spring of 2008, Berek called me out of the blue. "Please help me," he said in a quavering voice. He was ready. And, wonder of wonders, Marian Bereska in Radomsko was ready to tell his story as well.

Thus, the next chapter of that tale opened in a packed banquet hall at the Warsaw Marriott Hotel as Marian Bereska—a tall, slightly stooped man in a rough tweed coat—walked up to the podium. It was August 2011, and I'd come to Poland to witness a special ceremony bestowing Israel's highest honor—the Righteous Among the Nations medal from Yad Vashem—on a group of Poles who rescued their Jewish neighbors, acquaintances, and even complete strangers during the Holocaust.

I'd been keen to meet a rescuer from my family's town ever since I listened to Berek Ofman's harrowing tale of surviving the German occupation sequestered in the bunker of the Bereskas' little house. I'd been crushed when Marian changed his mind at the last moment and declined to meet with Tomek and me in Radomsko several years earlier.

At the time, it appeared that Marian Bereska would carry his secret to the grave. For seventy years, he'd kept this story to himself. He hadn't told his wife, his children, or any of his neighbors or friends in the town where he'd lived his entire life. In the postwar years, under Communism, secrecy about the past had become a habit. Now he was standing in front of ambassadors from twenty-six countries plus international media, ready to tell his story to the whole world.

I took a seat between Szymon Bereska, a grandson of Marian Bereska, and Leo Ofman, the son of Regina and Berek Ofman—the survivors. Leo's very existence was predicated on the Bereskas' actions. His parents married two days after Radomsko was liberated, on January 16, 1945. Leo was born in a DP camp in Germany two years later, before his parents immigrated to the United States. This was Leo's first trip to his parents' native land. He'd traveled here from Arizona. Though he hadn't spoken Polish since his childhood, to his surprise and delight, he discovered that Polish rolled easily off his tongue.

Szymon Bereska, twenty-eight, was a doctoral student in philology at Warsaw University. It had taken him almost two decades, but Szymon had persevered in coaxing the tale out of his grandfather and finally convincing him that in democratic Poland it was safe—and moreover necessary—to tell his story.

Throughout 2009 I helped the Ofman family prepare Berek's statement to submit to Yad Vashem. In Poland, Szymon readied his grandfather's testimony, had it notarized, and sent it to Jerusalem for corroboration. It took Yad Vashem a year to make their final decision.

More Poles have received medals of the Righteous than people of any other nationality. Currently, the number from Poland is 6,266. It doesn't sound like a lot, the Israeli ambassador reminded us at the Warsaw ceremony, then added, "But when we ask, 'Why weren't there more?' to be honest, each and every one of us has to ask—in a world of broken moral order, would I have risked my own life and my family's lives to save a neighbor—a stranger?"

When I finally met Marian Bereska, I tried to ask why he and his mother had assumed the brutal risks of harboring fugitives during the occupation. He brushed off my query; the question had no meaning. The Bereskas did not view their neighbors through a crooked mirror. They saw people who needed their help. They responded. They said yes to young Berek, whom they knew and then they said yes to hiding four more strangers.

At a table in the hotel lobby, Marian carefully sketched out the dimensions of the bunker in my little black notebook: the trapdoor in the kitchen, the second door to the potato cellar. Five Jewish souls hidden under their roof, under their floor. He used his strong hands to demonstrate, occasionally using a cup or a spoon on the table to indicate where something happened, how close they came to disaster.

The day after the ceremony in Warsaw, on a bright summer morning, Szymon, Leo, and I drove the four hours from Warsaw to Radomsko, where Marian was scheduled to reveal his long-kept secret at a press conference. Leo, anxious for his first glimpse of the town he'd heard about his whole life, pushed the speed limit on the winding roads. Szymon cautioned him to slow down. We passed apple orchards and fat cows grazing next to sunflowers. En route, Szymon told us how he unraveled his grandfather's secret. "He often mentioned a cellar. . . . What cellar?" He heard the names Berek and Regina Ofman, and when Szymon was old enough to use the Internet, he found these names in the Memorial (Yizkor) Book of the Community of Radomsk. He started to piece it all together. He was immensely proud of his grandfather.

We joined Marian and Radomsko's mayor in the town hall to face a phalanx of eager, young reporters. My old friend Maciej Ziembinski was there to witness this moment as well.

The mayor, Anna Milczanowska, described how, in the eighties, Marian had been her boss at a city agency. At the time, young Anna was a Solidarity activist, and Marian, a civil engineer, belonged to the Communist Party. When the Communist secret police took an interest in her activities, Marian warned her and kept her under his protection. "I thought of him as my father after that," she said. The

Bereskas are the first family in Radomsko to be publicly identified as rescuers, the first to be recognized by Yad Vashem. The reporters—none of them older than thirty—listened with intense fascination to Marian's tale. After he spoke, the mayor told all assembled, "We wish to have more people like Marian Bereska in our community . . . so helpful, so open, so brave."

Marian, Szymon, Leo, and I walked the streets of the little town. We ate heavenly barley soup with Maciej, the mayor, and her staff at a local restaurant. We walked through the cemetery, past the tzaddik's tomb and my great-grandmother's grave. We ended the emotional day at the Radomsko train station, where Szymon and I caught the express back to Warsaw. Leo stayed the night in Radomsko at Marian's house.

The Radomsko train station had been renovated and refurbished; its streamlined modern curves glowed with fresh white paint. As we boarded, I looked out the window for a last glimpse of Marian, the Polish rescuer, and Leo, the Jewish survivor's son—himself a father and grandfather—standing side by side on the platform. They had only met for the first time the day before, and yet they already knew each other so well.

This image now becomes part of our collective memory, a link to a time when, as the yizkor tells us, a Polish Catholic painted the zodiac on the ceiling of Radomsko's Great Synagogue and a Polish Jewish tinsmith designed the spires of the town's cathedral.

ACKNOWLEDGMENTS

There are many thanks due on this long (and yes, crooked) road to publication.

Cheryl Holtzman was my partner and muse for this "Polish quandary," and her words are an essential part of the text. I remain in awe of her humor, creativity, courage, and fashion smarts. Thanks also to her family—Henry Holtzman, Anna Holtzman, Max Blitz.

Berek Ofman told me his amazing story and trusted me to help him prepare his testimony to gain recognition for his rescuers. Thanks to the entire Ofman family. In Radomsko, my deep thanks to Marian Bereska, Szymon Bereska, and to Maciej Ziembinski, one of the saviors of Atlantis.

Special thanks to Ester Wilhelm Tepper, who generously shared her story of survival in the Radomsko ghetto, as well as her love for Jewish culture and history.

Dorit Cypis's heartfelt gift for a writer to attend the Bearing Witness Retreat launched this project. Rabbi Don Singer, my teacher, challenged me with a koan about Polish-Jewish reconciliation. Over the years, he's sustained me with friendship, stories, songs, and conversations while walking creek-side trails.

Tomek Cebulski was the best translator and guide to Poland that this wandering Jew could ever have, as well as a dear friend, a partner in dialogue, and a historian-on-call. Tomek and his wife, Sylwia, are my warm hosts in Krakow, and now parents of little Helenka, who entered this world since my last trip to Poland.

Donna Pall helped me feel the weight and texture of my images. My grandmother told me to "tell my dreams to three smart people." Donna is definitely one of them.

A sheynem dank, biz hundert un tsvantsik to Gloria Berkenstat Freund—my Radomsko landsman—who translated the Radomsk Yizkor from Yiddish to English and posted it online for me and others to find.

Gassho to Bernie Glassman, Zen Peacemaker Order, to all the peacemakers who attended the Bearing Witness Retreat at Auschwitz-Birkenau in November 2000. Special thanks to Debra Unger for permission to quote from her father's letter and to Allan Whiteman for many invaluable insights over the years. Thanks to One by One (especially Monika Heidig), an organization bringing together in dialogue descendants of Holocaust survivors, perpetrators, and bystanders.

For the Bearing Witness Retreat, I followed the Zen practice of assembling a *mala*, or beads strung together and worn like a necklace. "Each bead represents a person who supports that peacemaker's vision and work." Thanks to my mala: Larry Steinman; Ruth Solomon; Matt Solomon; Ken and Rhonda Steinman; Charlotte Hildebrand; Beth Thielen, Anne Kalik, Irene Borger; Susan Banyas; Rob and Barbara Pressman; Judith Teitelman and Aaron Paley; Chris Rauschenberg and Janet Stein; Anne Germanacos; Richard Katkov and Miriam Mulder; Sarah Jacobus; Erica and Bill Clark; Meredith Monk; Lanny Harrison; Suzanne Edison; Louis and Paula Loomis; Regina O'Melveney; Donna Frazier; Linda and Dick Lange; Joan Kreiss.

Dziękuję bardzo to Kostek Gebert, who answered my questions about Polish history with utmost patience, offered a phenomenal depth of cultural understanding (plus hot tea and walks in Lazienki Park); Staszek and Monika Krajewski, who shared their wisdom and the warmth of their home; Rabbi Michael Shudrich, who offered insights into Jewish life in Poland today.

My dear friend Joanna Klass introduced me to astonishing theater in Wroclaw, Warsaw, and Krakow (Boska Komedia), as well as to twenty-four-hour herring and vodka kiosks, wine bars on the Vistula, art salons in the beautiful flat she shares with her husband, artist Wojtek Szasner—canny guide to the Warsaw flea market. Dorota

Golebiewska, who translated at the Bearing Witness Retreat and at Wannsee, has been a touchstone in Warsaw, as was Robert Gadek in Krakow. The playwright Malgorzata Sikorska-Miszczuk rescued me from the labyrinthine depths of the Warsaw train station on a frigid December day and provided hospitality and literary camaraderie. Poet Adam Zagajewski, through his writing and his friendship, has offered glimpses of illumination for this beginner at mysticism. In Lublin, the Grodzka Gate team—Tomasz Pietrasiewicz and Witek Dabrowski, inspired me with their daring creative work and walked me through crooked streets to attend the most moving Passover seder of my life. Krzysztof Czyżewski of the Borderland Foundation (Fundacja Pogranicze), thank you for your vision that sees beyond borders, your dedication and quiet strength. Barbara Kirshenblatt-Gimblett, author, folklorist, Polish food detective, thanks for friendship over the years of writing. Thanks to Alex Dunai, historian and genealogist in L'viv, Regina Kopilevich, guide to the mysteries of Vilnius, and to Ewa Wroczyńska, creator of the Tykocin Purim play.

My cousin Laura Mendley helped fill in gaps in family history; my cyberlandsleit CRARG (Czestochowa Radomsk Area Research Group) and the indefatigable and dedicated Dan Kazez provided a gold mine of archival information about Nowo-Radomsk. Thanks to Elizabeth Karpowicz, another Radomsko descendant, for assistance with Polish translation.

My colleagues at the Los Angeles Institute for Humanities at the University of Southern California offered critique and encouragement after my talk there. Special thanks to the late Michael Henry Heim, Priscilla Heim, Jack Miles, Jonathan Kirsch, Leo Braudy, Jon Wiener, Steve Ross, Barbara Isenberg, and Rabbi Leonard Beerman.

For financial support, thanks to August Maymudes and the Yablon Family Foundation for providing a writing fellowship. I am also indebted to the Adam Mickiewicz Institute for travel support in Poland and to the California Arts Council for a crucially timed nonfiction writing fellowship. I could not have written this book without uninterrupted writing retreats at Blue Mountain Center in the Adirondacks, Mesa Refuge in Point Reyes, California, and Ucross Foundation in Sheridan, Wyoming. My colleagues at the Library Foundation of Los Angeles have supported the time I have taken to research this project. Ken Brecher, Library Foundation president and friend, has been steadfast in support of my creative work at LFLA and also at the Sundance Institute's writing program.

I had quiet time for editing at Beth Thielen's home in Chatham, New York, and at Judy Munzig's in Ojai, California, plus a New York City retreat, thanks to Joan Kreiss and Roger Perlmutter.

Thanks to Dr. George Halasz for his pioneering work on generational transmission of trauma, to Richard Rodriguez for communing with St. Jude on behalf of *The Crooked Mirror*, to Lawrence Weschler for spirited guidance into the Eastern European literary canon, to Erica Lehrer for sharing her research on postconflict memory and reconciliation. Susan Freudenheim, editor at the *Jewish Journal*, commissioned my essay about the ceremony for the Righteous. Thanks to Alan Lockwood for sharing my love of Polish literature and ice-cold zubrovka. Other dear friends have provided support of various kinds over the years: Judith Nies, Sara Rimer, Annie Reiner, and Lynn Swanson.

I'm fortunate to work with my terrific agent, Betsy Amster, a gifted editor and dear friend, who was steadfast in her support over many years and piloted *The Crooked Mirror* home. Anne Dubuisson Anderson helped with my proposal, and Donna Frazier Glynn read a draft of my manuscript with a poet's insight.

To my brilliant editor, Amy Caldwell, and the great team at Beacon—what a blessing that this book found its way to your hands, your house.

My parents, Anne and Norman Steinman; grandparents Rebecca and Harry Steinman, Sarah and Louis Weiskopf; and uncle Albert Weiskopf have all passed away, but they are all in this book. As are the next generations: Jennifer Solomon, Matt Solomon, Jonathan Steinman, Sarah Rebecca Steinman, Hannah Steinman, Claire Aviva Onderwater, Alice Damascus Onderwater, Ari Onderwater, Henry Huckleberry Solomon, and Tuesday Anne Solomon.

My husband, Lloyd Hamrol, accompanied me to Our Lady of Czestochowa, read the entire manuscript aloud to me, cooked too many great meals to count, weathered my moods, and never wavered in his love and support.

Deep bow.

SELECTED BIBLIOGRAPHY

Ackerman, Diane. *The Zookeeper's Wife: A War Story*. New York: W. W. Norton, 2007.

Améry, Jean. *At the Mind's Limits: Contemplations by a Survivor on Auschwitz and Its Realities*. Bloomington: University of Indiana Press, 1980.

Appiah, Kwame Anthony. *The Honor Code: How Moral Revolutions Happen*. New York: W. W. Norton, 2010.

Bakan, David. *Sigmund Freud and the Jewish Mystical Tradition*. Boston: Beacon Press, 1957.

Bartana, Yael. *A Cookbook for Political Imagination*. Warsaw: Zacheta National Gallery of Art and Sternberg Press, 2011.

Bauer, Yehuda. *Rethinking the Holocaust*. New Haven, CT: Yale University Press, 2001.

Borowski, Tadeusz. *This Way to the Gas, Ladies and Gentlemen*. New York: Penguin Books, 1987.

Botsford, Keith. *Józef Czapski: A Life in Translation*. The Cahiers Series 10. London: Sylph Editions, 2009.

Browning, Christopher R. *Ordinary Men: Reserve Police Battalion 101 and the Final Solution in Poland*. New York: HarperCollins, 1992.

Czapski, Joseph. *The Inhuman Land*. New York: Sheed & Ward, 1952.

Czyzewski, Krzysztof. *The Path of the Borderland (Sciezka pogranicza)*. Sejny, Poland: Borderland Publishing House, 2001.

Dabrowska, Anna, ed. *Lights in the Darkness: The Righteous among the Nations; Testimonies*. Lublin: Osrodek Brama Grodzka, 2008.

Davies, Norman. *1795 to the Present*. Vol. 2 of *God's Playground: A History of Poland*. New York: Columbia University Press, 1982.

———. *Heart of Europe: The Past in Poland's Present*. Oxford, UK: Oxford University Press, 2001.

———. *Rising '44: The Battle for Warsaw*. New York: Viking, 2003.

————. *No Simple Victory: World War II in Europe, 1939–1945.* New York: Viking, 2006.

Desbois, Patrick. *The Holocaust by Bullets: A Priest's Journey to Uncover the Truth Behind the Murder of 1.5 Million Jews.* New York: Palgrave MacMillan, 2008.

Dwork, Deborah, and Robert Jan Van Pelt. *Auschwitz.* New York: W. W. Norton, 2006.

Freund, Gloria Berkenstat, project coordinator and trans. *Memorial Book of the Community of Radomsk and Vicinity (Radomsko, Poland).* Translation of *Sefer yizkor le-kehilat Radomsk ve-ha-seviva.* Tel Aviv, 1967. http://www.jewishgen.org/.

Gilbert, Martin. *The Righteous: The Unsung Heroes of the Holocaust.* New York: Henry Holt, 2003.

Glassman, Bernie. *Bearing Witness: A Zen Master's Lessons in Making Peace.* New York: Bell Tower Press, 1999.

Glatstein, Jacob. *The Glatstein Chronicles.* New Haven, CT: Yale University Press, 2010.

Glowacka, Dorota, and Joanna Zylinska, eds. *Imaginary Neighbors: Mediating Polish-Jewish Relations after the Holocaust.* Lincoln: University of Nebraska Press, 2007.

Gombrowicz, Witold. *Polish Memories.* Translated by Bill Johnston. New Haven, CT: Yale University Press, 2004.

Gross, Jan T. *Fear: Anti-Semitism in Poland after Auschwitz.* New York: Random House, 2006.

————. *The Neighbors: The Destruction of the Jewish Community in Jedwabne, Poland.* Princeton, NJ: Princeton University Press, 2001.

Grossman, Vasily. *The Road: Stories, Journalism, and Essays.* Translated by Robert and Elizabeth Chandler with Olga Mukovnikova. New York: New York Review of Books, 2010.

Haenel, Yannick. *Jan Karski: Roman.* Paris: Editions Gallimard, 2009.

Heilbrunn, Stefania. *Children of Dust and Heaven: A Collective Memoir.* Capetown, South Africa: printed by author, 1978.

————. *Children of Dust and Heaven: A Diary from Nazi Occupation through the Holocaust.* With an introduction by Ester Wilhelm Tepper. A collective memoir of residents of Radomsko written by a Holocaust survivor and also based on the diary of a young girl from Radomsko, Miriam Caszczewacki. Pacific Palisades, CA: Remember Point, 2012. Kindle edition.

Herling, Gustaw. *Volcano and Miracle: A Selection from* The Journal Written at Night. Translated by Ronald Strom. New York: Penguin Books, 1996.

Heschel, Abraham Joshua. *The Earth Is the Lord's: The Inner World of the Jew in Eastern Europe.* Woodstock, VT: Jewish Lights, 1995.

Hoffman, Eva. *After Such Knowledge: Memory, History, and the Legacy of the Holocaust.* New York: PublicAffairs, 2004.

————. *Shtetl.* New York: PublicAffairs, 2007.

Jabès, Edmond. *The Book of Questions II and III*. Translated by Rosmarie Waldrop. Middleton, CT: Wesleyan University Press, 1977.

Karski, Jan. *Story of a Secret State*. Boston: Houghton Mifflin, 1944.

Kassow, Samuel D. *Who Will Write Our History? Rediscovering a Hidden Archive from the Warsaw Ghetto*. Reprinted. New York: Vintage Books, 2007.

Kirshenblatt, Mayer, and Barbara Kirshenblatt-Gimblett. *They Called Me Mayer July: Painted Memories of a Jewish Childhood in Poland before the Holocaust*. Berkeley: University of California Press, 2007.

Kowalczyk, August. *A Barbed Wire Refrain*. Translated by Witold Zbirohowski-Koscia. Oswiecim Poland: Auschwitz-Birkenau State Museum, 2001.

Krajewski, Monika. *Time of Stones*. Warsaw: Interpress, 1983.

Krajewski, Stanislaw. *Poland and the Jews: Reflections of a Polish Polish Jew*. Krakow: Wydawnictwo Austeria, 2005.

Krall, Hannah. *Shielding the Flame: An Intimate Conversation with Dr. Marek Edelman, the Last Surviving Leader of the Warsaw Ghetto Uprising*. Translated by Joanna Stasinska and Lawrence Weschler. New York: Henry Holt, 1987.

Kugelmass, Jack, and Jonathan Boyarin, eds. and trans. *From a Ruined Garden: The Memorial Books of Polish Jewry*. Bloomington: Indiana University Press, 1998.

Levi, Primo. *Moments of Reprieve: A Memoir of Auschwitz*. Translated by Ruth Feldman. New York: Penguin Books, 1987.

———. *The Drowned and the Saved*. Translated by Raymond Rosenthal. New York: Vintage Books, 1989.

Lifton, Betty Jean. *The King of Children: A Biography of Janusz Korczak*. New York: Schocken Books, 1988.

Lights in the Darkness: The Righteous Among the Nations Testimonies. Lublin, Poland: Ośrodek Brama Grodzka—Teatr NN, 2008.

MacMillan, Margaret. *Paris 1919: Six Months That Changed the World*. New York: Random House, 2003.

Mendelsohn, Daniel. *The Lost: A Search for Six of Six Million*. New York: Harper-Collins, 2006.

Mickiewicz, Adam. *Pan Tadeusz or the Last Foray in Lithuania: A History of the Nobility in the Years 1811 and 1812 in Twelve Books of Verse*. Translated by Leonard Kress. Perrysburg, OH: HarrowGate Press, 2006.

Milosz, Czeslaw. *The History of Polish Literature*. Berkeley: University of California Press, 1983.

———. *Native Realm: A Search for Self-Definition*. Translated by Catherine S. Leach. New York: Farrar, Straus & Giroux, 1968.

———. *New and Collected Poems, 1931–2001*. Translated by Robert Hass. New York: Ecco Press, 2003.

Moczarski, Kazimierz. *Conversations with an Executioner*. Englewood Cliffs, NJ: Prentice-Hall, 1981.

Nitecki, Alicia. *Recovered Land*. Amherst: University of Massachusetts Press, 1995.

Opdyke, Irene Gut. *In My Hands: Memories of a Holocaust Rescuer.* New York: Anchor Books, 2001.

Paulsson, Gunnar S. *Secret City: The Hidden Jews of Warsaw, 1940–1945.* New Haven, CT: Yale University Press, 2002.

Polonsky, Antony, and Joanna B. Michlic, eds. *The Neighbors Respond: The Controversy over the Jedwabne Massacre in Poland.* Princeton, NJ: Princeton University Press, 2004.

Reid, Anna. *Borderland: A Journey through the History of Ukraine.* Boulder, CO: Westview Press, 2000.

Ringelblum, Emmanuel. *Polish-Jewish Relations During the Second World War.* Translated by Dafna Allon, Danuta Dabrowska, and Dana Keren. Evanston, IL: Northwestern University Press, 1974.

Roth, Joseph. *The Radetsky March.* Translated by Joachim Neugroschel. New York: Overlook Press, 2002.

———. *The Wandering Jews.* Translated by Michael Hofmann. London: Grant Books, 2001.

Rozewicz, Tadeusz. *Sobbing Superpower: Collected Poems of Tadeusz Rozewicz.* Translated by Joanna Trzeciak. New York: W. W. Norton, 2011.

Schama, Simon. *Landscape and Memory.* New York: Knopf, 1996.

Scharf, Rafael F. *Poland, What Have I to Do with Thee? Essays without Prejudice.* London: Vallentine Mitchell, 1998.

Schulz, Bruno. *The Street of Crocodiles.* Translated by Celina Wieniewska. New York: Penguin Books, 1977.

Segel, Harold B., ed. *Polish Romantic Drama: Three Plays in English Translation.* Polish Theater Archive. 2nd revised edition. New York: Routledge, 1997, p. 40 (*quote of Jan Kott*).

Shandler, Jeffrey, ed. *Awakening Lives: Autobiographies of Jewish Youth in Poland before the Holocaust.* New Haven, CT: Yale University Press/YIVO Institute for Jewish Research, 2002.

Sherwin, Byron L. *Sparks Amidst the Ashes: The Spiritual Legacy of Polish Jewry.* Oxford, UK: Oxford University Press, 1997.

Snyder, Timothy. *Bloodlands: Europe between Hitler and Stalin.* New York: Basic Books, 2010.

Steinberg, Paul. *Speak You Also: A Survivor's Reckoning.* New York: Henry Holt, 2003.

Steinlauf, Michael C. *Bondage to the Dead: Poland and the Memory of the Holocaust.* Syracuse, NY: Syracuse University Press, 1997.

Szewc, Piotr. *Annihilation.* Translated by Ewa Hryniewicz-Yarbrough. Normal, IL: Dalkey Archive Press, 1987.

Szymborska, Wislawa. *Poems New and Collected: 1957–1977.* Translated by Stanislaw Baranczak and Clare Cavanagh. New York: Harcourt, 1998.

Tec, Nechama. *When Light Pierced the Darkness: Christian Rescue of Jews in Nazi-Occupied Poland.* Oxford, UK: Oxford University Press, 1986.

Tulli, Magdalena. *Dreams and Stones*. Translated by Bill Johnston. New York: Archipelago Books, 2004.

Wat, Aleksander. *My Century: The Odyssey of a Polish Intellectual*. Edited and translated by Richard Lourie. New York: New York Review of Books, 2003.

Webber, Jonathan, and Chris Schwarz. *Rediscovering Traces of Memory: The Jewish Heritage of Polish Galicia*. Bloomington, IN: Indiana University Press, 2009.

Weschler, Lawrence. *The Passion of Poland: From Solidarity through the State of War*. New York: Pantheon Books, 1982.

Wiesenthal, Simon. *The Sunflower: On the Possibilities and Limits of Forgiveness*. New York: Schocken Books, 1998.

Wisenberg, S. L. *Holocaust Girls: History, Memory, and Other Obsessions*. Lincoln: University of Nebraska Press, 2002.

Wood, E. Thomas, and Stanislaw M. Jankowski. *Karski: How One Man Tried to Stop the Holocaust*. New York: John Wiley & Sons, 1994

Yerushalmi, Yosef Hayim. *Zakhor: Jewish History and Jewish Memory*. Seattle: University of Washington Press, 1983.

Young, James E. *The Texture of Memory: Holocaust Memorials and Meaning*. New Haven, CT: Yale University Press, 1993.

Zagajewski, Adam. *Mysticism for Beginners*. Translated by Clare Cavanagh. New York: Farrar, Straus & Giroux, 1997.

―――. *Another Beauty*. Translated by Clare Cavanagh. New York: Farrar, Straus & Giroux, 2000.

―――. *Two Cities: On Exile, History, and the Imagination*. Translated by Lillian Vallee. Athens: University of Georgia Press, 2002.

―――. *Without End: New and Selected Poems*. New York: Farrar, Straus & Giroux, 2003.

―――. *A Defense of Ardor: Essays*. Translated by Clare Cavanagh. New York: Farrar, Straus & Giroux, 2004.

Zimmerman, Jack, and Virginia Coyle. *The Practice of Council*. Ojai, CA: Ojai Foundation, 1991.